The Feminine Image In Literature

HAYDEN HUMANITIES SERIES

F. PARVIN SHARPLESS, *Series Editor*
Chairman, English Department
Germantown Friends School
Philadelphia, Pennsylvania

THE FEMININE IMAGE IN LITERATURE
Barbara Warren

THE MYTH OF THE FALL: LITERATURE OF INNOCENCE AND EXPERIENCE
F. Parvin Sharpless

The Feminine Image In Literature

BARBARA WARREN

HAYDEN BOOK COMPANY, INC.

Rochelle Park, New Jersey

Library of Congress Cataloging in Publication Data

Warren, Barbara, 1947-   comp.
  The feminine image in literature.

  (Hayden humanities series)
    1. Women—Literary collections. I. Title.
PN 6071.W7W3   808.8'0352   73-11928
ISBN 0-8104-5068-2

Printed in the United States of America

3   4   5   6   7   8   9   PRINTING

75 76 77 78   YEAR

Preface

The Hayden Humanities Series uses the term "humanities" in both a narrower and broader sense than in many examples of current curriculum structuring. We see humanities texts neither as conglomerations of stuff from literature, art, music, history, and philosophy purporting to express the spirit of a given time or place, nor as collections of readings supposedly illuminating vaguely suggested themes or subjects. Rather, we see them as focusing on the abiding ideas and values that men have wrestled with and lived by, as reflected through literature (broadly defined) and as informed by a variety of man-centered disciplines: psychology, sociology, anthropology, religion, philosophy, history.

The texts in this series deal with the significant human concerns upon which all human actions, great or small, social or individual, are based, whether we know it and admit it or not. These concerns are the stuff of all literature, yesterday and today; and they provide a background for recognizing, understanding, and defining the issues of the moment that claim our attention and wonder.

The approach in these texts is thematic, since such a structure has proved useful in traditional teaching units and in newer elective programs. But again there is a difference. The weakness of the thematic approach has been its tendency to yield units which are impossibly vague or impossibly broad, or both. What we have tried to do is declare and define an idea or issue thoughtfully and deeply so that others may test that declaration and definition through what they read and know, and find dealing with it a cumulative, organic experience, allowing growth and change.

In contrast to most thematically arranged anthologies, these texts do not pretend a faceless editor or the illusion of authorial objectivity or distance. The compiler has a voice and a point of view, and a conviction that he knows what he is talking about. The introductory essay both introduces and interprets; it defines an idea or issue—in this case *The Feminine Image in Literature*—and then tries to see it in the round by explaining its past, asserting its continuing vitality and viability, and suggesting some of the things that can be done with it.

This approach takes us far beyond the usual "knowing about" or "talking about" to which literature is too often reduced. We believe the themes have lasting value as organizing constructs for making sense out of our world and for comprehending how the literary artist makes sense out of it. The themes also have a coherence that such thematic structures as, say, "Man and Society" or "Man and the Environment" or "War and Peace" cannot possibly have. One import of both these observations is that the question of "modern" literature vs. "classical" or "traditional" makes little real sense. Literature, by our lights, is always new and renewable. Forever is now. The idiom and the cultural demands and expectations may be different, but the underlying human concerns that the artist is examining are timeless and universal—and that's what counts.

The reader is not expected to agree with everything in the introduction, but is urged to consider it carefully; a casual reading won't do. The argument needs to be understood, and then questions must be raised about validity, emphasis, application, ramification, relevance to experience, and ultimate usefulness in ordering ideas, feelings, beliefs, and values. The defining essay should be a point of departure and a point of return. Along with the headnotes and questions for each group of selections, it serves as a guide for analysis and discussion, not as a gospel to be ingested, remembered, and regurgitated.

There is no attempt in these texts at coverage of literary periods or schools of writing, but there is a variety of genres, modes, backgrounds, times, and writers. Certain long works have been excerpted; enough has been included from any work to feed the thematic demands and yet not misrepresent the total piece. The aim throughout has been to show how widely diffused in our literature the central concern of each text has been and still is.

The Feminine Image in Literature is divided into four parts. At the end of each are two groupings of suggestions for further reading. The first lists selections from *Short Story Masterpieces* (Albert

Erskine and Robert Penn Warren, Editors; Dell), an excellent and inexpensive collection of stories that are particularly appropriate for this text. Reference is made to these stories in the Study Questions at the end of each part. The second grouping lists a variety of additional works, pieces too long for inclusion in a text of this size, and further material from books already included in part.

The Study Questions are framed as a continuing dialogue about the matters raised in the selections. They are meant to direct attention to the specific images and experiences that support the introductory essay and illustrate the general observations made at the beginning of each part. They are not framed to be answered one at a time, but rather to be the focus of continuing discussion and response.

F. PARVIN SHARPLESS
Series Editor

Contents

The Feminine Image In Literature

Introduction

Why have a literature course based on "the feminine" rather than "the human" experience? For centuries, the human experience has been synonymous with the masculine experience, and the collective image of humanness has been one-sided and incomplete. Woman's experience has interested man only as it has involved himself, and he has defined her experience on the basis of his encounters with the women in both his real life and his fantasy life. Man's interpretation of woman's nature has created stereotypes that have served as models for generations of women, but man's understanding has been that of subject analyzing object; woman has not been defined as a subject in her own right.° Before woman can know and accept her human identity, apart from being the object of man's fantasies and desires, she must understand the nature of the images that have been projected upon her; she must separate herself from the man-created myths. Man, in turn, must understand why he has created these myths and what they reveal about himself.

In order for our humanness to find unique expression through our sexual identities, we must see ourselves and others as subjects—as important individuals with the capacity for creative actions and relationships in the outside world. We must transcend the stereotypes that society would impose upon us and refuse to be satisfied with being merely the objects of other people's desires. We need to learn that the definition of "the feminine" is an essential part of the definition of "the human" and that "the human" is greater than merely "the masculine" or "the feminine" alone. We need to understand that the sexual role isolated from the conscious, individual identity turns a person into a mannequin or a monster.

Girls must be encouraged to identify with the best that humanity has produced. They must consider the world of action and achievement as much their birthright as it is that of boys. They must assume their share of responsibility for this world and not allow themselves to be taken care of by men who view them as helpless playthings.

°Simone de Beauvoir elaborates on this point in Chapter IX of *The Second Sex* (H. M. Parshley, ed. and trans. New York: Bantam, 1970), and in the book's "Conclusion," which is included in this anthology. Working out meaningful definitions of "subject" and "object" and understanding the complex interaction of the two should be a central concern of a course on woman/man relationships. Simply defined, a subject has an internal reality apart from what it appears to be in the outside world; it has a will and can act; it is an essential being. An object has no inner life, no identity apart from what it appears to be in the outside world; it has no will of its own but is a slave to the will of others; it is passive; it is acted upon; it is an inessential thing.

The movement from childhood into maturity is a movement into consciousness of ourselves as subjects—a consciousness that lifts us rather brutally from a stage of development in which we are cared for by other people to one in which we must take care of ourselves. No one leaves the world of childhood irresponsibility easily; indeed, who would not be tempted to stay in the child's world forever if the reality of the outside world permitted it, even encouraged it as the highest fulfillment of one's nature? For too long, girls have been educated for passivity and expected to remain helpless children. Girls, like boys, must prepare to work in the outside world, support themselves, and assume responsibility for their actions, thus earning the right to be called fully human, essential individuals.°

The world is very much in need of the feminine contribution to consciousness, and women and men need to understand and value the unique nature of this contribution, which goes far beyond the fulfillment of biological functions. The conventional, reason-limited masculinity that dominates the world is out of touch with the feminine side of human nature, and lacks a quality of consciousness necessary for the fully human, individuated self. Men must turn to women to get back in touch with the vital but neglected part of their own natures.° Call this missing dimension Feeling, Eros, or Soul; it is whatever men have ardently worshipped in women over the ages—something that they were not conscious of in themselves, something that prevents one from treating other people as objects, something that makes one incapable of slaughtering masses of people for political reasons. Isolated from the feminine element, the masculine element results in the great collective stupidity of purely rational, ego-centered, narcissistic minds that can understand human experience only as the manipulation of objects in the external world.

A course on "the feminine experience" is for potential men as well as potential women; woman's search for her identity is also man's search for his. It is a search for the complex individual who feels and thinks, who values both Eros and Logos,° who transcends being an object

---

°Simone de Beauvoir writes: "The individual who is a subject, who is himself, if he has the courageous inclination toward transcendence, endeavors to extend his grasp on the world: he is ambitious, he acts." From *The Second Sex*, p. 604.

°"Feminine" and "masculine" describe qualities of consciousness, of human response, independent of sex. A person may be a female without being feminine in the way she relates to the world, just as a person may be a male without relating to the world in a masculine way; but a person cannot become a fully conscious, complete human being (an individuated woman or man) without accepting and integrating the feminine and masculine qualities of her/his nature. Both are essential elements or "superior functions" of humanness.

°Carl Jung defines Eros as "psychic relationship" and Logos as "objective or factual interest." Eros is considered the feminine function and Logos the masculine function. [See the selections from *C. G. Jung: Psychological Reflections*, which are included in this anthology.]

manipulated by unconscious forces inside or outside himself. It is a search for a human sexuality which expresses itself in subject-to-subject relationships. The search for identity is a process of uniting the feminine and masculine elements within the individual psyche, of transforming warring opposites into an androgynous whole.° But it is not an objective intellectual process that involves only the assimilation of facts; it is not concerned with knowledge removed from the context of real life experiences.

In "sex education" courses, we can learn "the facts of life," the information that explains how our sexuality can be acted out physically. But where do we learn about the relationships which provide the motivation and the context for sexual behavior? The "sexologists," the scientific observers and recorders of physiological responses, offer a great deal of technical information about how the body functions when it experiences strong emotions, but they tell us nothing about what the persons involved are feeling about themselves and each other. This subjective dimension of experience should be the concern of a literature course; it is what we must consider if we are to understand how to live with "the objective facts" of our physical natures.°

We need to talk about what is happening to us in the context of the life situation, of human encounters, and we need to carry on dialogues with members of the opposite sex. Literature, not sex manuals, provides the appropriate texts for such discussions. Literature brings to consciousness those subtle truths of human life that are learned through interacting with the world—learning experiences that involve understanding oneself as a subject who is both solitary and social. Serious writers are concerned with the subjective responses of the total person, not just the physical spasms that can be recorded on a machine. Knowing how another person's sexual components are put together and how they operate when connected with ours is not very useful knowledge when all we want to know is how to approach the person gracefully without being rejected, and how to build a relationship. It is the complexity of living with and expressing our sexuality within the context of our humanity that is the issue for those of us who want to experience ourselves and others as subjects, not as mechanical objects to be turned on and off.

°"Androgynous" means having both feminine and masculine characteristics. This psychological union of opposites is a goal of what Jung calls "the individuation process." [See the selections by Jung and M. Esther Harding included in this anthology.]

°"Subjective" refers to what is internal, invisible, pertaining to the mind or soul, the psychological or spiritual experiences of a person—how a person experiences himself as a being separate from the outside world and yet as an actor in that world. "Objective" refers to what is external, visible, pertaining to the world of things, and considered as independent of the perceiving mind although perceptible by the mind—what a person perceives as existing outside himself.

Becoming an individual human being who is subject rather than object is a matter of understanding the subjective as well as the objective contents of our experiences, and as a learning process it should be encouraged: it involves the vital self-knowledge that we must learn how to teach ourselves. This anthology sets up a thesis that we should challenge in terms of our own experiences. What is offered is a concept of the androgynous mind (or psyche) as a means of understanding human behavior and of resolving the conflict that exists between the sexes. We must decide whether this concept is supported by the reality of our own lives, whether it helps us to make sense out of our own experiences. For the psychoanalyst Carl Jung, it is not a philosophical theory but a psychological reality; it has no meaning unless grounded in the subjective experiences of individuals—in our dreams and in our daily activities. Virginia Woolf describes this psychological reality as "a plan of the soul so that in each of us two powers preside, one male, one female":

> ... and in the man's brain, the man predominates over the woman, and in the woman's brain, the woman predominates over the man. The normal and comfortable state of being is that when the two live in harmony together, spiritually cooperating. If one is a man, still the woman part of the brain must have effect; and a woman also must have intercourse with the man in her. Coleridge perhaps meant this when he said that a great mind is androgynous. It is when this fusion takes place that the mind is fully fertilised and uses all its faculties. Perhaps a mind that is purely masculine cannot create, any more than a mind that is purely feminine. ... But it would be well to test what one meant by man-womanly, and conversely by woman-manly, by pausing and looking at a book or two.°

Let us follow Woolf's suggestion and turn to some works of literature which can offer insights into what is meant by "man-womanly" and "woman-manly." The essays, poems, and stories in this anthology (as well as the recommended selections from *Short Story Masterpieces*°) present a variety of feminine images—created by both men and women—and explore some of the problems that face woman in her quest for identity as an individuated self within social structures that pressure her with images of what she "ought" to be. The organization of the material forms a progression of consciousness from a subject-object, unisexual point of view to a subject-subject, bisexual state of awareness. The central thesis

---

°*A Room of One's Own* (New York: Harbinger ed.), p. 102. The complete essay (Chapter Six) is included in this anthology.
°Edited by Robert Penn Warren and Albert Erskine (New York: Dell Publishing Co., Inc., 1968). This book is to be used in conjunction with *The Feminine Image in Literature* anthology.

is that to be human is to go through a process of growth in consciousness which leads to an awareness of the complex, androgynous nature of the individual; the process involves bringing to consciousness the unconscious elements within our psyches, and experiencing projected images as realities that exist inside ourselves.° The thematic organization of the selections is based on the premise that one's sexual identity is a vital, inseparable part of one's total identity and is developed and defined by the degree of consciousness one achieves. According to this assumption, the definition of "womanly" and "manly" varies with the level of consciousness attained by each individual and changes as a person moves from a primitive, unconscious state to a more sophisticated, more highly conscious state of awareness.° Woman's grievance against a man-dominated society is rooted in that society's insistence that she be satisfied with a primitive, unconscious or semiconscious level of existence.

In reading and discussing the works that follow, keep in mind that the issue for all of us, as growing human beings, is not whether we are fulfilling our feminine and masculine roles (as if these were absolute states into which we were born), but whether we are increasing our consciousness in a creative way; whether we are learning through our own lives the meaning of "man-womanly" and "woman-manly" and becoming self-confident, unique individuals with something to contribute to the world of relationships and work; whether we are becoming fully aware of ourselves as complex subjects and not merely the slaves of unconscious impulses that we do not understand and cannot control.

°A psychological explanation of the projection process is given by M. Esther Harding in Chapters 1 and 2 of *The Way of All Women,* 1st rev. ed. (New York, 1970), pp. 7–11, 49. [Part of Chapter 1 is included in this anthology.] Simply put, projection is seeing in another person qualities that exist within oneself.

°M. Esther Harding defines the development of consciousness in terms of three stages: "the naive, the sophisticated and the conscious." [See Chapter 1 of *The Way of All Women,* in this anthology.]

PART I

The Phantom Lady
and the Marble/Plastic Doll

The Phantom Lady and the Marble/Plastic Doll

One of the most interesting creatures to appear in masculine monologues is "the phantom lady," a spiritual being who causes the hero endless suffering and remorse and who leaves him "alone and palely loitering" on some "cold hill side." Whether she is viewed as seductress, "femme fatale," succubus, or divine muse, she is essentially the man's most vital spirit, his soul, without which he is inwardly dead, merely existing, wandering lost in a gray world. She is his Fate—a living hell or a divine madness—and he is not fully alive without her.

As the man's supreme ideal, his ultimate desire, an image with which he compares all living women, this "phantom lady" is a barrier between himself and actual experience. He can only waste away in a fantasy world if he seeks her as a real woman, for he will never find her in the flesh; she is an imaginary creature of his own making who will always elude him in the outside world because she is a part of his own psyche—he must unite with her inside himself. This is the nature of ideal images, dream-lovers, and inner spirits when they are projected onto people in the outside world. Eventually, they vanish from external reality because they are not part of that world; flesh-and-blood reality is contrary to their essence.

The "phantom lady" is always bigger and better and more perfect than life, and she always embodies what is missing in the outward reality of the man's life—that is why she is an airy substance like all things that are purely intellectual in nature and spiritual in source. Men see her everywhere; she appears and disappears at whim. Monologues about her keep pouring from masculine pens—always a bit melodramatic, overly sentimental, almost hysterical in tone. Every woman learns that the "femme fatale" is the only kind of woman that will capture the devoted lover. Yet, as a flesh-and-blood woman, a reality that will not evaporate overnight, she does not exist. One fleeting, alluring, ecstatic moment she is there in an embrace like paradise and then she is gone, and the man is back on the cold ground again, desolately loitering, waiting for her to reappear, but with something sensational to write about. In fact, he is composing a poem while he waits, and the experience he had will be much more vivid and alive on paper than it was in reality. He will make it sound as if something big really happened, but the point is that nothing happened or could happen, considering the kind of man he was—out of touch with "the phantom" inside himself and the wildness of his own nature. These are the men who write genteel pornography, meaning that all experience begins and ends in their heads. Flesh-and-blood reality cannot arouse them—only their fantasies about what they would like this reality to be.

Perhaps the hardest thing for any woman to overcome when she becomes conscious of herself in relation to men is the temptation to try to live up to this fictitious lady, to "imitate art," to become a complete artifice that will always be able to lure and fascinate the man she wants to keep away from that "cold hill side." Her motivation for this role-playing is usually, at the start, a desire to be loved. Having been brought up to have little sense of or respect for her own unique worth, having been discouraged from seeking her own identity regardless of what anyone thought, and having been made to feel that whatever value she has is based solely upon her appearance, her manners, and her ability to make men love her and to keep their love, she thinks she is doing what is right, even though it may not be good for her or for the man.

In trying to fulfill the artistic, romantic ideal, a woman gives up the reality of her own identity and creates for herself an inner void—her own gray world of "living death"—for she does not exist outside the man's image of her, or his worship of her. She is defined only by his poetic descriptions of her, by the images that he projects onto her. If she shows her true self, she will shatter those images, and he must search elsewhere for inspiration, for another woman who will start him writing poems again.

It is important to understand how man has viewed his most intimate soul, embodied in this elusive feminine spirit, for one loves and pursues nothing more passionately than one's own deepest self in its most beautiful, idealized form. The selections in Part I offer the "phantom lady" in a variety of poses, beginning with the spiritual and ending with the materialistic counterpart: "the marble/plastic doll." Both are products of the same fantasizing process in man; the more aesthetic man will choose an invisible spiritual ideal, while the philistine man will choose a visible physical ideal. The man on the "cold hill side" is concerned about his woman's nature, her wildness. The man with his eyes glued to the centerfold of *Playboy* magazine is concerned about his woman's physical measurements and sexy appearance. Both are doing the same thing: masturbating in their heads.

The selections in Part I depict the split in the nature of the man who views woman either as object of spiritual love or as object of lust. Neither extreme describes woman as she experiences herself, but only as man experiences some reality inside himself that he falsely believes he can find in the outside world. This is not to say that woman does not have a spiritual or a physical nature, that she does not experience love and lust; but she does not experience them in masculine terms, in the way men would have her experience them. Worshipped as spirit, woman becomes a goddess who embodies the noblest qualities of man's nature; she functions as man's soul, as a source of divine inspiration. Worshipped as flesh, she becomes man's plaything, valued for her physical beauty and for the pleasure man experiences in possessing her as a very visible sexual object. She functions as a temptress who lures man into "sin," even though he may spend a great deal of time composing seduction arguments intended to overcome her reluctance to succumb to his will—as though love-making were just an idea or the end product of a logical argument, as though relationships and feelings were based on infallible reasoning. Whatever man's ideal of woman, it reflects more about what he has neglected, denied, or repressed in his own nature than about the true nature of woman as she experiences herself. Man is really describing the feminine dimension of his own nature. What man seeks in woman is what he longs to be united with inside himself.

One wonders how much life among flesh-and-blood people is passing man by while he is out on that hillside or sitting home with a copy of *Playboy*. The central question to be considered in the discussion of the works in Part I is the degree to which man's idealized image of woman, "the woman of his dreams," creates a barrier between himself and actual experience, keeps him from growing and finding his individual identity through an interaction with real people in the outside world, and ultimately prevents him from making creative contributions to that world. Does the man who lives only in his fantasies of "the way things should be," in his projections onto external reality, waste away in pursuit of these images? Can he ever find the ideal embodied in a flesh-and-blood person, in someone with whom he can have a real relationship for a prolonged period of time? What is the effect of such projections on women, on the way they view themselves and their purpose in life? What happens to the woman who tries to live up to man's ideals? Define the nature of each type of woman depicted in Part I; consider the nature of the man who is worshipping this woman and the nature of his particular kind of worship.

Discuss the difference between artifice and reality. Why would anyone choose to play a part rather than to be herself? Is it a conscious choice? Do we try to live out the reality of our lives as we actually experience it, or do we try to make our lives "imitate art" to fulfill some ideal? How do men and women remove their masks and get in touch with what is underneath the objective appearance? What insights do these works offer into the conflict between men and women, into the essential feminine quality that man longs to possess and to be united with? What is the significance of the private images that people hold of their "ideal mate"? Discuss personal fantasies aside from those offered in these works. What is the impetus behind poetic monologues?

LA BELLE DAME SANS MERCI

John Keats (1795–1821)

AH, WHAT can ail thee, wretched wight,
  Alone and palely loitering?
The sedge is withered from the lake,
  And no birds sing.

Ah, what can ail thee, wretched wight,   5
  So haggard and so woe-begone?
The squirrel's granary is full,
  And the harvest's done.

I see a lily on thy brow,
  With anguish moist and fever dew;   10
And on thy cheek a fading rose
  Fast withereth too.

I met a Lady in the meads
  Full beautiful, a faery's child;
Her hair was long, her foot was light,   15
  And her eyes were wild.

I set her on my pacing steed,
  And nothing else saw all day long;
For sideways would she lean, and sing
  A faery's song.   20

I made a garland for her head,
  And bracelets too, and fragrant zone;°
She looked at me as she did love,
  And made sweet moan.

She found me roots of relish sweet,   25
  And honey wild, and manna dew,
And sure in language strange she said,
  I love thee true.

She took me to her elfin grot,°
  And there she gazed and sighèd deep,   30
And there I shut her wild sad eyes—
  So kissed to sleep.

°*zone*: sash   °*grot*: cave

And there we slumbered on the moss,
    And there I dreamed, ah woe betide°
The latest° dream I ever dreamed   35
    On the cold hill side.

I saw pale kings, and princes too,
    Pale warriors, death-pale were they all;
Who cried—"La Belle Dame sans Merci
    Hath thee in thrall!"°   40

I saw their starved lips in the gloom
    With horrid warning gapèd wide,
And I awoke, and found me here
    On the cold hill side.

And this is why I sojourn here   45
    Alone and palely loitering,
Though the sedge is withered from the lake,
    And no birds sing.

THE PHANTOM HORSEWOMAN

Thomas Hardy (1840–1928)

Queer are the ways of a man I know:
        He comes and stands
        In a careworn craze,
        And looks at the sands
        And the seaward haze   5
        With moveless hands
        And face and gaze,
        Then turns to go . . .
And what does he see when he gazes so?

They say he sees as an instant thing   10
        More clear than to-day,
        A sweet soft scene
        That once was in play
        By that briny green;
        Yes, notes alway   15

°*betide*: befall   °*latest*: last   °*thrall*: servitude

From *Collected Poems* by Thomas Hardy. Reprinted by permission of The Macmillan Company, New York; the Hardy Estate; Macmillan London and Basingstoke; and The Macmillan Company of Canada, Limited.

Warm, real, and keen,
What his back years bring—
A phantom of his own figuring.

Of this vision of his they might say more:
Not only there   20
Does he see this sight,
But everywhere
In his brain—day, night,
As if on the air
It were drawn rose bright—   25
Yea, far from that shore
Does he carry this vision of heretofore:

A ghost-girl-rider. And though, toil-tried,
He withers daily,
Time touches her not,   30
But she still rides gaily
In his rapt thought
On that shagged and shaly
Atlantic spot,
And as when first eyed   35
Draws rein and sings to the swing of the tide.

"SHE WAS A PHANTOM OF DELIGHT..."

William Wordsworth (1770–1850)

She° was a Phantom of delight
When first she gleamed upon my sight;
A lovely Apparition, sent
To be a moment's ornament;
Her eyes as stars of Twilight fair;   5
Like Twilight's, too, her dusky hair;
But all things else about her drawn
From May-time and the cheerful Dawn;
A dancing Shape, an Image gay,
To haunt, to startle, and way-lay.   10

I saw her upon nearer view,
A Spirit, yet a Woman too!

°*She*: refers to Mary Hutchinson, whom Wordsworth knew from childhood and married in 1802.

Her household motions light and free,
And steps of virgin-liberty;
A countenance in which did meet   15
Sweet records, promises as sweet;
A Creature not too bright or good
For human nature's daily food;
For transient sorrows, simple wiles,
Praise, blame, love, kisses, tears, and smiles.   20

And now I see with eye serene
The very pulse of the machine;
A Being breathing thoughtful breath,
A Traveller between life and death;
The reason firm, the temperate will,   25
Endurance, foresight, strength, and skill;
A perfect Woman, nobly planned,
To warn, to comfort, and command;
And yet a Spirit still, and bright
With something of angelic light.   30

LIGEIA

Edgar Allan Poe (1809–1849)

> And the will therein lieth, which dieth not. Who knoweth the mysteries of the
> will, with its vigor? For God is but a great will pervading all things by nature of
> its intentness. Man doth not yield himself to the angels, nor unto death utterly,
> save only through the weakness of his feeble will.
>
> *Joseph Glanvill°*

I cannot, for my soul, remember how, when, or even precisely
where, I first became acquainted with the lady Ligeia. Long years have
since elapsed, and my memory is feeble through much suffering. Or,
perhaps, I cannot *now* bring these points to mind, because, in truth,
the character of my beloved, her rare learning, her singular yet placid
cast of beauty, and the thrilling and enthralling eloquence of her low
musical language, made their way into my heart by paces so steadily and
stealthily progressive that they have been unnoticed and unknown. Yet
I believe that I met her first and most frequently in some large, old,
decaying city near the Rhine. Of her family—I have surely heard her
speak. That it is of a remotely ancient date cannot be doubted. Ligeia!
Ligeia! Buried in studies of a nature more than all else adapted to
deaden impressions of the outward world, it is by that sweet word alone
—by Ligeia—that I bring before mine eyes in fancy the image of her

---

°*Joseph Glanvill*: English clergyman and philosopher (1636–1680); it isn't certain
whether Poe wrote the passage and attributed it to Glanvill.

who is no more. And now, while I write, a recollection flashes upon me that I have *never known* the paternal name of her who was my friend and my betrothed, and who became the partner of my studies, and finally the wife of my bosom. Was it a playful charge on the part of my Ligeia? or was it a test of my strength of affection, that I should institute no inquiries upon this point? or was it rather a caprice of my own—a wildly romantic offering on the shrine of the most passionate devotion? I but indistinctly recall the fact itself—what wonder that I have utterly forgotten the circumstances which originated or attended it? And, indeed, if ever that spirit which is entitled *Romance*—if ever she, the wan and the misty-winged *Ashtophet°* of idolatrous Egypt, presided as they tell, over marriages ill-omened, then most surely she presided over mine.

There is one dear topic, however, on which my memory fails me not. It is the *person* of Ligeia. In stature she was tall, somewhat slender, and, in her latter days, even emaciated. I would in vain attempt to portray the majesty, the quiet ease, of her demeanor, or the incomprehensible lightness and elasticity of her footfall. She came and departed as a shadow. I was never made aware of her entrance into my closed study save by the dear music of her low sweet voice, as she placed her marble hand upon my shoulder. In beauty of face no maiden ever equalled her. It was the radiance of an opium-dream—an airy and spirit-lifting vision more wildly divine than the phantasies which hovered about the slumbering souls of the daughters of Delos. Yet her features were not of that regular mould which we have been falsely taught to worship in the classical labors of the heathen. 'There is no exquisite beauty,' says Bacon, Lord Verulam, speaking truly of all the forms and *genera* of beauty, 'without some *strangeness* in the proportion.' Yet, although I saw that the features of Ligeia were not of a classic regularity—although I perceived that her loveliness was indeed 'exquisite,' and felt that there was much of 'strangeness' pervading it, yet I have tried in vain to detect the irregularity and to trace home my own perception of 'the strange.' I examined the contour of the lofty and pale forehead—it was faultless—how cold indeed that word when applied to a majesty so divine!—the skin rivalling the purest ivory, the commanding extent and repose, the gentle prominence of the regions above the temples; and then the raven-black, the glossy, the luxuriant and naturally-curling tresses, setting forth the full force of the Homeric epithet, 'hyacinthine!' I looked at the delicate outlines of the nose—and nowhere but in the graceful medallions of the Hebrews had I beheld a similar perfection. There were the same luxurious smoothness of surface, the same scarcely perceptible tendency to the aquiline, the same harmoniously curved nostrils speaking the free spirit. I regarded the sweet mouth. Here was indeed the triumph of all things

---

°*Ashtophet*: probably Poe's invention

heavenly—the magnificent turn of the short upper lip—the soft, voluptuous slumber of the under—the dimples which sported, and the color which spoke—the teeth glancing back, with a brilliancy almost startling, every ray of the holy light which fell upon them in her serene and placid, yet most exultingly radiant of all smiles. I scrutinized the formation of the chin—and here, too, I found the gentleness of breadth, the softness and the majesty, the fullness and the spirituality, of the Greek—the contour which the god Apollo revealed but in a dream, to Cleomenes, the son of the Athenian. And then I peered into the large eyes of Ligeia.

For eyes we have no models in the remotely antique. It might have been, too, that in these eyes of my beloved lay the secret to which Lord Verulam alludes. They were, I must believe, far larger than the ordinary eyes of our own race. They were even fuller than the fullest of the gazelle eyes of the tribe of the valley of Nourjahad. Yet it was only at intervals—in moments of intense excitement—that this peculiarity became more than slightly noticeable in Ligeia. And at such moments was her beauty—in my heated fancy thus it appeared perhaps—the beauty of beings either above or apart from the earth—the beauty of the fabulous Houri° of the Turk. The hue of the orbs was the most brilliant of black, and, far over them, hung jetty lashes of great length. The brows, slightly irregular in outline, had the same tint. The 'strangeness,' however, which I found in the eyes, was of a nature distinct from the formation, or the color, or the brilliancy of the features, and must, after all, be referred to the *expression*. Ah, word of no meaning! behind whose vast latitude of mere sound we intrench our ignorance of so much of the spiritual. The expression of the eyes of Ligeia! How for long hours have I pondered upon it! How have I, through the whole of a midsummer night, struggled to fathom it! What was it—that something more profound than the well of Democritus—which lay far within the pupils of my beloved? What *was* it? I was possessed with a passion to discover. Those eyes! those large, those shining, those divine orbs! they became to me twin stars of Leda, and I to them devoutest of astrologers.

There is no point, among the many incomprehensible anomalies of the science of mind, more thrillingly exciting than the fact—never, I believe, noticed in the schools—that, in our endeavors to recall to memory something long forgotten, we often find ourselves *upon the very verge* of remembrance, without being able, in the end, to remember. And thus how frequently, in my intense scrutiny of Ligeia's eyes, have I felt approaching the full knowledge of their expression—felt it approaching—yet not quite be mine—and so at length entirely depart! And

---

°*Houri*: One of the dark-eyed maidens in the Mohammedan paradise who are eternally young and beautiful. Each true believer is promised seventy-two houris.

(strange, oh strangest mystery of all!) I found, in the commonest objects of the universe, a circle of analogies to that expression. I mean to say that, subsequently to the period when Ligeia's beauty passed into my spirit, there dwelling as in a shrine, I derived, from many existences in the material world, a sentiment such as I felt always aroused within me by her large and luminous orbs. Yet not the more could I define that sentiment, or analyze, or even steadily view it. I recognized it, let me repeat, sometimes in the survey of a rapidly-growing vine—in the contemplation of a moth, a butterfly, a chrysalis, a stream of running water. I have felt it in the ocean; in the falling of a meteor. I have felt it in the glances of unusually aged people. And there are one or two stars in heaven—(one especially, a star of the sixth magnitude, double and changeable, to be found near the large star in Lyra) in a telescopic scrutiny of which I have been made aware of the feeling. I have been filled with it by certain sounds from stringed instruments, and not unfrequently by passages from books. Among innumerable other instances, I well remember something in a volume of Joseph Glanvill, which (perhaps merely from its quaintness—who shall say?) never failed to inspire me with the sentiment;—'And the will therein lieth, which dieth not. Who knoweth the mysteries of the will, with its vigor? For God is but a great will pervading all things by nature of its intentness. Man doth not yield him to the angels, nor unto death utterly, save only through the weakness of his feeble will.'

Length of years, and subsequent reflection, have enabled me to trace, indeed, some remote connection between this passage in the English moralist and a portion of the character of Ligeia. An *intensity* in thought, action, or speech, was possibly, in her, a result, or at least an index, of that gigantic volition which, during our long intercourse, failed to give other and more immediate evidence of its existence. Of all the women whom I have ever known, she, the outwardly calm, the ever-placid Ligeia, was the most violently a prey to the tumultuous vultures of stern passion. And of such passion I could form no estimate, save by the miraculous expansion of those eyes which at once so delighted and appalled me—by the almost magical melody, modulation, distinctness and placidity of her very low voice—and by the fierce energy (rendered doubly effective by contrast with her manner of utterance) of the wild words which she habitually uttered.

I have spoken of the learning of Ligeia: it was immense—such as I have never known in woman. In the classical tongues was she deeply proficient, and as far as my own acquaintance extended in regard to the modern dialects of Europe, I have never known her at fault. Indeed upon any theme of the most admired, because simply the most abstruse of the boasted erudition of the academy, have I *ever* found Ligeia at fault? How singularly—how thrillingly, this one point in the nature of my wife has forced itself, at this late period only, upon my attention! I said her knowledge was such as I have never known in woman—but where breathes the man who has traversed, and successfully, *all* the wide areas of moral, physical, and mathematical science? I saw not then what I now clearly perceive, that the acquisitions of Ligeia were gigantic, were astounding; yet I was sufficiently aware of her infinite supremacy to resign myself, with a childlike confidence, to her guidance through the chaotic world of metaphysical investigation at which I was most busily occupied during the earlier years of our marriage. With how vast a triumph—with how vivid a delight—with how much of all that is ethereal in hope—did I *feel,* as she bent over me in studies but little sought—but less known—that delicious vista by slow degrees expanding before me, down whose long, gorgeous, and all untrodden path, I might at length pass onward to the goal of a wisdom too divinely precious not to be forbidden!

How poignant, then, must have been the grief with which, after some years, I beheld my well-grounded expectations take wings to themselves and fly away! Without Ligeia I was but as a child groping benighted. Her presence, her readings alone, rendered vividly luminous the many mysteries of the transcendentalism in which we were immersed. Wanting the radiant lustre of her eyes, letters, lambent and golden, grew duller than Saturnian lead. And now those eyes shone less and less frequently upon the pages over which I pored. Ligeia grew ill. The wild eyes blazed with a too—too glorious effulgence; the pale fingers became of the transparent waxen hue of the grave, and the blue veins upon the lofty forehead swelled and sank impetuously with the tides of the most gentle emotion. I saw that she must die—and I struggled desperately in spirit with the grim Azrael.° And the struggles of the passionate wife were, to my astonishment, even more energetic than my own. There had been much in her stern nature to impress me with the belief that, to her, death would have come without its terrors;—but not so. Words are impotent to convey any just idea of the fierceness of resistance with which she wrestled with the Shadow. I groaned in anguish at the pitiable spectacle. I would have soothed—I would have reasoned; but, in the intensity of her wild desire for life,—for life—*but* for life— solace and reason were alike the uttermost of folly. Yet not until the last instance, amid the most convulsive writhings of her fierce spirit, was shaken the external placidity of her demeanor. Her voice grew more gentle—grew more low—yet I would not wish to dwell upon the wild meaning of the quietly uttered words. My brain reeled as I hearkened entranced, to a melody more than mortal—to assumptions and aspirations which mortality had never before known.

° *Azrael*: the Mohammedan angel of death

That she loved me I should not have doubted; and I might have been easily aware that, in a bosom such as hers, love would have reigned no ordinary passion. But in death only, was I fully impressed with the strength of her affection. For long hours, detaining my hand, would she pour out before me the overflowing of a heart whose more than passionate devotion amounted to idolatry. How had I deserved to be so blessed by such confessions?—how had I deserved to be so cursed with the removal of my beloved in the hour of her making them? But upon this subject I cannot bear to dilate. Let me say only, that in Ligeia's more than womanly abandonment to a love, alas! all unmerited, all unworthily bestowed, I at length recognized the principle of her longing with so wildly earnest a desire for the life which was now fleeing so rapidly away. It is this wild longing—it is this eager vehemence of desire for life—*but* for life—that I have no power to portray—no utterance capable of expressing.

At high noon of the night in which she departed, beckoning me, peremptorily, to her side, she bade me repeat certain verses composed by herself not many days before. I obeyed her.—They were these:

> Lo! 't is a gala night
>   Within the lonesome latter years!
> An angel throng, bewinged, bedight
>   In veils, and drowned in tears,
> Sit in a theatre, to see
>   A play of hopes and fears,
> While the orchestra breathes fitfully
>   The music of the spheres.
>
> Mimes, in the form of God on high,
>   Mutter and mumble low,
> And hither and thither fly—
>   Mere puppets they, who come and go
> At bidding of vast formless things
>   That shift the scenery to and fro,
> Flapping from out their Condor wings
>   Invisible Woe!
>
> That motley drama!—oh, be sure
>   It shall not be forgot!
> With its Phantom chased forever more,
>   By a crowd that seize it not,
> Through a circle that ever returneth in
>   To the self-same spot,
> And much of Madness and more of Sin
>   And Horror the soul of the plot.

But see, amid the mimic rout,
  A crawling shape intrude!
A blood-red thing that writhes from out
  The scenic solitude!
It writhes!—it writhes!—with mortal pangs
  The mimes become it food,
And the seraphs sob at vermin fangs
  In human gore imbued.

Out—out are the lights—out all!
  And over each quivering form,
The curtain, a funeral pall,
  Comes down with the rush of a storm,
And the angels, all pallid and wan,
  Uprising, unveiling, affirm
That the play is the tragedy, 'Man,'
  And its hero the Conqueror Worm.

'O God!' half shrieked Ligeia, leaping to her feet and extending her arms aloft with a spasmodic movement, as I made an end of these lines—'O God! O Divine Father!—shall these things be undeviatingly so?—shall this Conqueror be not once conquered? Are we not part and parcel in Thee? Who—who knoweth the mysteries of the will with its vigor? Man doth not yield him to the angels, *nor unto death utterly,* save only through the weakness of his feeble will.'

And now, as if exhausted with emotion, she suffered her white arms to fall, and returned solemnly to her bed of death. And as she breathed her last sighs, there came mingled with them a low murmur from her lips. I bent to them my ear and distinguished, again, the concluding words of the passage in Glanvill—'*Man doth not yield him to the angels, nor unto death utterly, save only through the weakness of his feeble will.*'

She died;—and I, crushed into the very dust with sorrow, could no longer endure the lonely desolation of my dwelling in the dim and decaying city by the Rhine. I had no lack of what the world calls wealth. Ligeia had brought me far more, very far more than ordinarily falls to the lot of mortals. After a few months, therefore, of weary and aimless wandering, I purchased, and put in some repair, an abbey, which I shall not name, in one of the wildest and least frequented portions of fair England. The gloomy and dreary grandeur of the building, the almost savage aspect of the domain, the many melancholy and time-honored memories connected with both, had much in unison with the feelings of utter abandonment which had driven me into that remote and unsocial region of the country. Yet although the external abbey, with its verdant decay hanging about it, suffered but little alteration, I gave way, with a child-like perversity, and perchance with a faint hope of alleviating my sorrows, to a display of more than regal magnificence within.—For such follies, even in childhood, I had imbibed a taste and now they came back to me as if in the dotage of grief. Alas, I feel how much even of incipient madness might have been discovered in the gorgeous and fantastic draperies, in the solemn carvings of Egypt, in the wild cornices and furniture, in the Bedlam patterns of the carpets of tufted gold! I had become a bounden slave in the trammels of opium, and my labors and my orders had taken a coloring from my dreams. But these absurdities I must not pause to detail. Let me speak only of that one chamber, ever accursed, whither in a moment of mental alienation, I led from the altar as my bride—as the successor of the unforgotten Ligeia—the fair-haired and blue-eyed Lady Rowena Trevanion, of Tremaine.

There is no individual portion of the architecture and decoration of that bridal chamber which is not now visibly before me. Where were the souls of the haughty family of the bride, when, through thirst of gold, they permitted to pass the threshold of an apartment so bedecked, a maiden and a daughter so beloved? I have said that I minutely remember the details of the chamber—yet I am sadly forgetful on topics of deep moment—and here there was no system, no keeping, in the fantastic display, to take hold upon the memory. The room lay in a high turret of the castellated abbey, was pentagonal in shape, and of capacious size. Occupying the whole southern face of the pentagon was the sole window —an immense sheet of unbroken glass from Venice—a single pane, and tinted of a leaden hue, so that the rays of either the sun or moon, passing through it, fell with a ghastly lustre on the objects within. Over the upper portion of this huge window, extended the trellice-work of an aged vine, which clambered up the massy walls of the turret. The ceiling, of gloomy-looking oak, was excessively lofty, vaulted, and elaborately fretted with the wildest and most grotesque specimens of a semi-Gothic, semi-Druidical device. From out the most central recess of this melancholy vaulting, depended, by a single chain of gold with long links, a huge censer of the same metal, Saracenic in pattern, and with many perforations so contrived that there writhed in and out of them, as if endued with a serpent vitality, a continual succession of parti-colored fires.

Some few ottomans and golden candelabra, of Eastern figure, were in various stations about—and there was the couch, too—the bridal couch— of an Indian model, and low, and sculptured of solid ebony, with a pall-like canopy above. In each of the angles of the chamber stood on end a gigantic sarcophagus of black granite, from the tombs of the kings over against Luxor, with their aged lids full of immemorial sculpture. But in the draping of the apartment lay, alas! the chief phantasy of all. The lofty walls, gigantic in height—even unproportionably so—were hung from summit to foot, in vast folds, with a heavy and massive-looking tapestry—tapestry of a material which was found alike as a carpet on the floor, as a covering for the ottomans and the ebony bed, as a canopy for the bed, and as the gorgeous volutes of the curtains which partially shaded the window. The material was the richest cloth of gold. It was spotted all over, at irregular intervals, with arabesque figures, about a foot in diameter, and wrought upon the cloth in patterns of the most jetty black. But these figures partook of the true character of the arabesque only when regarded from a single point of view. By a contrivance now common, and indeed traceable to a very remote period of antiquity, they were made changeable in aspect. To one entering the room, they bore the appearance of simple monstrosities; but upon a farther advance, this appearance gradually departed; and step by step, as the visitor moved his station in the chamber, he saw himself surrounded by an endless succession of the ghastly forms which belong to the superstition of the Norman, or arise in the guilty slumbers of the monk. The phantasmagoric effect was vastly heightened by the artificial introduction of a strong continual current of wind behind the draperies—giving a hideous and uneasy animation to the whole.

In halls such as these—in a bridal chamber such as this—I passed, with the Lady of Tremaine, the unhallowed hours of the first month of our marriage—passed them with but little disquietude. That my wife dreaded the fierce moodiness of my temper—that she shunned me and loved me but little—I could not help perceiving; but it gave me rather pleasure than otherwise. I loathed her with a hatred belonging more to demon than to man. My memory flew back, (oh, with what intensity of regret!) to Ligeia, the beloved, the august, the beautiful, the entombed. I revelled in recollections of her purity, of her wisdom, of her lofty, her ethereal nature, of her passionate, her idolatrous love. Now, then, did my spirit fully and freely burn with more than all the fires of her own. In the excitement of my opium dreams (for I was habitually fettered in the shackles of the drug) I would call aloud upon her name, during the silence of the night, or among the sheltered recesses of the glens by day, as if, through the wild eagerness, the solemn passion, the consuming ardor of my longing for the departed, I could restore her to the pathway she had abandoned—ah, *could* it be forever?—upon the earth.

About the commencement of the second month of the marriage, the Lady Rowena was attacked with sudden illness, from which her recovery was slow. The fever which consumed her rendered her nights uneasy; and in her perturbed state of half-slumber, she spoke of sounds, and of motions, in and about the chamber of the turret, which I concluded had no origin save in the distemper of her fancy, or perhaps in the phantasmagoric influences of the chamber itself. She became at length convalescent—finally well. Yet but a brief period elapsed, ere a second more violent disorder again threw her upon a bed of suffering; and from this attack her frame, at all times feeble, never altogether recovered. Her illnesses were, after this epoch, of alarming character, and of more alarming recurrence, defying alike the knowledge and the great exertions of her physicians. With the increase of the chronic disease which had thus, apparently, taken too sure hold upon her constitution to be eradicated by human means, I could not fail to observe a similar increase in the nervous irritation of her temperament, and in her excitability by trivial causes of fear. She spoke again, and now more frequently and pertinaciously, of the sounds—of the slight sounds—and of the unusual motions among the tapestries, to which she had formerly alluded.

One night, near the closing in of September, she pressed this distressing subject with more than usual emphasis upon my attention. She had just awakened from an unquiet slumber, and I had been watching, with feelings half of anxiety, half of vague terror, the workings of her emaciated countenance. I sat by the side of her ebony bed, upon one of the ottomans of India. She partly arose, and spoke, in an earnest low whisper, of sounds which she *then* heard, but which I could not hear—of motions which she *then* saw, but which I could not perceive. The wind was rushing hurriedly behind the tapestries, and I wished to show her (what, let me confess it, I could not *all* believe) that those almost inarticulate breathings, and those very gentle variations of the figures upon the wall, were but the natural effects of that customary rushing of the wind. But a deadly pallor, overspreading her face, had proved to me that my exertions to reassure her would be fruitless. She appeared to be fainting, and no attendants were within call. I remembered where was deposited a decanter of light wine which had been ordered by her physicians, and hastened across the chamber to procure it. But, as I stepped beneath the light of the censer, two circumstances of a startling nature attracted my attention. I had felt that some palpable although invisible object had passed lightly by my person; and I saw that there lay upon the golden carpet, in the very middle of the rich lustre thrown from the censer, a shadow—a faint, indefinite shadow of angelic aspect—such as might be fancied for the shadow of a shade. But I was wild with the excitement of an immoderate dose of opium, and heeded these things but little, nor spoke of them to Rowena. Having found the wine, I recrossed the chamber, and poured out a goblet-ful, which I held to the lips of the fainting lady. She had now partially recovered, however, and took the vessel herself, while I sank upon an ottoman near me, with my eyes fastened upon her person. It was then that I became distinctly aware of a gentle foot-fall upon the carpet, and near the couch; and in a second thereafter, as Rowena was in the act of raising the wine to her lips, I saw, or may have dreamed that I saw, fall within the goblet, as if from some invisible spring in the atmosphere of the room, three or four large drops of a brilliant and ruby colored fluid. If this I saw—not so Rowena. She swallowed the wine unhesitatingly, and I forbore to speak to her of a circumstance which must, after all, I considered, have been but the suggestion of a vivid imagination, rendered morbidly active by the terror of the lady, by the opium, and by the hour.

Yet I cannot conceal it from my own perception that, immediately subsequent to the fall of the ruby-drops, a rapid change for the worse took place in the disorder of my wife; so that, on the third subsequent night, the hands of her menials prepared her for the tomb, and on the fourth, I sat alone, with her shrouded body, in that fantastic chamber which had received her as my bride.—Wild visions, opium-engendered, flitted, shadow-like, before me. I gazed with unquiet eye upon the sarcophagi in the angles of the room, upon the varying figures of the drapery, and upon the writhing of the parti-colored fires in the censer overhead. My eyes then fell, as I called to mind the circumstances of a former night, to the spot beneath the glare of the censer where I had seen the faint traces of the shadow. It was there, however, no longer; and breathing with greater freedom, I turned my glances to the pallid and rigid figure upon the bed. Then rushed upon me a thousand memories of Ligeia—and then came back upon my heart, with the turbulent violence of a flood, the whole of that unutterable woe with which I had regarded *her* thus enshrouded. The night waned; and still, with a bosom full of bitter thoughts of the one only and supremely beloved, I remained gazing upon the body of Rowena.

It might have been midnight, or perhaps earlier, or later, for I had taken no note of time, when a sob, low, gentle, but very distinct, startled me from my revery.—I *felt* that it came from the bed of ebony—the bed of death. I listened in an agony of superstitious terror—but there was no repetition of the sound. I strained my vision to detect any motion in the corpse—but there was not the slightest perceptible. Yet I could not have been deceived. I *had* heard the noise, however faint, and my soul was awakened within me. I resolutely and perseveringly kept my attention riveted upon the body. Many minutes elapsed before any circumstance occurred tending to throw light upon the mystery. At length it became evident that a slight, a very feeble, and barely noticeable tinge of color had flushed up within the cheeks, and along the sunken small veins of the eyelids. Through a species of unutterable horror and awe, for which the language of mortality has no sufficiently energetic expression, I felt my heart cease to beat, my limbs grow rigid where I sat. Yet a sense of duty finally operated to restore my self-possession. I could no longer doubt that we had been precipitate in our preparations—that Rowena still lived. It was necessary that some immediate exertion be made; yet the turret was altogether apart from the portion of the abbey tenanted by the servants—there were none within call—I had no means of summoning them to my aid without leaving the room for many minutes—and this I could not venture to do. I therefore struggled alone in my endeavors to call back the spirit still hovering. In a short period it was certain, however, that a relapse had taken place; the color disappeared from both eyelid and cheek, leaving a wanness even more than that of marble; the lips became doubly shrivelled and pinched up in the ghastly expression of death; a repulsive clamminess and coldness overspread rapidly the surface of the body; and all the usual rigorous stiffness immediately supervened. I fell back with a shudder upon the couch from which I had been so startlingly aroused, and again gave myself up to passionate waking visions of Ligeia.

An hour thus elapsed when (could it be possible?) I was a second time aware of some vague sound issuing from the region of the bed. I listened—in extremity of horror. The sound came again—it was a sigh. Rushing to the corpse, I saw—distinctly saw—a tremor upon the lips. In a minute afterward they relaxed, disclosing a bright line of the pearly teeth. Amazement now struggled in my bosom with the profound awe which had hitherto reigned there alone. I felt that my vision grew dim, that my reason wandered; and it was only by a violent effort that I at length succeeded in nerving myself to the task which duty thus once more had pointed out. There was now a partial glow upon the forehead and upon the cheek and throat; a perceptible warmth pervaded the whole frame; there was even a slight pulsation at the heart. The lady *lived;* and with redoubled ardor I betook myself to the task of restoration. I chafed and bathed the temples and the hands, and used every exertion which experience, and no little medical reading, could suggest. But in vain. Suddenly, the color fled, the pulsation ceased, the lips resumed the expression of the dead, and, in an instant afterward, the whole body took upon itself the icy chilliness, the livid hue, the intense rigidity, the sunken outline, and all the loathsome peculiarities of that which has been, for many days, a tenant of the tomb.

And again I sunk into visions of Ligeia—and again, (what marvel that I shudder while I write?) *again* there reached my ears a low sob from the region of the ebony bed. But why shall I minutely detail the unspeakable horrors of that night? Why shall I pause to relate how, time after time, until near the period of the gray dawn, this hideous drama of revification was repeated; how each terrific relapse was only into a sterner and apparently more irredeemable death; how each agony wore the aspect of a struggle with some invisible foe; and how each struggle was succeeded by I know not what of wild change in the personal appearance of the corpse? Let me hurry to a conclusion.

The greater part of the fearful night had worn away, and she who had been dead, once again stirred—and now more vigorously than hitherto, although arousing from a dissolution more appalling in its utter hopelessness than any. I had long ceased to struggle or to move, and remained sitting rigidly upon the ottoman, a helpless prey to a whirl of violent emotions, of which extreme awe was perhaps the least terrible, the least consuming. The corpse, I repeat, stirred, and now more vigorously than before. The hues of life flushed up with unwonted energy into the countenance—the limbs relaxed—and, save that the eyelids were yet pressed heavily together, and that the bandages and draperies of the grave still imparted their charnel character to the figure, I might have dreamed that Rowena had indeed shaken off, utterly, the fetters of Death. But if this idea was not, even then, altogether adopted, I could at least doubt no longer, when, arising from the bed, tottering, with feeble steps, with closed eyes, and with the manner of one bewildered in a dream, the thing that was enshrouded advanced boldly and palpably into the middle of the apartment.

I trembled not—I stirred not—for a crowd of unutterable fancies connected with the air, the stature, the demeanor of the figure, rushing hurriedly through my brain, had paralyzed— had chilled me into stone. I stirred not—but gazed upon the apparition. There was a mad disorder in my thoughts—a tumult unappeasable. Could it, indeed, be the *living* Rowena who confronted me? Could it indeed be Rowena *at all*—the fair-haired, the blue-eyed Lady Rowena Trevanion of Tremaine? Why, *why* should I doubt it? The bandage lay heavily about the mouth—but then might it not be the mouth of the breathing Lady of Tremaine? And the cheeks—there were the roses as in her noon of life—yes, these might indeed be the fair cheeks of the living Lady of Tremaine. And the chin, with its dimples, as in health, might it not be hers?—but *had she then grown taller since her malady?* What inexpressible madness seized me with that thought? One bound, and I had reached her feet! Shrinking from my touch, she let fall from her head, unloosened, the ghastly cerements which had confined it, and there streamed forth, into the rushing atmosphere of the chamber, huge masses of long and dishevelled hair; *it was blacker than the raven wings of the midnight!* And now slowly opened *the eyes* of the figure which stood before me. 'Here then, at least,' I shrieked aloud, 'can I never—can I never be mistaken—these are the full, and the black, and the wild eyes—of my lost love—of the lady–of the LADY LIGEIA.'

A SONG OF PRAISE

Countee Cullen (1903–1946)

(for one who praised his lady's being fair)

You have not heard my love's dark throat,
    Slow-fluting like a reed,
Release the perfect golden note
    She caged there for my need.

Her walk is like the replica   5
    Of some barbaric dance
Wherein the soul of Africa
    Is winged with arrogance.

And yet so light she steps across
    The ways her sure feet pass,   10
She does not dent the smoothest moss
    Or bend the thinnest grass.

My love is dark as yours is fair,
    Yet lovelier I hold her
Than listless maids with pallid hair,   15
    And blood that's thin and colder.

You-proud-and-to-be-pitied one,
    Gaze on her and despair;
Then seal your lips until the sun
    Discovers one as fair.   20

THE CRYSTAL CABINET

William Blake (1757–1827)

The Maiden caught me in the Wild,
Where I was dancing merrily;
She put me into her Cabinet
And Lock'd me up with a golden Key.

This Cabinet is form'd of Gold   5
And Pearl & Crystal shining bright,
And within it opens into a World
And a little lovely Moony Night.

Another England there I saw,
Another London with its Tower,   10
Another Thames & other Hills,
And another pleasant Surrey Bower,

Another Maiden like herself,
Translucent, lovely, shining clear,
Threefold each in the other clos'd—   15
O, what a pleasant trembling fear!

O, what a smile! a threefold Smile
Fill'd me, that like a flame I burn'd;
I bent to Kiss the lovely Maid,
And found a Threefold Kiss return'd.   20

I strove to seize the inmost Form
With ardor fierce & hands of flame,
But burst the Crystal Cabinet,
And like a Weeping Babe became—

A weeping Babe upon the wild,   25
And Weeping Woman pale reclin'd,
And in the outward air again
I fill'd with woes the passing Wind.

ADAM'S CURSE

William Butler Yeats (1865–1939)

We sat together at one summer's end,
That beautiful mild woman, your close friend,
And you and I, and talked of poetry.
I said: 'A line will take us hours maybe;
Yet if it does not seem a moment's thought,   5
Our stitching and unstitching has been naught.

Better go down upon your marrow-bones
And scrub a kitchen pavement, or break stones
Like an old pauper, in all kinds of weather;
For to articulate sweet sounds together   10
Is to work harder than all these, and yet

Be thought an idler by the noisy set
Of bankers, schoolmasters, and clergymen
The martyrs call the world.'

And thereupon
That beautiful mild woman for whose sake   15
There's many a one shall find out all heartache
On finding that her voice is sweet and low
Replied: 'To be born woman is to know—
Although they do not talk of it at school—
That we must labour to be beautiful.'   20

I said: 'It's certain there is no fine thing
Since Adam's fall but needs much labouring.
There have been lovers who thought love should be
So much compounded of high courtesy
That they would sigh and quote with learned looks   25
Precedents out of beautiful old books;
Yet now it seems an idle trade enough.'

We sat grown quiet at the name of love;
We saw the last embers of daylight die,
And in the trembling blue-green of the sky   30
A moon, worn as if it had been a shell
Washed by time's waters as they rose and fell
About the stars and broke in days and years.

I had a thought for no one's but your ears:
That you were beautiful, and that I strove   35
To love you in the old high way of love;
That it had all seemed happy, and yet we'd grown
As weary-hearted as that hollow moon.

ALL THINGS TO ALL MEN°

M. Esther Harding (1888–1971)

In childhood we are taught certain stories and myths telling of the origin of the world and of mankind and giving a general view of life and

---

°The essay by M. Esther Harding (which is taken from the first chapter of her book *The Way of All Women*) offers a psychological interpretation of why men are attracted to certain types of women and sets up a framework for understanding human behavior. Her observations are based on the psychological discoveries of Carl Jung and on her own experience as a psychotherapist.

From *The Way of All Women* by M. Esther Harding. Reprinted with permission of the C. G. Jung Foundation.

of conduct. It is as though they said: "This is the way things came into being, and this shows their essential nature and relationship." These legends and tales which appeal so immediately to the child are for the most part as old as historical man and hark back to the infancy of the race. The views they express, insofar as they are still binding today, must represent something deeply embedded in the mind of man. Man has corrected and refined these beliefs in certain realms; in other spheres they remain powers in the background, determining his conduct. In no way are these unseen and unrecognized forces more strikingly manifested than in man's general attitude toward woman.

"In the beginning"—according to the record in Genesis—"God created the heaven and the earth" with all that they contained. The summit of his creation was mankind—"male and female created He them." In this statement is expressed a belief in divine creation, but the statement is also intended to account for the simple fact that mankind is *both* male and female. The first chapter of Genesis contains, however, another and a better known version of the making of man: it is the story of Adam's sleep and of the creation of Eve by the removal of one of his ribs. This story shows woman conceived of as a part of man, taken out of his side while he is unconscious. It is a myth which represents woman as an unconscious part of man, wholly secondary to him, without any living spirit or soul of her own. This myth illustrates an attitude fundamental in man's view of woman. If the story had been told by women we should have had a different account of the creation. For instance, in a school examination paper the question was set: "Give an account of the creation of man." A little girl wrote: "First God created Adam. Then He looked at him and said, 'I think if I tried again I could do better.' Then He created Eve." Here we have a perfectly naive feminine version of the story.

There is a great discrepancy, I admit, between a myth hallowed by age and religious tradition and this school child's version of it. But from the psychological point of view they are nonetheless valid examples of the rift between two attitudes. This rift is illustrated, on the one hand, by man's still prevalent way of regarding woman and, on the other, by the worst exaggeration of the feminist movement.

Where does the truth lie? Is it to be found somewhere between the two points of view or is it necessary to approach the whole subject from an entirely different angle?

The first condition for an impartial investigation into the relationships between men and women is to rule out old assumptions of the superiority or the inferiority of one to the other. We must not hold the view that woman is man's inferior, nor must we take our stand on the little girl's version of the creation and assume that man is a creature who has not yet evolved to the female standard. This latter view is secretly held by many women, but they never express it directly, for to do so would be heresy. Indeed, the majority of women who hold it most firmly would deny it if challenged. But if we talk with them we can see this assumption underlying such simple comments as: "Men are so stupid," "Men, poor things, they can't help it," "They are all children," and so on. The implication is that women are wiser and more adult than men, but this is kept secret. It is not only not talked about, it is not even formulated, and the women who say such things about men do not really *think* them in their heads.

It is not the woman who resembles the aggressive woman of the feminist movement who makes such comments.° She is too concerned with trying to be man's equal and so discounts all differences, physiological as well as psychological. She never depreciates man, for her aim is to be like a man, equal to a man, no whit his inferior. She no longer has any standpoint for criticism of him, because she has sold her birthright, her feminine inheritance, her uniqueness, by cancelling the difference arising from the fact that she is female. It is only the very feminine women who in secret speak so condescendingly of men. Such women are strong in their feminine position; they make no attempt to rival men; they do not want an individual position in the world, for they are wanted by men who, indeed, are even willing to support them.

Just what, then, is the difference between the woman who is the man's woman and the woman who is not the man's woman? Men have often commented upon it. Their attention has been caught by the latter type of woman only because of her competition, which threatens them in business or in the professions, or because of her insistence on her political rights. But their deeper interest has been in the man's woman, primarily on account of what she has meant to them personally. She has been repeatedly portrayed in plays and novels and we can sense her peculiar influence in lyric poetry which so often celebrates her. She figures in myths and legends, but she is always shown from the man's point of view. And even when, as in these modern days, attempts are made to give a more objective picture of human beings, we find that such women are still described, for the most part, from the masculine point of view. There is, for instance, no outstanding autobiography written by a woman of this type which presents to our closer scrutiny her own inner experience of life. For these women most often present themselves to us solely in terms of their external experience; they recount outer events and the part they played in them but fail to convey a picture of their inner experience. Possibly they are not sufficiently aware of themselves to be able to give a picture of what their subjective life is like. For this type of woman is generally very unselfconscious; she does not analyze herself or her motives;

°Harding is referring to the feminist movement of the early part of the 20th century. (*All Things to All Men* was written in 1933.)

she just *is;* and for the most she is inarticulate. Furthermore she has, as a rule, no urge to make herself understood by a large audience. Her interest and her life lie in her relation to one man or perhaps to two or three men; hers is a *personal* interest, not one which concerns itself with a larger group. Hence it is that women of this type, numerous as they are—for, indeed, they may be considered to make up the primary type of womanhood—have never been interpreted truly. Their silence has become their "mystery." A mass of literature has grown up about them which purports to explain them, but the explanation is always based on the man's idea of the woman; it is never the woman's interpretation of herself.

C. G. Jung faced this problem more effectively than any other psychologist. Not only did he analyze the problem of the significance of woman from the point of view of the man, but he, alone among psychologists, clearly differentiated between this subjective significance and the objective reality of the woman herself and defined clearly the type which can most readily carry for the man the significance of his own subjective and unconscious values. But here Jung's further discussion of the subject necessarily meets a blank wall. He, as a man, can tell us relatively little of the woman herself and of her part in the proceeding. Only from the point of view of an observer can he tell us what value, if any, *she* gains from carrying the image of the man's unconscious values and from associating with the man who thus glorifies her.

Such a woman, who is peculiarly adapted through her own natural gifts to be man's partner, in the fashion implied in the Genesis idyl, is the primary type of woman *in nature.* She is the female human animal, whose whole attention is focussed instinctively on her mate. She adapts herself to his wishes, makes herself beautiful in his eyes, charms him, pleases him. These things are naturally a manifestation of the fundamental biological relation between the sexes. But where these instinctive reactions appear in modern women the aim of Mother Nature is masked, in accordance with the conventional code, while the woman herself may be quite unaware of the hidden meaning of her actions.

Primitive woman was doubtless quite content with the role the Genesis myth assigned to her, for in primitive situations, where the biological aim is the sole guide in life, that the woman shall be attractive to the man and shall call forth and hold his interest is all that is important for life and for her. Even until today some women have remained almost as unconscious as their most remote ancestress and are still content to be only man's helpmeet and counterpart. But humanity at large has moved since those days toward a greater consciousness, chiefly through the emergence of a conscious and personal ego whose aims have conflicted with the simple urges which Mother Nature first implanted in our breasts. Thus, as woman has evolved and become more aware of herself as a separate entity—an ego—a conflict has arisen within her psyche between the individual values which she has attained and the ancient, collective, feminine trends—and conflict is the beginning of consciousness.

There are three typical stages of development through which the human being passes in the gradual evolution of consciousness. These may be called the *naive,* the *sophisticated* and the *conscious.* The first, or naive, is related to nature only. It is a way of functioning which is entirely unselfconscious. It is, so to speak, the state of man before the Fall, when he was entirely innocent and at one with himself. In this stage there is hardly any differentiation between conscious and unconscious, for selfconsciousness has not arisen. The individual lives in a primitive union with nature, a state broken only by the emergence of the ego. This is a change of great importance in the development of the personality and is a definite step toward consciousness.

From this point the individual enters the period of sophistication. The natural powers within him and the resources of the world without are gradually explored and exploited, and the capacities and powers thus gained are organized under the leadership of the ego. Personal aggrandizement and the satisfaction of the ego arise and form a new life-motive. The lust for power comes to occupy an increasing place. But at this point a new factor may come into the picture. The selfishness of the power attitude may obtrude itself on consciousness. Love perhaps arises which will dispute the dominant position of the ego, or some other value which transcends personal considerations may replace those formerly held. This change in emphasis inaugurates a gradual redemption of the personality from the dominance of the ego, and the third stage—the stage of consciousness—begins.

In the innocent play of domestic animals we may see certain ways of acting which we recognize as fundamentally masculine or feminine. The arts and wiles which the female uses to attract the male are so nearly akin to the ways of a pretty woman that we cannot help smiling. These things are manifestations of primitive femininity. They can be seen too in tiny children. A little girl, while still quite young, begins to act in a different way from a little boy. Where he is independent and aggressive, she is coy and winsome. She begins very early in life to gain her ends through coaxing or merely through being adorable. Her whole way of functioning is in relation to someone else from whom she may attract attention or care or love. In many grown women we see the same process at work. The woman herself is doubtless unaware of what she is doing. She may have no deeper motive than eagerness to *please,* to do what is expected of her, to fulfill another person's ideal of her. This other person is usually a man. She rarely stops to ask what she herself wants or how she feels. She is content if he is content, provided his contentment is only to be attained through her. In this way she makes of herself a sort of mirror which reflects the man's mood, his half-unrealized feelings. If he is sad, she is melancholy. If he is joyous, she bubbles with mirth. And, indeed, so subtle is her unconscious, or half-unconscious, intuition of his mood that often she will react to it while he himself is still unaware of what his mood is. So it is that he seems to discover what should be his own feeling *in her*. For men tend to be exceedingly unconscious of their own feeling moods. Even though a man may have suffered an intense personal loss he is very likely to react to it as an almost *impersonal* emergency, requiring a practical adaptation only, and to remain entirely unaware that he has also a feeling reaction to it as a *personal* experience. All he knows is that he feels out of harmony with himself. In this state he goes to see a woman such as we have been describing. She senses his mood almost before he speaks to her. Regardless of what she had been thinking or feeling before his arrival she now reflects the feeling of which he is unaware. If he has had a blow which he does not recognize as an emotional one, it is melancholy she reflects—a great vague, contentless yearning. As he does not know what there is to be sorry about, her melancholy cannot have much point or content, but this very vagueness allows his own sorrow or regret to find a place in her. He can project his unconscious feeling on to her, and no matter what it may be it can flow into her and so find its own form, undisturbed by any preconceptions on her part. He feels his personal sorrow raised to the level of a universal grief and is relieved of his own pain in contemplating the pain of mankind. By his contact with her he has gained a contact with his own feeling, and through the generalization of her mood he has found a way of adapting to his own grief which, left unrealized, might have overwhelmed him.

So it is that a man can find in such a woman an image or picture of the other part of himself, otherwise unknown to him, which indeed he does not recognize as belonging to himself. This image seems to be in her; he perceives it, but as though it were her feeling, not his own. When a subjective content is experienced in this way it is commonly spoken of as *projected*. The fact that its subjective source is not recognized means that it is in a sense *unconscious*. When projected by a man upon a woman it is like a mirage, an illusion, concealing the woman who is there; his own unconscious feeling-contents meet him in personified form. The sum of these contents make up the unrecognized part of man's psyche and when brought together into a whole constitute the man's feminine soul,° which

---

° *Soul* is here used in a psychological, not a theological, sense. When Jung speaks of the *soul* he is concerned "with the psychological recognition of the existence of a semiconscious psychic complex, having partial autonomy of function. . . . The autonomy of the soul-complex naturally lends support to the notion of an invisible, personal entity that apparently lives in a world very different from ours." (*Two Essays on Analytical Psychology*, pp. 188–189.) The reader is referred to Jung's discussion of this whole subject in the *Two Essays* and to the definitions of soul and soul-image in the chapter "Definitions" in *Psychological Types*. Wherever in

exercises over him an irresistible fascination and appears variously as *La Desirée* or *La Belle Dame sans Merci*. This feminine soul of the man Jung has called *anima*.°

Men with the same inherited background have anima figures which are strangely similar, so that the anima herself can be recognized by her characteristics, which are universal and collective. In imaginative writings, especially in novels and plays the anima is often drawn unmistakably. Anima figures form the central characters in such imaginative stories as *She* by Rider Haggard, *Green Mansions* by W. H. Hudson, and many others. She-who-must-be-obeyed and the Bird Girl represent the anima of their authors. They have certain characteristics in common: they are only part human (each is both more and less than a real woman), they carry feeling values, and each has a quality which makes her lightest word a command, absolutely binding on the hero.

These are portrayals of the anima herself, the collective soul of man, which we feel to be non-human, but many women, both in fiction and in real life, show certain anima characteristics which are more or less modified by human traits. For although it is true that a man's anima as a rule becomes apparent to him only when it is projected onto a woman, yet the anima herself is not a real woman. She represents rather a collective, or universalized, picture of woman as she has appeared through the centuries of human experience *in relation to man*. This last factor is important. All that a man sees is colored for him by his own subjective contents. And inasmuch as woman, throughout the ages, has been to man the symbol of his unknown feminine soul, his eyes have been peculiarly blinded when he has looked at her. A man without a soul is but half a man; consequently when his soul is projected onto another human being it is as though half of himself were in her. The woman becomes enormously important as well as enormously attractive to him. He longs to get into relation with her, for by so doing he will come into relation once more with his own soul, which is otherwise lost to him.

Certain women have a peculiar aptitude for reflecting the man's anima. However, not all women have this gift. Those who are so endowed form a definite group, although naturally the women comprising it differ markedly from one another in many particulars, for this group makes up a large proportion of womanhood throughout the world and contains women of many qualities. Yet there are certain characteristics held by all

---

this book technical terms have been used, the author has endeavored to use them in the sense in which Jung has defined them, either in the chapter on definitions referred to or scattered throughout his other writings. [Author's note.]

° Jung put the "-a" ending on the Latin word for mind, feeling, will (a person's spirit or soul) to signify the feminine nature of a man's unconscious ("the anima") and the "-us" ending on the same word to signify the masculine nature of a woman's unconscious ("the animus"). Simply put, the anima is the woman within man, and the animus is the man within woman; they personify psychological bisexuality.

these women in common—a fact which justifies our speaking of them as forming a distinct anima type.

The general characteristics of the anima woman change as she passes through the different stages of psychological development. In the first, or naive, stage she is a natural, instinctive creature. She manifests in her every action the innocent functioning of feminine instinct. Her whole attention is directed, albeit without her conscious knowledge, to the effects she produces on men. She is completely naive. She has no conscious critique of her own actions and motives; she has no objective standard or criterion at all. It never occurs to her to judge herself by an external standard, or, indeed, to view herself as object. She is just female creature, as unconscious of herself and as innocent as the domestic animals. If a man projects his anima onto her, she is unaware of it. She simply lives what she feels and what she is. She is related to herself and to her own instinctive satisfactions, just as the animals are. She is a nature product. And for this reason she never knows beforehand what she wants. She is ambiguous. "She will and she won't." The opposites in her sleep side by side, so that she has a certain bivalent quality, like nature. The man senses his soul in her and seeks to be united with her. His anima is also, like nature, bivalent. So her ambiguity fits in with his need.

In time the ego awakes in her and the second stage of development begins. She finds that by living instinctively she attracts the attention of a man or of men. The man, finding in her a symbol or picture of his soul, wants a close relationship with her so that he may be reunited to his own soul. Because of this urgent need he is willing to give her almost anything she asks. She wants a relationship with him too, or perhaps we should say "Nature in her" wants it for biological ends. But because she is, as a rule, unaware of this natural urge within her she acts as though she were indifferent, with the result that the man pays further court to her. Then if her ego comes to consciousness she makes a discovery, namely that this seeming indifference makes her more desirable from the man's point of view; and she begins to use it as a definite trick, of which she is at least partly aware, to attract the man's attention and gifts. Or perhaps the woman is truly indifferent and cold. She may really not want the man's attentions but she realizes that the power she has over him is a great asset. If she then, either deliberately or half-unconsciously, begins to exploit the man's projection using his need to her own advantage, the flirt gradually emerges, who in her worst aspect becomes the "gold digger."

Ego development in the anima woman, however, may show itself in a much more adapted and social form. For instance, a woman may use her charm and the attraction she has for men in a socially desirable and acceptable way, which is yet a conscious use of her gifts to attain an end. If she is married she develops skill in managing her husband and the whole situation between them. She is always at hand, she always anticipates his wishes, she makes home so pleasant that he of necessity has to fall in with her plans and do what is expected of him. A woman of this type makes what is popularly called a "wise wife." Her ego orientation is not directed to such purely personal and selfish ends as in the case of the flirt and the gold digger, but to ends which are seemingly legitimate, namely making her husband happy and her marriage a success. The danger of this orientation becomes apparent, however, when we sense a subtle emphasis on the possessive pronoun. It is *her* husband, *her* marriage! In order to keep her husband happy such a woman almost inevitably has to reserve a part of her reactions. She gives him only as much of her feelings as is calculated to be good for him, and by skillful management she keeps him unaware not only of a certain lack of reality in her reactions but also of the fact that life is humdrum and dull. If, however, she should be ill or obliged to be away from home it may be that the husband will wake up and begin to find life apart from his all-loving wife far more interesting than when he was perpetually lapped about by her solicitous care. Then he becomes aware that her kindness and unselfishness are not all they seemed, and the egocentric attitude behind her mask of the "good wife" peeps out.'

If such a woman is to develop beyond the stage of egocentricity something more is needed than the refinement of her desires for personal success and happiness. Her natural capacity to attract the man's anima projection gives her an importance and power which are in a certain sense fictitious, for she has done nothing to merit them. They depend solely on the man's illusion. It is like a fortune put into her hands for which she has not had to work. To sacrifice this power requires real devotion to a purpose or value which is superior to her own ego. Redemption from primitive instinct, on the one hand, and the domination of the egotistic attitude, on the other, demand first that the woman become aware of her own instinct and of the part she plays in relation to the man. If she truly loves him or if a deeper relation to life develops within her, then the whole current of her desire may be diverted toward a non-personal goal— to one which supersedes the goal of personal satisfaction and superiority. Thus a fresh step is made in the conscious development of the individual—a step toward individuation.°

°It is necessary here to distinguish between the use of the terms *collective, individual,* and *personal*. As far as possible Jung's usage has been followed. For example, in *Psychological Types* Jung says that "men who in public life are extremely energetic, bold, obstinate, willful, and inconsiderate" may at home "appear good-natured, mild, accommodating, even weak" (p. 589). He asks "which, then, is the true character, the real personality?" and answers, "According to my view . . . such a man has no real character at all, i.e., he is not *individual* but *collective*, i.e., he corresponds with general circumstances and expectations. . . . He is an individual, of course, like every being: but an unconscious one. Through his more or less complete identification with the attitude of the moment, he at least deceives others, and also

It is the primitive, feminine element in woman which catches the projection of the man's anima in actual life. There is in all women a streak or thread of this primitive femininity, although in some women it may be almost entirely repressed and in others kept out of sight by a conscious effort. Our Western education of girls seeks to eradicate its manifestations as far as possible; hence with the majority of our women it remains a trend, a factor of their psychology, but not the dominating one. This trend, however, is the ruling factor in the personality of certain women and girls who make up the groups of anima women. It is interesting to note how such a woman functions in life and how she affects those around her.

When a woman of marked anima type comes into a community, all the young men, unmarried and married alike, are immediately fascinated by her. Their heads are turned and they cannot say too much in her praise, while they vie with each other in showing her attentions. The women, however, have a different opinion of her. At first they are merely cold and aloof but soon become critical and blame her for the defections of their husbands and lovers. They usually make the mistake of criticizing her to their men and are horrified to find that the men defend her. Or if masculine courage is lacking for that—and it takes a courage of no mean order for a man to defend a woman when feminine public opinion condemns her—the men compensate for what they consider injustice and prejudice on the part of their women by redoubling their attentions to her. This merely adds to the feminine fury against the "depraved woman," the "hussy." But what of the woman herself? She will say: "I only want to be left alone, to go my own way and live my own life. I do not set out to attract men, and I certainly do not want to estrange them from their wives and sweethearts. Why do all the women shun me and mistrust me? I am lonely and want a woman friend. I want to be good. But wherever I go men follow me, they offer to see me home and even make improper advances to me. Is it my fault? I do not want it. But the poor things are so unhappy I simply must comfort them as far as I can; only a woman with a heart of stone could do less. But I always send them home to their wives or sweethearts. Can I help it if they come back?" Such, at all events, is her way of putting the case.

Now here are three different estimates of the same situation. The man's estimate is based on the value he finds through being able to project his anima and in that way to make a relation to his own unconscious. The wives, on the other hand, hate one who acts the part of anima, as they

_____

often himself, as to his real character. He puts on a *mask*. ... A man who is identified with this mask I would call 'personal' (as opposed to 'individual') " (p. 590). "The psychological individual is characterized by its peculiar, unique psychology. . . . The psychological individual, or individuality, has an a priori unconscious existence. ... A conscious process of differentiation is required to bring the individuality to consciousness" (pp. 560–61). [Author's note.]

think, shamelessly. Their resistance to her is doubtless strengthened because they would all like to have her power over men, but their moral code prevents them from exercising even such powers as they have. It is a case of "they could if they would but they dare not." And their involuntary renunciation makes them bitter as it did the fox who called the grapes sour.

Meanwhile the woman herself remains quite unconscious of what she is doing. She feels herself to be entirely innocent. Her actions and their results have no connection. She cannot see herself as a whole. When talking with such a woman one gets a sense of the most amazing ambiguity and of the extraordinary ambivalence of her every word and action. She does not know in the least that she invites the attentions of the men who flock around her or that she plays them off one against another. She just *is*. And no one is more amazed at the result of her actions than she herself. I remember once seeing a girl of this type who was saying goodby to a group of admirers clustered around her. She shook hands with all but one. As it gradually dawned on him that she was passing him by, he looked more and more crestfallen and slipped away from the group to open the door for her. As she came out he said in the greatest dejection, "Aren't you going to say goodby to me?" "Oh, I thought you were going to see me home," she replied. Needless to say the young man went with her, although up to that moment he had had no intention of leaving the party so early. But—and here we come to the interesting part of the incident— the girl had had no intention of asking him to leave with her. Her oversight of him had been purely accidental, it was not till she saw his dejected attitude that it occurred to her to ask him to accompany her. Further, she had no idea that he would interpret her action as singling him out from her admirers. She was later both hurt and puzzled to discover that he had construed her action as encouragement and that, on this basis, he expected her to accept a greater intimacy with him. She was more puzzled to find that the other admirers were jealous of the preference she had unwittingly shown him.

A girl of this type will say the most provocative things and will allow herself to become involved in a compromising situation with one whom, perhaps, she really dislikes, only to be amazed and hurt when he takes her words and actions at their face value. Or perhaps she wishes to dismiss an admirer. She really wants to be rid of him, but instead of taking a definite stand, telling him plainly that she does not like his attentions, she compromises, puts him off. She runs away, as it were, but always gives him a final glance over her shoulder, with a "come hither" look in her eye. If one challenges this attitude she defends it by saying, "It would be so cruel to dismiss him finally; I am only trying to get him to accept the idea of separation gradually." It never occurs to her that she is like the good lady who, on being told that the puppy's tail had been docked, said, "Oh, how cruel to cut it all off at once. Why didn't they do it a bit at a time so that the puppy could get used to it?" The anima woman is kind, but her kindness is cruelty, and her innocent goodness makes her act as the most sophisticated man-killer would. For this type of woman is a nature product, and nature is always bivalent—good and bad, kind and cruel.

All these ways of acting are purely feminine; they are collective, not individual, and occur whenever masculine interests and desires—masculine libido in short—are brought into contact with feminine libido. Women in whom this way of functioning is strong find the same attitude in *all* the men they meet. To them all men are alike. Therefore *all* men may find in such a woman a collective feminine attitude which can accept every man and his masculine libido no matter what form it takes. Such a woman is truly "all things to all men." . . .

Women who function primarily as the anima of men are not by any means all alike in character or personality, but beneath their external differences a fundamental similarity in psychological attitude and reaction can be found which accounts for the effect they produce in life and especially on men. Three kinds of women will be described who apparently are poles asunder, as different from each other as women could be, and yet on deeper investigation it will become clear that they all have a basic attitude to life which is characteristic of the anima woman and differentiates her from others.

First, we have the innocent flower-like maiden who is generally fair and pretty, who always suggests innocence and who, regardless of what her age may be, invariably plays the part of a child. She is the heroine of many books. She is always pure and good; she may be sinned against, but she never sins. She is man's good angel. Dora in *David Copperfield* is just such a person. She is ignorant of the world and its ways, yet she is often engaged in trying to reform some reprobate who, whatever his faults may be, has at least ventured into the struggle of life instead of remaining on the outskirts as she has done. Such a girl is glorified out of all semblance to reality by the projection of the man's anima, for when he sees his anima—his soul—in her, she becomes to him an "angel child." To one who is not under this illusion, she appears a dull enough little thing. Her education is often defective and generally consists of a knowledge of how to dress and how to hold her tongue, though in the latter accomplishment she may be deficient! She rarely has anything to offer in the way of achievement, yet her charm and good looks and her "influence for good" undoubtedly have their place in the world. Under this flower-like innocence, however, one may often glimpse a "something" which suggests that the girl is not so innocent and disinterested as she appears. Her gestures seem to hint that she perhaps fancies herself in the role of guardian angel, or she shows a tendency, scarcely recognized by herself, to seek the center of the stage. The dreams and fantasies of such girls may unmistakably show the ego trend in the unconscious. One girl dreamed that she was dressed like little Lord Fauntleroy coming down a wide staircase into a large hall where a group of people, all gazing at her in silent admiration, awaited her. The analysis of such a girl often reveals deeply hidden away a cherished fantasy of herself as a princess. In real life women of this type nearly always select from their group of admirers the important men as recipients of their favors and, as a rule, make what is called a good marriage. All these things indicate that the ego which is so conspicuously absent from the conscious personality is not entirely missing but is in the unconscious, so that an ego trend poisons, as it were, the purity of the girl's motives in every situation.

The flower-like anima girl is doomed to be a child to the end of her days. Childishness may be charming enough while she is still young; it may be tolerable even through her thirties; but after that it becomes pathetic or boresome, for she goes through life as the mummy of a child in a painted casket. She is condemned to be a perpetual Ophelia, counting her flowers while others around her are concerned with the possibly tragic destiny of men and states. Novelists have recognized that this type of woman must always be young and have, indeed, resorted to the device of keeping her eternally youthful by making her die early—a fate, which strange to say, frequently happens to her in real life.

The next instance is apparently the exact opposite of the child anima. She is dark, full-blooded, passionate; she lives all of her feelings and instincts entirely uncensored. The innocent flower-like girl has no consciousness of her own instinct, she may well be entirely cold or un-awakened, but this woman is passion personified. Her tempestuous moods lure and hold the man. He never knows where he will find her from one day to the next—whether he will be received with passionate embraces or with a stiletto! Such a woman lives exactly as she feels, without any calculation as to the effects of her action, and she always feels strongly. She personifies "Nature, red in tooth and claw." Kipling's line, "The female of the species is more deadly than the male," characterizes her. Apart from the violence of her reactions to men, she may be domestically minded; she may wish to "be good" and to live a quiet and ordered life; but ever and again men come around her and something within her is stirred and acts automatically, quite regardless of her own conscious wishes in the matter. Carmen is a good example of the passionate anima woman, but with her the ego trend in the unconscious is dominant for she delights to gain power over men in order to flaunt them.

A woman of this kind whether egotistic or not is enormously attractive to certain types of men. It is as though her abandonment to her emotions releases in them their over-restrained feelings and permits them to experience that irrationality of nature which they have held under too rational a rule. They may not even need to abandon themselves to their more irrational passions; for many a man it may be sufficient to have the woman abandon herself. For, in her abandonment, it is as though for a little while his untamed irrational anima finds release.

Finally, there is the woman who stands in marked contrast to both the flower-like anima girl and the passionate anima woman. She is cold and distant and unreachable. By her very passivity she releases the man, in certain instances, from a too great intensity. She is usually without emotional expression and is utterly impersonal. She gives no indication of her own wishes, answers a question either by silence or by a cold phrase which may have various interpretations.

Galsworthy, in portraying Irene in the *Forsyte Saga,* has drawn a woman of this type with great skill. It has been said that Irene was frigid to the wrong man and glowing to the right man, but this does not alter the fact that she played the cold anima to Soames. Irene could not by will power, it is true, give a sexual response to Soames, whom she did not love, but she failed nonetheless to live up to what was required of her by the law of relatedness. She lived for several years in marriage with him and made herself into a statue. In spite of the fact that the responsibility for the related side of life belongs principally to the woman, Irene withheld her feeling reactions in all the episodes of everyday life and so gave Soames no opportunity to develop a better kind of relationship with her. She continued in the marriage and did nothing about it. Even in the final scene (which doubtless rouses the indignation of every male reader of the book) when Soames forced her to an unwelcome intimacy she still maintained the passive role of the injured wife. Why didn't she fight him? But this would have meant taking a stand, something of which she was hardly capable. She preferred to maintain the role of injured innocence. As a result of her passivity, Soames was virtually tied to a corpse through all the years of his marriage. I hold no brief for Soames. He is not painted in attractive colors. But one must ask why Irene did not play the game *or* end the situation. The answer is that she was afraid. As Soames' wife she had a home and a position of wealth. If she left him she would have had to support herself and face the condemnation of society. This she was not strong enough to face alone. She needed the support of Bossiny and the strength born of her love for him, in order to free herself from her bondage. By remaining with Soames she could get what she wanted without giving anything in return. Her action depended on an unconscious ego-power motive.

When we come close to such a woman to find out what she is really like we shall probably discover that, like her sisters described above, she is entirely innocent of any conscious wish to tyrannize over the man. She is probably a very nebulous person who is not clearly conscious of her own wishes, quite unable to say what she feels at any moment and liable, as Irene was, to be thrust into a marriage which she only subsequently discovers is distasteful to her. She probably spends most of her time in a half-twilight state—not fully aware of what is going on around her—never really rousing herself to make a definite decision which she is prepared to stand by. She has perhaps assumed her cold, distant manner as a convenient shield between herself and reality, having found it to be the most effective armor against those importunate persons and circumstances, irritating because always recalling to her the obligation to wake up and make a decision. She too is bivalent—she will and she won't; and rather than rouse herself to definite action she will endure anything. Here again we have this ambiguous quality of the anima woman.

These typical anima women are, in each instance, naive and unconscious. They act in this way because this is the way "it" acts in them. Such a woman is a nature product and in this stage of consciousness, at all events, is innocent of any deliberate attempt to gain power over the man whom her charms have attracted. She does not realize that her power over him is due to his anima projection which her own nebulous quality has mirrored. For him the relation with her is weighted through his anima; while for her the situation holds the possibility of the fulfillment of her biological needs, an aspect, however, which is frequently neglected. Beyond that it holds the possibilities of personal satisfaction because of the fictitious position of importance she occupies on account of his absorption in her.

The woman, however, may grow tired of carrying the man's anima. She may become increasingly aware that her husband does not really love *her* but is always seeing something over her shoulder, as it were. She may say that she does not want this any longer and that she wishes to be loved for herself but that she cannot prevent his seeing her as other than she is. This "cannot," however, is not altogether true. If she would show herself in her true colors by giving her reaction at the time, he would soon begin to discriminate between her and his anima. If asked why she does not do this, she will almost invariably admit that she is afraid of losing him. In other words she is not really prepared to give up the advantages she gains by carrying his anima projection, although she may also want greater liberty in order to develop her own personality. For to play the anima role means to act, think and feel *only* as feminine being. It is a role which is entirely collective, representing a biological and instinctive reaction to the male.

But woman is, after all, not only a nature product, not only an instinctive feminine creature; she is also a human being. In the Western world, at all cultural levels above the peasant, there is present, at least potentially, an ego, a center of consciousness which says "I" and which prevents the woman from being *only* nature. Yet if she lives only as anima, the ego remains relatively unconscious. If this is the case, her actions are all tinged by ego-power motives which can be unmasked by looking below the surface. Thus every woman who neglects her real reaction in too great compliance to the wishes of the man plays to catch the projection of the man's anima. She has a motive, although, it is true, the motive may be an unconscious one. No reaction is over-ridden except by a stronger one; action follows the strongest motive. If a woman allows her wish or impulse to be over-ridden, there must be a stronger motive at work than her conscious wish. If, in complying with the man's wishes, she represses her own desire, she does it in order to catch the man's anima—in the last analysis to catch the man—and her motive is the wish for power or prestige or support, even though she herself may not be aware of this fact.

When this ego motive, latent in the unconscious, becomes dominant and rises to consciousness in any one of these women, she embarks on the second stage in the evolution of consciousness. The naive woman becomes the sophisticated woman of the world. She is frankly intent on power and superiority and exploits men for money or for prestige or for the satisfaction of her instincts. The flirt, the gold digger, the scalphunter, the courtesan are all types of the anima woman who has gone wrong, as it were, whose natural gifts have been organized under the ego. These women are, or become, almost always cold and aloof. Even the passionate type learns to use her instinct for the gaining of power. She does not give herself even to her own passion, for the deepest interest lies elsewhere.

Some readers may be disturbed because so often the so-called lower types of women have been chosen as illustrations. Naturally extreme cases are chosen in order to point out a particular psychological trend. They have also been chosen because they show unmistakably the traits of character which always exist to some degree in the woman who reacts only as anima, even though the characteristics may be so completely masked that the woman herself remains unaware of their existence.

But these two stages of consciousness, the naive state and the sophisticated or ego state, do not represent the psychological condition in all women. In the naive state consciousness is diffuse, not clearly centered, and the natural impulses and instincts function unchecked by any development of individual conscious aims in the woman herself. In the sophisticated stage the individual aims of the woman, which in many cases may even go contrary to the natural impulses or biological aims, come to the fore and gradually dominate consciousness. In the third stage both the natural impulses and the dominance of ego-power are superseded by a newly recognized value or object which the woman accepts as of greater worth and significance than either the biological urge or the impulse to acquire personal power and satisfaction. This may be called a suprapersonal value or object because it is accepted by the individual as being above personal needs and wishes, thus claiming complete and unconditional allegiance. . . .

The anima woman must find her suprapersonal value, not through an intellectually accepted ideal but through a deeper experience of her own nature which leads her into relation to the woman's spirituality, the feminine principle itself. Jung has used the old Greek philosophic concept of Eros or relatedness to express this feminine principle, in contrast to the Logos which is the masculine principle dealing with factual knowledge and wisdom.

The Marble/Plastic Doll

PLAYBOY

Richard Wilbur (1921–   )

High on his stockroom ladder like a dunce
The stock-boy sits, and studies like a sage
The subject matter of one glossy page,
As lost in curves as Archimedes once.

Sometimes, without a glance, he feeds himself.   5
The left hand, like a mother-bird flight,
Brings him a sandwich for a sidelong bite,
And then returns it to a dusty shelf.

What so engrosses him? The wild décor
Of this pink-papered alcove into which   10
A naked girl has stumbled, with its rich
Welter of pelts and pillows on the floor,

Amidst which, kneeling in a supple pose,
She lifts a goblet in her farther hand,
As if about to toast a flower-stand   15
Above which hovers an exploding rose

Fired from a long-necked crystal vase that rests
Upon a tasseled and vermilion cloth
One taste of which would shrivel up a moth?
Or is he pondering her perfect breasts?   20

Nothing escapes him of her body's grace
Or of her floodlit skin, so sleek and warm

And yet so strangely like a uniform,
But what now grips his fancy is her face,

And how the cunning picture holds her still 25
At just that smiling instant when her soul,
Grown sweetly faint, and swept beyond control,
Consents to his inexorable will.

MISS TEMPTATION

Kurt Vonnegut, Jr. (1922–   )

Puritanism had fallen into such disrepair that not even the oldest spinster thought of putting Susanna ° in a ducking stool; not even the oldest farmer suspected that Susanna's diabolical beauty had made his cow run dry.

Susanna was a bit-part actress in the summer theater near the village, and she rented a room over the firehouse. She was a part of village life all summer, but the villagers never got used to her. She was forever as startling and desirable as a piece of big-city fire apparatus.

Susanna's feathery hair and saucer eyes were as black as midnight. Her skin was the color of cream. Her hips were like a lyre, and her bosom made men dream of peace and plenty for ever and ever. She wore barbaric golden hoops on her shell-pink ears, and around her ankles were chains with little bells on them.

She went barefoot and slept until noon every day. And, as noon drew near, the villagers on the main street would grow as restless as beagles with a thunderstorm on the way.

At noon, Susanna would appear on the porch outside her room. She would stretch languidly, pour a bowl of milk for her black cat, kiss the cat, fluff her hair, put on her earrings, lock her door, and hide the key in her bosom.

And then, barefoot, she would begin her stately, undulating, titillating, tinkling walk—down the outside stairway, past the liquor store, the insurance agency, the real-estate office, the diner, the American Legion post, and the church, to the crowded drugstore. There she would get the New York papers.

She seemed to nod to all the world in a dim, queenly way. But the only person she spoke to during her daily walk was Bearse Hinkley, the seventy-two-year-old pharmacist.

°*Susanna:* See the story of Susanna in the Apocrypha.

The old man always had her papers ready for her.

"Thank you, Mr. Hinkley. You're an angel," she would say, opening a paper at random. "Now, let's see what's going on back in civilization." While the old man would watch, fuddled by her perfume, Susanna would laugh or gasp or frown at items in the paper—items she never explained.

Then she would take the papers, and return to her nest over the firehouse. She would pause on the porch outside her room, dip her hand into her bosom, bring out the key, unlock the door, pick up the black cat, kiss it again, and disappear inside.

The one-girl pageant had a ritual sameness until one day toward the end of summer, when the air of the drugstore was cut by a cruel, sustained screech from a dry bearing in a revolving soda-fountain stool.

The screech cut right through Susanna's speech about Mr. Hinkley's being an angel. The screech made scalps tingle and teeth ache. Susanna looked indulgently in the direction of the screech, forgiving the screecher. She found that the screecher wasn't a person to be indulged.

The screech had been made by the stool of Cpl. Norman Fuller, who had come home the night before from eighteen bleak months in Korea. They had been eighteen months without war—but eighteen months without cheer, all the same. Fuller had turned on the stool slowly, to look at Susanna with indignation. When the screech died, the drugstore was deathly still.

Fuller had broken the enchantment of summer by the seaside—had reminded all in the drugstore of the black, mysterious passions that were so often the mainsprings of life.

He might have been a brother, come to rescue his idiot sister from the tenderloin;° or an irate husband, come to a saloon to horsewhip his wife back to where she belonged, with the baby. The truth was that Corporal Fuller had never seen Susanna before.

He hadn't consciously meant to make a scene. He hadn't known, consciously, that his stool would screech. He had meant to underplay his indignation, to make it a small detail in the background of Susanna's pageant—a detail noticed by only one or two connoisseurs of the human comedy.

But the screech had made his indignation the center of the solar system for all in the drugstore—particularly for Susanna. Time had stopped, and it could not proceed until Fuller had explained the expression on his granite Yankee face.

Fuller felt his skin glowing like hot brass. He was comprehending destiny. Destiny had suddenly given him an audience, and a situation about which he had a bitter lot to say.

Fuller felt his lips move, heard the words come out. "Who do you think you are?" he said to Susanna.

°*tenderloin*: vice-ridden section of any large city

"I beg your pardon?" said Susanna. She drew her newspapers about herself protectively.

"I saw you come down the street like you were a circus parade, and I just wondered who you thought you were," said Fuller.

Susanna blushed gloriously. "I—I'm an actress," she said.

"You can say that again," said Fuller. "Greatest actresses in the world. American women."

"You're very nice to say so," said Susanna uneasily.

Fuller's skin glowed brighter and hotter. His mind had become a fountain of apt, intricate phrases. "I'm not talking about theaters with seats in 'em. I'm talking about the stage of life. American women act and dress like they're gonna give you the world. Then, when you stick out your hand, they put an ice cube in it."

"They do?" said Susanna emptily.

"They do," said Fuller, "and it's about time somebody said so." He looked challengingly from spectator to spectator, and found what he took to be dazed encouragement. "It isn't fair," he said.

"What isn't?" said Susanna, lost.

"You come in here with bells on your ankles, so's I'll have to look at your ankles and your pretty pink feet," said Fuller. "You kiss the cat, so's I'll have to think about how it'd be to be that cat," said Fuller. "You call an old man an angel, so's I'll have to think about what it'd be like to be called an angel by you," said Fuller. "You hide your key in front of everybody, so's I'll have to think about where that key is," said Fuller.

He stood. "Miss," he said, his voice full of pain, "you do everything you can to give lonely, ordinary people like me indigestion and the heebie-jeebies, and you wouldn't even hold hands with me to keep me from falling off a cliff."

He strode to the door. All eyes were on him. Hardly anyone noticed that his indictment had reduced Susanna to ashes of what she'd been moments before. Susanna now looked like what she really was—a muddle-headed nineteen-year-old clinging to a tiny corner of sophistication.

"It isn't fair," said Fuller. "There ought to be a law against girls acting and dressing like you do. It makes more people unhappy than it does happy. You know what I say to you, for going around making everybody want to kiss you?"

"No," piped Susanna, every fuse in her nervous system blown.

"I say to you what you'd say to me, if I was to try and kiss you," said Fuller grandly. He swung his arms in an umpire's gesture for "out." "The hell with you," he said. He left, slamming the screen door.

He didn't look back when the door slammed again a moment later, when the patter of running bare feet and the wild tinkling of little bells faded away in the direction of the firehouse.

That evening, Corporal Fuller's widowed mother put a candle on the table, and fed him sirloin steak and strawberry shortcake in honor of his homecoming. Fuller ate the meal as though it were wet blotting paper, and he answered his mother's cheery questions in a voice that was dead.

"Aren't you glad to be home?" said his mother, when they'd finished their coffee.

"Sure," said Fuller.

"What did you do today?" she said.

"Walked," he said.

"Seeing all your old friends?" she said.

"Haven't got any friends," said Fuller.

His mother threw up her hands. "No friends?" she said. "You?"

"Times change, ma," said Fuller heavily. "Eighteen months is a long time. People leave town, people get married——"

"Marriage doesn't kill people, does it?" she said.

Fuller didn't smile. "Maybe not," he said. "But it makes it awful hard for 'em to find any place to fit old friends in."

"Dougie isn't married, is he?"

"He's out west, ma—with the Strategic Air Command," said Fuller. The little dining room became as lonely as a bomber in the thin, cold stratosphere.

"Oh," said his mother. "There must be somebody left."

"Nope," said Fuller. "I spent the whole morning on the phone, ma. I might as well have been back in Korea. Nobody home."

"I can't believe it," she said. "Why, you couldn't walk down Main Street without being almost trampled by friends."

"Ma," said Fuller hollowly, "after I ran out of numbers to call, you know what I did? I went down to the drugstore, ma, and just sat there by the soda fountain, waiting for somebody to walk in—somebody I knew maybe just even a little. Ma," he said in anguish, "all I knew was poor old Bearse Hinkley. I'm not kidding you one bit." He stood, crumpling his napkin into a ball. "Ma, will you please excuse me?"

"Yes. Of course," she said. "Where are you going now?" She beamed. "Out to call on some nice girl, I hope?"

Fuller threw the napkin down. "I'm going to get a cigar!" he said. "I don't know any girls. They're all married too."

His mother paled. "I—I see," she said. "I—I didn't even know you smoked."

"Ma," said Fuller tautly, "can't you get it through your head? I been away for eighteen months, ma—eighteen months!"

"It is a long time, isn't it?" said his mother, humbled by his passion. "Well, you go get your cigar." She touched his arm. "And please don't feel so lonesome. You just wait. Your life will be so full of people again, you won't know which one to turn to. And, before you know it, you'll meet some pretty young girl, and you'll be married too."

"I don't intend to get married for some time, mother," said Fuller stuffily. "Not until I get through divinity school."

"Divinity school!" said his mother. "When did you decide that?"

"This noon," said Fuller.

"What happened this noon?"

"I had kind of a religious experience, ma," he said. "Something just made me speak out."

"About what?" she said, bewildered.

In Fuller's buzzing head there whirled a rhapsody of Susannas. He saw again all the professional temptresses who had tormented him in Korea, who had beckoned from makeshift bed-sheet movie screens, from curling pin-ups on damp tent walls, from ragged magazines in sand-bagged pits. The Susannas had made fortunes, beckoning to lonely Corporal Fullers everywhere—beckoning with stunning beauty, beckoning the Fullers to come nowhere for nothing.

The wraith of a Puritan ancestor, stiff-necked, dressed in black, took possession of Fuller's tongue. Fuller spoke with a voice that came across the centuries, the voice of a witch hanger, a voice redolent with frustration, self-righteousness, and doom.

"What did I speak out against?" he said. "Temp-ta-tion."

Fuller's cigar in the night was a beacon warning carefree, frivolous people away. It was plainly a cigar smoked in anger. Even the moths had sense enough to stay away. Like a restless, searching red eye, it went up and down every street in the village, coming to rest at last, a wet, dead butt, before the firehouse.

Bearse Hinkley, the old pharmacist, sat at the wheel of the pumper, his eyes glazed with nostalgia—nostalgia for the days when he had been young enough to drive. And on his face, for all to see, was a dream of one more catastrophe, with all the young men away, when an old man or nobody would drive the pumper to glory one more time. He spent warm evenings there, behind the wheel—and had for years.

"Want a light for that thing?" he said to Corporal Fuller, seeing the dead cigar between Fuller's lips.

"No, thanks, Mr. Hinkley," he said. "All the pleasure's out of it."

"Beats me how anybody finds any pleasure in cigars in the first place," said the old man.

"Matter of taste," said Fuller. "No accounting for tastes."

"One man's meat's another man's poison," said Hinkley. "Live and let live, I always say." He glanced at the ceiling. Above it was the fragrant nest of Susanna and her black cat. "Me? All my pleasures are looking at what used to be pleasures."

Fuller looked at the ceiling, too, meeting the unmentioned issue squarely. "If you were young," he said, "you'd know why I said what I said to her. Beautiful, stuck-up girls give me a big pain."

"Oh, I remember that," said Hinkley. "I'm not so old I don't remember the big pain."

"If I have a daughter, I hope she isn't beautiful," said Fuller. "The beautiful girls at high school—by God, if they didn't think they were something extra-special."

"By God, if I don't think so, too," said Hinkley.

"They wouldn't even look at you if you didn't have a car and an allowance of twenty bucks a week to spend on 'em," said Fuller.

"Why should they?" said the old man cheerfully. "If I was a beautiful girl, I wouldn't." He nodded to himself. "Well—anyway, I guess you came home from the wars and settled that score. I guess you told her."

"Ah-h-h," said Fuller. "You can't make any impression on them."

"I dunno," said Hinkley. "There's a fine old tradition in the theater: The show must go on. You know, even if you got pneumonia or your baby's dying, you still put on the show."

"I'm all right," said Fuller. "Who's complaining? I feel fine."

The old man's white eyebrows went up. "Who's talking about you?" he said. "I'm talking about her."

Fuller reddened, mousetrapped by egoism. "She'll be all right," he said.

"She will?" said Hinkley. "Maybe she will. All I know is, the show's started at the theater. She's supposed to be in it and she's still upstairs."

"She is?" said Fuller, amazed.

"Has been," said Hinkley, "ever since you paddled her and sent her home."

Fuller tried to grin ironically. "Now, isn't that too bad?" he said. His grin felt queasy and weak. "Well, good-night, Mr. Hinkley."

"Good-night, soldier boy," said Hinkley. "Good-night."

As noon drew near on the next day, the villagers along the main street seemed to grow stupid. Yankee shopkeepers made change lackadaisically, as though money didn't matter any more. All thoughts were of the great cuckoo clock the firehouse had become. The question was: Had Corporal Fuller broken it or, at noon, would the little door on top fly open, would Susanna appear?

In the drugstore, old Bearse Hinkley fussed with Susanna's New York papers, rumpling them in his anxiety to make them attractive. They were bait for Susanna.

Moments before noon, Corporal Fuller—the vandal himself—came into the drugstore. On his face was a strange mixture of guilt and sore-headedness. He had spent the better part of the night awake, reviewing his grievances against beautiful women. *All they think about is how beautiful they are,* he'd said to himself at dawn. *They wouldn't even give you the time of day.*

He walked along the row of soda-fountain stools and gave each empty stool a seemingly idle twist. He found the stool that had screeched so loudly the day before. He sat down on it, a monument of righteousness. No one spoke to him.

The fire siren gave its perfunctory wheeze for noon. And then, hearselike, a truck from the express company drove up to the firehouse. Two men got out and climbed the stairs. Susanna's hungry black cat jumped to the porch railing and arched its back as the expressmen disappeared into Susanna's room. The cat spat when they staggered out with Susanna's trunk.

Fuller was shocked. He glanced at Bearse Hinkley, and he saw that the old man's look of anxiety had become the look of double pneumonia—dizzy, blind, drowning.

"Satisfied, corporal?" said the old man.

"I didn't tell her to leave," said Fuller.

"You didn't leave her much choice," said Hinkley.

"What does she care what I think?" said Fuller. "I didn't know she was such a tender blossom."

The old man touched Fuller's arm lightly. "We all are, corporal—we all are," he said. "I thought that was one of the few good things about sending a boy off to the Army. I thought that was where he could find out for sure he wasn't the only tender blossom on earth. Didn't you find that out?"

"I never thought I was a tender blossom," said Fuller. "I'm sorry it turned out this way, but she asked for it." His head was down. His ears were hot crimson.

"She really scared you stiff, didn't she?" said Hinkley.

Smiles bloomed on the faces of the small audience that had drawn near on one pretext or another. Fuller appraised the smiles, and found that the old man had left him only one weapon—utterly humorless good citizenship.

"Who's afraid?" he said stuffily. "I'm not afraid. I just think it's a problem somebody ought to bring up and discuss."

"It's sure the one subject nobody gets tired of," said Hinkley.

Fuller's gaze, which had become a very shifty thing, passed over the magazine rack. There was tier upon tier of Susannas, a thousand square feet of wet-lipped smiles and sooty eyes and skin like cream. He ransacked his mind for a ringing phrase that would give dignity to his cause.

"I'm thinking about juvenile delinquency!" he said. He pointed to the magazines. "No wonder kids go crazy."

"I know I did," said the old man quietly. "I was as scared as you are."

"I told you, I'm not afraid of her," said Fuller.

"Good!" said Hinkley. "Then you're just the man to take her papers to her. They're paid for." He dumped the papers in Fuller's lap.

Fuller opened his mouth to reply. But he closed it again. His throat had tightened, and he knew that, if he tried to speak, he would quack like a duck.

"If you're really not afraid, corporal," said the old man, "that would be a very nice thing to do—a Christian thing to do."

As he mounted the stairway to Susanna's nest, Fuller was almost spastic in his efforts to seem casual.

Susanna's door was unlatched. When Fuller knocked on it, it swung open. In Fuller's imagination, her nest had been dark and still, reeking of incense, a labyrinth of heavy hangings and mirrors, with somewhere a Turkish corner, with somewhere a billowy bed in the form of a swan.

He saw Susanna and her room in truth now. The truth was the cheerless truth of a dirt-cheap Yankee summer rental—bare wood walls, three coat hooks, a linoleum rug. Two gas burners, an iron cot, an icebox. A tiny sink with naked pipes, a plastic drinking glass, two plates, a murky mirror. A frying pan, a saucepan, a can of soap powder.

The only harem touch was a white circle of talcum powder before the murky mirror. In the center of the circle were the prints of two bare feet. The marks of the toes were no bigger than pearls.

Fuller looked from the pearls to the truth of Susanna. Her back was to him. She was packing the last of her things into a suitcase.

She was now dressed for travel—dressed as properly as a missionary's wife.

"Papers," croaked Fuller. "Mr. Hinkley sent 'em."

"How very nice of Mr. Hinkley," said Susanna. She turned. "Tell him——" No more words came. She recognized him. She pursed her lips and her small nose reddened.

"Papers," said Fuller emptily. "From Mr. Hinkley."

"I heard you," she said. "You just said that. Is that all you've got to say?"

Fuller flapped his hands limply at his sides. "I'm—I—I didn't mean to make you leave," he said. "I didn't mean that."

"You suggest I stay?" said Susanna wretchedly. "After I've been denounced in public as a scarlet woman? A tart? A wench?"

"Holy smokes, I never called you those things!" said Fuller.

"Did you ever stop to think what it's like to be me?" she said. She patted her bosom. "There's somebody living inside here, too, you know."

"I know," said Fuller. He hadn't known, up to then.

"I have a soul," she said.

"Sure you do," said Fuller, trembling. He trembled because the room was filled with a profound intimacy. Susanna, the golden girl of a thousand tortured daydreams, was now discussing her soul, passionately, with Fuller the lonely, Fuller the homely, Fuller the bleak.

"I didn't sleep a wink last night because of you," said Susanna.

"Me?" He wished she'd get out of his life again. He wished she were in black and white, a thousandth of an inch thick on a magazine page. He wished he could turn the page and read about baseball or foreign affairs.

"What did you expect?" said Susanna. "I talked to you all night. You know what I said to you?"

"No," said Fuller, backing away. She followed, and seemed to throw off heat like a big iron radiator. She was appallingly human.

"I'm not Yellowstone Park!" she said. "I'm not supported by taxes! I don't belong to everybody! You don't have any right to say anything about the way I look!"

"Good gravy!" said Fuller.

"I'm so tired of dumb toots like you!" said Susanna. She stamped her foot and suddenly looked haggard. "I can't help it if you want to kiss me! Whose fault is that?"

Fuller could now glimpse his side of the question only dimly, like a diver glimpsing the sun from the ocean floor. "All I was trying to say was, you could be a little more conservative," he said.

Susanna opened her arms. "Am I conservative enough now?" she said. "Is this all right with you?"

The appeal of the lovely girl made the marrow of Fuller's bones ache. In his chest was a sigh like the lost chord. "Yes," he said. And then he murmured, "Forget about me."

Susanna tossed her head. "Forget about being run over by a truck," she said. "What makes you so mean?"

"I just say what I think," said Fuller.

"You think such mean things," said Susanna, bewildered. Her eyes widened. "All through high school, people like you would look at me as if they wished I'd drop dead. They'd never dance with me, they'd never talk to me, they'd never even smile back." She shuddered. "They'd just go slinking around like small-town cops. They'd look at me the way you did—like I'd just done something terrible."

The truth of the indictment made Fuller itch all over. "Probably thinking about something else," he said.

"I don't think so," said Susanna. "You sure weren't. All of a sudden, you started yelling at me in the drugstore, and I'd never even seen you before." She burst into tears. "What is the matter with you?"

Fuller looked down at the floor. "Never had a chance with a girl like you—that's all," he said. "That hurts."

Susanna looked at him wonderingly. "You don't know what a chance is," she said.

"A chance is a late-model convertible, a new suit, and twenty bucks," said Fuller.

Susanna turned her back to him and closed her suitcase. "A chance is a girl," she said. "You smile at her, you be friendly, you be glad she's a girl." She turned and opened her arms again. "I'm a girl. Girls are shaped this way," she said. "If men are nice to me and make me happy, I kiss them sometimes. Is that all right with you?"

"Yes," said Fuller humbly. She had rubbed his nose in the sweet reason that governed the universe. He shrugged. "I better be going. Good-by."

"Wait!" she said. "You can't do that—just walk out, leaving me feeling so wicked." She shook her head. "I don't deserve to feel wicked."

"What can I do?" said Fuller helplessly.

"You can take me for a walk down the main street, as though you were proud of me," said Susanna. "You can welcome me back to the human race." She nodded to herself. "You owe that to me."

Cpl. Norman Fuller, who had come home two nights before from eighteen bleak months in Korea, waited on the porch outside Susanna's nest, with all the village watching.

Susanna had ordered him out while she changed, while she changed for her return to the human race. She had also called the express company and told them to bring her trunk back.

Fuller passed the time by stroking Susanna's cat. "Hello, kitty, kitty, kitty, kitty," he said, over and over again. Saying, "Kitty, kitty, kitty, kitty," numbed him like a merciful drug.

He was saying it when Susanna came out of her nest. He couldn't stop saying it, and she had to take the cat away from him, firmly, before she could get him to look at her, to offer his arm.

"So long, kitty, kitty, kitty, kitty, kitty, kitty," said Fuller.

Susanna was barefoot, and she wore barbaric hoop earrings, and ankle bells. Holding Fuller's arm lightly, she led him down the stairs, and began her stately, undulating, titillating, tinkling walk past the liquor store, the insurance agency, the real-estate office, the diner, the American Legion post, and the church, to the crowded drugstore.

"Now, smile and be nice," said Susanna. "Show you're not ashamed of me."

"Mind if I smoke?" said Fuller.

"That's very considerate of you to ask," said Susanna. "No, I don't mind at all."

By steadying his right hand with his left, Corporal Fuller managed to light a cigar.

TO HIS COY° MISTRESS

Andrew Marvell (1621–1678)

Had we but world enough, and time,
This coyness, lady, were no crime.
We would sit down, and think which way
To walk, and pass our long love's day.
Thou by the Indian Ganges' side   5
Should'st rubies find: I by the tide
Of Humber° would complain. I would
Love you ten years before the Flood,
And you should, if you please, refuse
Till the conversion of the Jews.   10
My vegetable° love should grow
Vaster than empires, and more slow.
An hundred years should go to praise
Thine eyes, and on thy forehead gaze:
Two hundred to adore each breast: 15
But thirty thousand to the rest;
An age at least to every part,
And the last age should show your heart.
For, lady, you deserve this state,°
Nor would I love at lower rate.   20
    But at my back I always hear
Time's wingèd chariot hurrying near:
And yonder all before us lie
Deserts of vast eternity.
Thy beauty shall no more be found;   25
Nor, in thy marble vault, shall sound
My echoing song: then worms shall try
That long-preserved virginity,
And your quaint honour turn to dust,
And into ashes all my lust.   30
The grave's a fine and private place,
But none, I think, do there embrace.
    Now, therefore, while the youthful hue
Sits on thy skin like morning dew,
And while thy willing soul transpires°   35
At every pore with instant° fires,
Now let us sport us while we may;

°*Coy*: modest   °*Humber*: river, Eastern England, on which town of Hull is located
°*vegetable*: full of growing   °*state*: royal concern   °*transpires*: comes out (like
   breathing)   °*instant*: eager

And now, like amorous birds of prey,
Rather at once our Time devour,
Than languish in his slow-chapped° power.   40
Let us roll all our strength and all
Our sweetness up into one ball,
And tear our pleasures with rough strife
Thorough ° the iron gates of life.
Thus, though we cannot make our sun   45
Stand still, yet we will make him run.

THE STRENGTH OF GOD

Sherwood Anderson (1876–1941)

The Reverend Curtis Hartman was pastor of the Presbyterian
Church of Winesburg, and had been in that position ten years. He was
forty years old, and by his nature very silent and reticent. To preach,
standing in the pulpit before the people, was always a hardship for him
and from Wednesday morning until Saturday evening he thought of
nothing but the two sermons that must be preached on Sunday. Early
on Sunday morning he went into a little room called a study in the bell
tower of the church and prayed. In his prayers there was one note that
always predominated. "Give me strength and courage for Thy work,
O Lord!" he pleaded, kneeling on the bare floor and bowing his head in
the presence of the task that lay before him.

The Reverend Hartman was a tall man with a brown beard. His
wife, a stout, nervous woman, was the daughter of a manufacturer of
underwear at Cleveland, Ohio. The minister himself was rather a favorite
in the town. The elders of the church liked him because he was quiet and
unpretentious and Mrs. White, the banker's wife, thought him scholarly
and refined.

The Presbyterian Church held itself somewhat aloof from the other
churches of Winesburg. It was larger and more imposing and its minister
was better paid. He even had a carriage of his own and on summer
evenings sometimes drove about town with his wife. Through Main Street
and up and down Buckeye Street he went, bowing gravely to the people,
while his wife, afire with secret pride, looked at him out of the corners
of her eyes and worried lest the horse become frightened and run away.

For a good many years after he came to Winesburg things went
well with Curtis Hartman. He was not one to arouse keen enthusiasm

---

°*chapped*: chopped   °*Thorough*: through

From *Winesburg, Ohio.* Copyright 1919 by B. W. Huebsch, Inc., renewed 1947 by
Eleanor Copenhaver Anderson. Reprinted by permission of The Viking Press, Inc.

among the worshippers in his church but on the other hand he made no enemies. In reality he was much in earnest and sometimes suffered prolonged periods of remorse because he could not go crying the word of God in the highways and byways of the town. He wondered if the flame of the spirit really burned in him and dreamed of a day when a strong sweet new current of power would come like a great wind into his voice and his soul and the people would tremble before the spirit of God made manifest in him. "I am a poor stick and that will never really happen to me," he mused dejectedly, and then a patient smile lit up his features. "Oh well, I suppose I'm doing well enough," he added philosophically.

The room in the bell tower of the church, where on Sunday mornings the minister prayed for an increase in him of the power of God, had but one window. It was long and narrow and swung outward on a hinge like a door. On the window, made of little leaded panes, was a design showing the Christ laying his hand upon the head of a child. One Sunday morning in the summer as he sat by his desk in the room with a large Bible opened before him, and the sheets of his sermon scattered about, the minister was shocked to see, in the upper room of the house next door, a woman lying in her bed and smoking a cigarette while she read a book. Curtis Hartman went on tiptoe to the window, and closed it softly. He was horror stricken at the thought of a woman smoking and trembled also to think that his eyes, just raised from the pages of the book of God, had looked upon the bare shoulders and white throat of a woman. With his brain in a whirl he went down into the pulpit and preached a long sermon without once thinking of his gestures or his voice. The sermon attracted unusual attention because of its power and clearness. "I wonder if she is listening, if my voice is carrying a message into her soul," he thought and began to hope that on future Sunday mornings he might be able to say words that would touch and awaken the woman apparently far gone in secret sin.

The house next door to the Presbyterian Church, through the windows of which the minister had seen the sight that had so upset him, was occupied by two women. Aunt Elizabeth Swift, a grey competent-looking widow with money in the Winesburg National Bank, lived there with her daughter Kate Swift, a school teacher. The school teacher was thirty years old and had a neat trim-looking figure. She had few friends and bore a reputation of having a sharp tongue. When he began to think about her, Curtis Hartman remembered that she had been to Europe and had lived for two years in New York City. "Perhaps after all her smoking means nothing," he thought. He began to remember that when he was a student in college and occasionally read novels, good although somewhat worldly women, had smoked through the pages of a book that had once fallen into his hands. With a rush of new determination he worked on his sermons all through the week and forgot, in his zeal to reach the ears and the soul of this new listener, both his embarrassment in the pulpit and the necessity of prayer in the study on Sunday mornings.

Reverend Hartman's experience with women had been somewhat limited. He was the son of a wagon maker from Muncie, Indiana, and had worked his way through college. The daughter of the underwear manufacturer had boarded in a house where he lived during his school days and he had married her after a formal and prolonged courtship, carried on for the most part by the girl herself. On his marriage day the underwear manufacturer had given his daughter five thousand dollars and he promised to leave her at least twice that amount in his will. The minister had thought himself fortunate in marriage and had never permitted himself to think of other women. He did not want to think of other women. What he wanted was to do the work of God quietly and earnestly.

In the soul of the minister a struggle awoke. From wanting to reach the ears of Kate Swift, and through his sermons to delve into her soul, he began to want also to look again at the figure lying white and quiet in the bed. On a Sunday morning when he could not sleep because of his thoughts he arose and went to walk in the streets. When he had gone along Main Street almost to the old Richmond place he stopped and picking up a stone rushed off to the room in the bell tower. With the stone he broke out a corner of the window and then locked the door and sat down at the desk before the open Bible to wait. When the shade of the window to Kate Swift's room was raised he could see, through the hole, directly into her bed, but she was not there. She also had arisen and had gone for a walk and the hand that raised the shade was the hand of Aunt Elizabeth Swift.

The minister almost wept with joy at this deliverance from the carnal desire to "peep" and went back to his own house praising God. In an ill moment he forgot, however, to stop the hole in the window. The piece of glass broken out at the corner of the window just nipped off the bare heel of the boy standing motionless and looking with rapt eyes into the face of the Christ.

Curtis Hartman forgot his sermon on that Sunday morning. He talked to his congregation and in his talk said that it was a mistake for people to think of their minister as a man set aside and intended by nature to lead a blameless life. "Out of my own experience I know that we, who are the ministers of God's word, are beset by the same temptations that assail you," he declared. "I have been tempted and have surrendered to temptation. It is only the hand of God, placed beneath my head, that has raised me up. As he has raised me so also will he raise you. Do not despair. In your hour of sin raise your eyes to the skies and you will be again and again saved."

Resolutely the minister put the thoughts of the woman in the bed out of his mind and began to be something like a lover in the presence of his wife. One evening when they drove out together he turned the horse out of Buckeye Street and in the darkness on Gospel Hill, above Waterworks Pond, put his arm about Sarah Hartman's waist. When he had eaten breakfast in the morning and was ready to retire to his study at the back of his house he went around the table and kissed his wife on the cheek. When thoughts of Kate Swift came into his head, he smiled and raised his eyes to the skies. "Intercede for me, Master," he muttered, "keep me in the narrow path intent on Thy work."

And now began the real struggle in the soul of the brown-bearded minister. By chance he discovered that Kate Swift was in the habit of lying in her bed in the evenings and reading a book. A lamp stood on a table by the side of the bed and the light streamed down upon her white shoulders and bare throat. On the evening when he made the discovery the minister sat at the desk in the study from nine until after eleven and when her light was put out stumbled out of the church to spend two more hours walking and praying in the streets. He did not want to kiss the shoulders and the throat of Kate Swift and had not allowed his mind to dwell on such thoughts. He did not know what he wanted. "I am God's child and he must save me from myself," he cried, in the darkness under the trees as he wandered in the streets. By a tree he stood and looked at the sky that was covered with hurrying clouds. He began to talk to God intimately and closely. "Please, Father, do not forget me. Give me power to go tomorrow and repair the hole in the window. Lift my eyes again to the skies. Stay with me, Thy servant, in his hour of need."

Up and down through the silent streets walked the minister and for days and weeks his soul was troubled. He could not understand the temptation that had come to him nor could he fathom the reason for its coming. In a way he began to blame God, saying to himself that he had tried to keep his feet in the true path and had not run about seeking sin. "Through my days as a young man and all through my life here I have gone quietly about my work," he declared. "Why now should I be tempted? What have I done that this burden should be laid on me?"

Three times during the early fall and winter of that year Curtis Hartman crept out of his house to the room in the bell tower to sit in the darkness looking at the figure of Kate Swift lying in her bed and later went to walk and pray in the streets. He could not understand himself. For weeks he would go along scarcely thinking of the school teacher and telling himself that he had conquered the carnal desire to look at her body. And then something would happen. As he sat in the study of his own house, hard at work on a sermon, he would become nervous and begin to walk up and down the room. "I will go out into the streets," he told himself and even as he let himself in at the church door he persistently denied to himself the cause of his being there. "I will not repair the hole in the window and I will train myself to come here at night and sit in the presence of this woman without raising my eyes. I will not be defeated in this thing. The Lord has devised this temptation as a test of my soul and I will grope my way out of darkness into the light of righteousness."

One night in January when it was bitter cold and snow lay deep on the streets of Winesburg Curtis Hartman paid his last visit to the room in the bell tower of the church. It was past nine o'clock when he left his own house and he set out so hurriedly that he forgot to put on his overshoes. In Main Street no one was abroad but Hop Higgins the night watchman and in the whole town no one was awake but the watchman and young George Willard, who sat in the office of the *Winesburg Eagle* trying to write a story. Along the street to the church went the minister, plowing through the drifts and thinking that this time he would utterly give way to sin. "I want to look at the woman and to think of kissing her shoulders and I am going to let myself think what I choose," he declared bitterly and tears came into his eyes. He began to think that he would get out of the ministry and try some other way of life. "I shall go to some city and get into business," he declared. "If my nature is such that I cannot resist sin, I shall give myself over to sin. At least I shall not be a hypocrite, preaching the word of God with my mind thinking of the shoulders and neck of a woman who does not belong to me."

It was cold in the room of the bell tower of the church on that January night and almost as soon as he came into the room Curtis Hartman knew that if he stayed he would be ill. His feet were wet from tramping in the snow and there was no fire. In the room in the house next door Kate Swift had not yet appeared. With grim determination the man sat down to wait. Sitting in the chair and gripping the edge of the desk on which lay the Bible he stared into the darkness thinking the blackest thoughts of his life. He thought of his wife and for the moment almost hated her. "She has always been ashamed of passion and has cheated me," he thought. "Man has a right to expect living passion and beauty in a woman. He has no right to forget that he is an animal and in me there is something that is Greek. I will throw off the woman of my bosom and seek other women. I will besiege this school teacher. I will fly in the face of all men and if I am a creature of carnal lusts I will live then for my lusts."

The distracted man trembled from head to foot, partly from cold, partly from the struggle in which he was engaged. Hours passed and a fever assailed his body. His throat began to hurt and his teeth chattered. His feet on the study floor felt like two cakes of ice. Still he would not give up. "I will see this woman and will think the thoughts I have never dared to think," he told himself, gripping the edge of the desk and waiting.

THE MARBLE/PLASTIC DOLL 61

Curtis Hartman came near dying from the effects of that night of waiting in the church, and also he found in the thing that happened what he took to be the way of life for him. On other evenings when he had waited he had not been able to see, through the little hole in the glass, any part of the school teacher's room except that occupied by her bed. In the darkness he had waited until the woman suddenly appeared sitting in the bed in her white night-robe. When the light was turned up she propped herself up among the pillows and read a book. Sometimes she smoked one of the cigarettes. Only her bare shoulders and throat were visible.

On the January night, after he had come near dying with cold and after his mind had two or three times actually slipped away into an odd land of fantasy so that he had by an exercise of will power to force himself back into consciousness, Kate Swift appeared. In the room next door a lamp was lighted and the waiting man stared into an empty bed. Then upon the bed before his eyes a naked woman threw herself. Lying face downward she wept and beat with her fists upon the pillow. With a final outburst of weeping she half arose, and in the presence of the man who had waited to look and to think thoughts the woman of sin began to pray. In the lamplight her figure, slim and strong, looked like the figure of the boy in the presence of the Christ on the leaded window.

Curtis Hartman never remembered how he got out of the church. With a cry he arose, dragging the heavy desk along the floor. The Bible fell, making a great clatter in the silence. When the light in the house next door went out he stumbled down the stairway and into the street. Along the street he went and ran in at the door of the *Winesburg Eagle*. To George Willard, who was tramping up and down in the office undergoing a struggle of his own, he began to talk half incoherently. "The ways of God are beyond human understanding," he cried, running in quickly and closing the door. He began to advance upon the young man, his eyes glowing and his voice ringing with fervor. "I have found the light," he cried. "After ten years in this town, God has manifested himself to me in the body of a woman." His voice dropped and he began to whisper. "I did not understand," he said. "What I took to be a trial of my soul was only a preparation for a new and more beautiful fervor of the spirit. God has appeared to me in the person of Kate Swift, the school teacher, kneeling naked on a bed. Do you know Kate Swift? Although she may not be aware of it, she is an instrument of God, bearing the message of truth."

Reverend Curtis Hartman turned and ran out of the office. At the door he stopped, and after looking up and down the deserted street, turned again to George Willard. "I am delivered. Have no fear." He held up a bleeding fist for the young man to see. "I smashed the glass of the window," he cried. "Now it will have to be wholly replaced. The strength of God was in me and I broke it with my fist."

THE FLEA

John Donne (1573–1631)

Mark but this flea, and mark in this,
How little that which thou deny'st me is;
It sucked me first, and now sucks thee,
And in this flea our two bloods mingled be;
Thou know'st that this cannot be said   5
A sin, nor shame, nor loss of maidenhead;
    Yet this enjoys before it woo,
    And pampered° swells with one blood made of two,
    And this, alas, is more than we would do.

Oh stay, three lives in one flea spare,   10
Where we almost, yea, more than married are.
This flea is you and I, and this
Our marriage bed, and marriage temple is;
Though parents grudge, and you, w'are met,
And cloistered in these living walls of jet.   15
    Though use make you apt to kill me,
    Let not to that, self-murder added be,
    And sacrilege, three sins in killing three.

Cruel and sudden, hast thou since
Purpled thy nail in blood of innocence?   20
Wherein could this flea guilty be,
Except in that drop which it sucked from thee?
Yet thou triumph'st and say'st that thou
Find'st not thyself, nor me the weaker now;
    'Tis true, then learn how false fears be: 25
    Just so much honor, when thou yield'st to me,
    Will waste, as this flea's death took life from thee.

SONG

William Blake (1757–1827)

Fresh from the dewy hill, the merry year
Smiles on my head, and mounts his flaming car;
Round my young brows the laurel wreathes a shade,
And rising glories beam around my head.

°*pampered*: glutted

My feet are wing'd, while o'er the dewy lawn   5
I meet my maiden, risen like the morn:
Oh bless those holy feet, like angels' feet;
Oh bless those limbs, beaming with heav'nly light!

Like as an angel glitt'ring in the sky
In times of innocence and holy joy;   10
The joyful shepherd stops his grateful song
To hear the music of an angel's tongue.

So when she speaks, the voice of Heaven I hear:
So when we walk, nothing impure comes near;
Each field seems Eden, and each calm retreat;   15
Each village seems the haunt of holy feet.

But that sweet village, where my black-ey'd maid
Closes her eyes in sleep beneath night's shade,
When'er I enter, more than mortal fire
Burns in my soul, and does my song inspire.   20

*   *   *

Do not be confused by the mythological framework of Blake's poetry; it will be further identified and defined as you move on to the study questions and discussions of other works. It is not necessary to recognize the mythic figures by name because, within the context of each of his poems, Blake identifies the characters through the imagery that he uses to describe them, through their behavior, and through what they say about themselves and each other. His characters can be understood in terms of the forces that we experience inside ourselves and in the outside world, and in our interactions with other individuals and with the institutions of society. He personifies all of our ideas and feelings, personal and collective—all the elements of human existence and experience, natural and man-made, unconscious and conscious. Blake's primary concern is the split in man that causes him to be at war with himself and with all other forms of life—the split between abstract thought and actual experience, between reason and imagination, spectres and reality. This split is expressed in the conflict between the Rationalist/Materialist who controls the surface of the world and is concerned with only the outward appearance of things, and the Thinking/Feeling Man of Imagination who lives inside himself and transforms the outer world through his intimate Experience/Understanding of the Reality beneath the external form, the Truth (or True Art) beneath all artifice.

Some key terms in Blake's symbolism:

1. *Albion* signifies Collective Humanity as it exists in the outside world; *Jerusalem* is this reality seen spiritually. The *Daughters of Albion* are Collective Womanhood or the Feminine Element of Humanity struggling to survive in the non-spiritual reality of the outside world.
2. *Urizen* is Reason, the Prince of Light, of Cold, Materialistic Consciousness. His female counterpart is *Ahania,* Woman misjudged as Sin or Plaything. *Bromion* is Urizen's Henchman, the Materialist, Warrior, and Rapist; he upholds Law and Puritanical Morality.
3. *Thel* is the Virgin, Woman untouched by Experience.
4. *Luvah* signifies Emotion, Love. *Vala,* the female counterpart, is Nature.
5. *Urthona* is Creativity, Poetic Energy, embodied as *Los,* which signifies Imagination, Prophecy (also Time). *Los's* female counterpart is *Enitharmon,* signifying Space. The child of Los is *Orc,* Revolutionary Energy.
6. *Beulah* is the State of Innocence (Childhood, Love).

*   *   *

VISIONS OF THE DAUGHTERS OF ALBION

William Blake

The Eye sees more than the Heart knows

THE ARGUMENT

I loved Theotormon,
And I was not ashamed;
I trembled in my virgin fears,
And I hid in Leutha's vale!

I plucked Leutha's flower,
And I rose up from the vale;
But the terrible thunders tore
My virgin mantle in twain.

VISIONS

Enslav'd, the Daughters of Albion weep; a trembling
   lamentation
Upon their mountains; in their valleys, sighs toward America.

For the soft soul of America, Oothoon, wander'd in woe,
Along the vales of Leutha seeking flowers to comfort her;
And thus she spoke to the bright Marygold of Leutha's vale: 5
"Art thou a flower? art thou a nymph? I see thee now a flower,
Now a nymph! I dare not pluck thee from thy dewy bed!"

The Golden nymph replied: "Pluck thou my flower,
    Oothoon the mild!
Another flower shall spring, because the soul of sweet delight
Can never pass away." She ceas'd, & clos'd her golden shrine.   10

Then Oothoon pluck'd the flower, saying: "I pluck thee
    from thy bed,
Sweet flower, and put thee here to glow between my breasts,
And thus I turn my face to where my whole soul seeks."

Over the waves she went in wing'd exulting swift delight,
And over Theotormon's reign took her impetuous course.   15

Bromion rent her with his thunders; on his stormy bed
Lay the faint maid, and soon her woes appall'd his thunders
    hoarse.

Bromion spoke: "Behold this harlot here on Bromion's bed,
And let the jealous dolphins sport around the lovely maid!
Thy soft American plains are mine, and mine thy north   20
    & south:
Stampt with my signet are the swarthy children of the sun;
They are obedient, they resist not, they obey the scourge;
Their daughters worship terrors and obey the violent.
Now thou maist marry Bromion's harlot, and protect the child
Of Bromion's rage, that Oothoon shal! put forth in nine   25
    moons' time."

Then storms rent Theotormon's limbs: he roll'd his
    waves around
And folded his black jealous waters round the adulterate pair.
Bound back to back in Bromion's caves, terror & meekness
    dwell:

At entrance Theotormon sits, wearing the threshold hard
With secret tears; beneath him sound like waves on a   30
    desert shore

The voice of slaves beneath the sun, and children
    bought with money,
That shiver in religious caves beneath the burning fires
Of lust, that belch incessant from the summits of the earth.

Oothoon weeps not; she cannot weep! her tears are locked up;
But she can howl incessant writhing her soft snowy limbs   35
And calling Theotormon's Eagles to prey upon her flesh.

"I call with holy voice! Kings of the sounding air,
Rend away this defiled bosom that I may reflect
The image of Theotormon on my pure transparent breast."

The Eagles at her call descend & rend their bleeding prey: 40
Theotormon severely smiles; her soul reflects the smile,
As the clear spring, mudded with feet of beasts, grows
    pure & smiles.

The Daughters of Albion hear her woes, & echo back her sighs.

"Why does my Theotormon sit weeping upon the threshold,
And Oothoon hovers by his side, persuading him in vain?   45
I cry: arise, O Theotormon! for the village dog
Barks at the breaking day; the nightingale has done lamenting;
The lark does rustle in the ripe corn, and the Eagle returns
From nightly prey and lifts his golden beak to the pure east,
Shaking the dust from his immortal pinions to awake   50
The sun that sleeps too long. Arise, my Theotormon, I am pure
Because the night is gone that clos'd me in its deadly black.

"They told me that the night & day were all that I could see;
They told me that I had five senses to inclose me up,
And they inclos'd my infinite brain into a narrow circle,   55
And sunk my heart into the Abyss, a red, round globe,
    hot burning,
Till all from life I was obliterated and erased.
Instead of morn arises a bright shadow, like an eye
In the eastern cloud; instead of night a sickly charnel house:
That Theotormon hears me not! to him the night and morn   60
Are both alike; a night of sighs, a morning of fresh tears,
And none but Bromion can hear my lamentations.

"With what sense is it that the chicken shuns the ravenous
    hawk?

With what sense does the tame pigeon measure out the
  expanse?
With what sense does the bee form cells? have not the   65
  mouse & frog
Eyes and ears and sense of touch? yet are their habitations
And their pursuits as different as their forms and as their joys.
Ask the wild ass why he refuses burdens, and the meek camel
Why he loves man: is it because of eye, ear, mouth, or skin,
Or breathing nostrils? No, for these the wolf and tiger have.   70
Ask the blind worm the secrets of the grave, and why her spires
Love to curl round the bones of death; and ask the
  rav'nous snake
Where she gets poison, & the wing'd eagle why he loves the sun;
And then tell me the thoughts of man, that have been
  hid of old.

"Silent I hover all the night, and all day could be silent   75
If Theotormon once would turn his loved eyes upon me.
How can I be defil'd when I reflect thy image pure?
Sweetest the fruit that the worm feeds on, & the soul
  prey'd on by woe,
The new wash'd lamb ting'd with the village smoke, &
  the bright swan
By the red earth of our immortal river. I bathe my wings,   80
And I am white and pure to hover round Theotormon's
  breast."

Then Theotormon broke his silence, and he answered:
"Tell me what is the night or day to one o'erflow'd with woe?
Tell me what is a thought, & of what substance is it made?
Tell me what is a joy, & in what gardens do joys grow?   85
And in what rivers swim the sorrows? and upon what
  mountains
Wave shadows of discontent? and in what houses dwell
  the wretched,
Drunken with woe forgotten, and shut up from cold despair?
Tell me where dwell the thoughts forgotten till thou
  call them forth?
Tell me where dwell the joys of old? & where the ancient loves,   90
And when will they renew again, & the night of oblivion past,
That I might traverse times & spaces far remote, and bring
Comforts into a present sorrow and a night of pain?
Where goest thou, O thought? to what remote land is
  thy flight?

If thou returnest to the present moment of affliction 95
Wilt thou bring comforts on thy wings, and dews and
   honey and balm,
Or poison from the desert wilds, from the eyes of the envier?"

Then Bromion said, and shook the cavern with his lamentation:

"Thou knowest that the ancient trees seen by thine eyes
   have fruit,
But knowest thou that trees and fruits flourish upon the earth   100
To gratify senses unknown? trees, beasts and birds unknown;
Unknown, not unperceiv'd, spread in the infinite microscope,
In places yet unvisited by the voyager, and in worlds
Over another kind of seas, and in atmospheres unknown:
Ah! are there other wars beside the wars of sword and fire?   105
And are there other sorrows beside the sorrows of poverty?
And are there other joys beside the joys of riches and ease?
And is there not one law for both the lion and the ox?
And is there not eternal fire and eternal chains
To bind the phantoms of existence from eternal life?"   110

Then Oothoon waited silent all the day and all the night;
But when the morn arose, her lamentation renew'd.
The Daughters of Albion hear her woes, & echo back
   her sighs.

"O Urizen! Creator of men! mistaken Demon of heaven!
Thy joys are tears, thy labour vain to form men to thine image.   115
How can one joy absorb another? are not different joys
Holy, eternal, infinite? and each joy is a Love.

"Does not the great mouth laugh at a gift, & the narrow
   eyelids mock
At the labour that is above payment? and wilt thou take
   the ape
For thy counsellor, or the dog for a schoolmaster to thy   120
   children?
Does he who contemns poverty and he who turns with
   abhorrence
From usury feel the same passion, or are they moved alike?
How can the giver of gifts experience the delights of the
   merchant?
How the industrious citizen the pains of the husbandman?
How different far the fat fed hireling with hollow drum,   125

THE MARBLE/PLASTIC DOLL   *69*

Who buys whole corn fields into wastes, and sings upon
    the heath!
How different their eye and ear! how different the world
    to them!
With what sense does the parson claim the labour of the
    farmer?
What are his nets & gins & traps; & how does he sur-
    round him
With cold floods of abstraction, and with forests of solitude,   130
To build him castles and high spires, where kings &
    priests may dwell;
Till she who burns with youth, and knows no fixed lot,
    is bound
In spells of law to one she loathes? and must she drag the chain
Of life in weary lust? must chilling, murderous thoughts
    obscure
The clear heaven of her eternal spring; to bear the wintry   135
    rage
Of a harsh terror, driv'n to madness, bound to hold a rod
Over her shrinking shoulders all the day, & all the night
To turn the wheel of false desire, and longings that
    wake her womb
To the abhorred birth of cherubs in the human form,
That live a pestilence & die a meteor, & are no more;   140
Till the child dwell with one he hates, and do the deed
    he loathes,
And the impure scourge force his seed into its unripe birth'
Ere yet his eyelids can behold the arrows of the day?

"Does the whale worship at they footsteps as the hungry dog;
Or does he scent the mountain prey because his nostrils wide   145
Draw in the ocean? does his eye discern the flying cloud
As the raven's eye? or does he measure the expanse like
    the vulture?
Does the still spider view the cliffs where eagles hide
    their young;
Or does the fly rejoice because the harvest is brought in?
Does not the eagle scorn the earth & despise the treasures   150
    beneath?
But the mole knoweth what is there, & the worm shall
    tell it thee.
Does not the worm erect a pillar in the mouldering
    church yard

And a palace of eternity in the jaws of the hungry grave?
Over his porch these words are written: 'Take thy bliss,
    O Man!
And sweet shall be thy taste, & sweet thy infant joys renew!'   155

"Infancy! fearless, lustful, happy, nestling for delight
In laps of pleasure: Innocence! honest, open, seeking
The vigorous joys of morning light; open to virgin bliss.
Who taught thee modesty, subtile modesty, child of night
    & sleep?
When thou awakest wilt thou dissemble all thy secret joys,   160
Or wert thou not awake when all this mystery was disclos'd?
Then com'st thou forth a modest virgin, knowing to dissemble,
With nets found under thy night pillow, to catch virgin joy
And brand it with the name of whore, & sell it in the night,
In silence, ev'n without a whisper, and in seeming sleep.   165
Religious dreams and holy vespers light thy smoky fires:
Once were thy fires lighted by the eyes of honest morn.
And does my Theotormon seek this hypocrite modesty,
This knowing, artful, secret, fearful, cautious, trembling
    hypocrite?
Then is Oothoon a whore indeed! and all the virgin joys   170
Of life are harlots, and Theotormon is a sick man's dream;
And Oothoon is the crafty slave of selfish holiness.

"But Oothoon is not so: a virgin fill'd with virgin fancies,
Open to joy and to delight where ever beauty appears;
If in the morning sun I find it, there my eyes are fix'd   175
In happy copulation; if in evening mild, wearied with work,
Sit on a bank and draw the pleasures of this free born joy.

"The moment of desire! the moment of desire! The virgin
That pines for man shall awaken her womb to enormous joys
In the secret shadows of her chamber: the youth shut up from   180
The lustful joy shall forget to generate & create an amorous
    image
In the shadows of his curtains and in the folds of his silent
    pillow.
Are not these the places of religion, the rewards of continence,
The self enjoyings of self denial? why dost thou seek religion?
Is it because acts are not lovely that thou seekest solitude   185
Where the horrible darkness is impressed with reflections
    of desire?

"Father of Jealousy, be thou accursed from the earth!
Why hast thou taught my Theotormon this accursed thing?
Till beauty fades from off my shoulders, darken'd and cast out,
A solitary shadow wailing on the margin of non-entity.   190

"I cry: Love! Love! Love! happy happy Love! free as
    the mountain wind!
Can that be Love that drinks another as a sponge drinks water,
That clouds with jealousy his nights, with weepings all the day,
To spin a web of age around him, grey and hoary, dark,
Till his eyes sicken at the fruit that hangs before his sight?   195
Such is self-love that envies all, a creeping skeleton
With lamplike eyes watching around the frozen marriage bed.

"But silken nets and traps of adamant will Oothoon spread,
And catch for thee girls of mild silver, or of furious gold.
I'll lie beside thee on a bank & view their wanton play   200
In lovely copulation, bliss on bliss, with Theotormon:
Red as the rosy morning, lustful as the first born beam,
Oothoon shall view his dear delight, nor e'er with jealous
    cloud
Come in the heaven of generous love, nor selfish blightings
    bring.

"Does the sun walk in glorious raiment on the secret floor   205
Where the cold miser spreads his gold; or does the
    bright cloud drop
On his stone threshold? does his eye behold the beam
    that brings
Expansion to the eye of pity? or will he bind himself
Beside the ox to thy hard furrow? does not that mild
    beam blot
The bat, the owl, the glowing tiger, and the king of night?   210
The sea fowl takes the wintry blast for a cov'ring to her limbs,
And the wild snake the pestilence to adorn him with
    gems & gold;
And trees & birds & beasts & men behold their eternal joy.
Arise, you little glancing wings, and sing your infant joy!
Arise, and drink your bliss, for every thing that lives is holy!"   215

Thus every morning wails Oothoon; but Theotormon sits
Upon the margin'd ocean conversing with shadows dire.

The Daughters of Albion hear her woes, & echo back her sighs.

WORKS IN *Short Story Masterpieces*

F. Scott Fitzgerald, *Winter Dreams*
John Cheever, *Torch Song*

OTHER SUGGESTED WORKS

Robert Graves, *The Portrait*
Robert Bridges, *The Philosopher to His Mistress*
Euripides, *Trojan Women*
Virginia Woolf, *A Room of One's Own,* Chapter Two
Sören Kierkegaard, *Diary of the Seducer,* from *Either/Or,* Volume I

QUESTIONS

1a. Why is the man in Keats's poem "alone and palely loitering . . .
on the cold hill side"? Where might he be instead? What is strange
about his behavior and about the situation in which we find him?

b. What is the nature of *La Belle Dame sans Merci?* What is the significance of her name? Discuss the images used to describe her. Why
does the man make a point of kissing shut "her wild, sad eyes"?
Why are they "wild sad eyes"?

c. Why does Keats's man dream of "pale kings, and princes"? What
has made them all "death pale"? Why are they starved? Is it for
something that La Belle Dame cannot provide? What is their "horrid
warning"?

2. Why is it significant that the "ghost-girl-rider" in Hardy's poem is
"a phantom of his own figuring"? Why does he waste away every
day while "time touches her not"? Compare this phantom lady with
La Belle Dame. What have they done to the men?

3. Why do both Wordsworth and Hardy use the word "phantom" to
describe their women? Does the man in Wordsworth's poem attempt
to confront an aspect of his woman that the man in Keats's poem
ignores? Why does he say "a Spirit, yet a Woman too!"? Why the
exclamation point, as if he has made some startling discovery? But
how does he go on to define her Womanhood? What does he mean
by "household motions light and free" and "steps of virgin-liberty"?
Why does he use the word "machine"? How can a machine have a
pulse? What is strange in the imagery of the last stanza of the poem?

4. What new element is introduced in Blake's poem *The Crystal Cabinet* and Poe's story *Ligeia?* What does Blake's man have that Keats's
man is lacking? What is the significance of his shattering "the
Crystal Cabinet"? What in the man's behavior or attitude shatters

it? What world does the cabinet represent? Compare it with the reality of the outside world. What is "the inmost Form" that he strives "to seize"? Is it the same thing that Keats's, Hardy's, Wordsworth's, and Poe's men are after? Why can't this "inmost Form" be possessed in the manner in which Blake's man seeks it? Why does he become "like a Weeping Babe" when "the Crystal Cabinet" is burst? Why is the woman now weeping and "pale reclined"? What has been lost and why? Compare Blake's with Keats's poem.

5. How does Poe turn fascination with La Belle Dame into a religion? How is love of this kind of woman a love of death, a death cult? Describe the nature of the passion depicted in *Ligeia*. What is the passion directed to? Why does this passion destroy life? Discuss the imagery used to describe Ligeia, and compare it with descriptions of women in the other works discussed. (In conjunction with the Poe story, read D. H. Lawrence's essay on Poe in *Studies in Classic American Literature*. Discuss what Lawrence says about love and knowledge in terms of the works in Part I.)

6. How is Ligeia's death like the breaking of "the Crystal Cabinet"? What is destructive about man's striving "to seize the inmost Form"? In Poe's man, what form does this striving take? What is he seeking? In what state is he left at the end of the story? Compare his final condition (and Ligeia's) with that of the men (and women) in the poems by Keats, Hardy, and Blake.

7. Compare Cullen's beloved with Poe's Ligeia. Discuss the nature of the imagery used to describe them both. What is unusual about these women? Why are Poe and Cullen so hostile toward fair-haired/skinned ladies? Why do they prefer dark ladies? What are they exulting?

8. In *Adam's Curse*, what insight does Yeats offer into the "phantom-lady" problem? What is "the old high way of love"? What is wrong with it? What is it missing? How is the man in Yeats's poem like the man in Poe's story in his attitude toward love and beauty? Why are the people "weary-hearted"? Why is the image of the "hollow moon" appropriate? What is "Adam's curse"? Is it also Eve's curse? What kind of beauty is the woman talking about in the second stanza?

9. Discuss M. Esther Harding's essay in terms of the works in Part I. Are her observations about the nature of man/woman relationships and of man's images of woman supported by the experiences of people in real life? Does she offer a meaningful psychological explanation of the "phantom-lady" problem? Does her theory of projection make sense in terms of your own experience?

10. What is the similarity between the man "palely loitering" in Keats's poem and the man in Wilbur's poem sitting with his eyes glued to

the centerfold of *Playboy* magazine? What are both men seeking and lacking? What are they both doing? Is the same kind of woman the object of their attention? Are both poems concerned with pornography? If so, what is pornography?

11. Compare Vonnegut's *Miss Temptation* and Anderson's *The Strength of God*. What is the significance of both of the men turning to religion when they are tempted by women? What can frustrated desire lead men to do? If man cannot have what he thinks he wants, what attitude does he take toward the object of his desire? What insight is offered into the nature of repression and religion in its most dishonest, superficial form?

12. Why does the man in Vonnegut's story view woman as the source of evil and temptation? Is man really tempted by forces outside himself? If so, why the long history of seduction poems, such as Andrew Marvell's *To His Coy Mistress* and John Donne's *The Flea*? What form does man as tempter assume? How does he go about getting the woman to succumb to his will? How is it different from the way in which woman supposedly seduces man? Are men tempted by beautiful bodies and women by grand ideas and sound arguments?

13. Compare the women in Vonnegut's and Anderson's stories and the way the men respond to them. In what ways are these women like the centerfold in *Playboy* magazine? What happens when the picture turns into flesh-and-blood reality? Why is Cpl. Fuller so upset with Susanna? How does she step out of the magazine and become an actual person? What important insights does she offer into the nature of man/woman relationships and the problem of being yourself—particularly if you are beautiful? (Refer back to the discussion of beauty in *Adam's Curse*. Compare Susanna with Yeats's beautiful woman.) Discuss the Cpl. Fuller-Susanna encounter in terms of experiences in real life: pre-conceived notions about the opposite sex that create barriers and keep people locked in their fantasy worlds.

14. On what image of woman are the seducers in Marvell's and Donne's poems basing their arguments? Do they believe in this image, or are they merely playing on the image that they believe the woman holds of herself? Whom does each poem tell us the most about—the one being seduced or the seducer? Discuss the nature of the deceit. (For a more detailed, philosophical study of man as seducer, see Sören Kierkegaard's *Diary of the Seducer* at the end of Volume I of *Either/Or*.)

15a. Compare the Marvell poem with Blake's *Song*. How are both men in the same predicament with regard to the women they love?

Describe the two kinds of love or feeling involved by comparing the angelic maiden in the beginning of Blake's poem with the "black-ey'd maid" at the end.

b. How is Blake's man split inside himself? Discuss the states through which he moves in each stanza. Why is he in a dangerous state in Stanzas 3 and 4? What change comes after the "But" in Stanza 5? Why is that "But" essential? How is what he thinks he should love (or the manner in which he expresses his love) different from what he really desires and needs? Compare the religious imagery of the first four stanzas with the imagery of the last stanza. Why does "more than mortal fire" burn in his soul when he is with his "black-ey'd maid"? Why is it significant that he avoids describing the fire as "heavenly"? How is Blake redefining the nature of religious experience? How might the preacher in Anderson's story profit from Blake's understanding of "True Religion"? Should there be a difference between "divine" and "mortal"? How can the fully mortal be "more than mortal"? What is the significance of ending with *"my song"* rather than an *"angel's song"*?

16a. Discuss how *Visions of the Daughters of Albion* shows the fall of woman from the man-made pedestal of purity and godliness into the man-made (reason-created) abyss of harlotry and sinfulness. If woman can be only one of two possible extremes—either a Virgin/Saint or a Whore/Devil—what happens when she passes from the first state to the second? Do these labels describe what woman is actually experiencing and who she really is? How is her experience of "loss of innocence" different from the way the rational world labels it? How does each extreme presuppose and depend upon the existence of the other? Why does man pretend that the two states are completely separate? Must experience be a destructive, defiling absolute? (Discuss the difference between Experience-in-Itself and Ideas-of-Experience.) Has woman no choice but to be Virgin or Whore, Saint or Devil? What in man's world misjudges her as sinful plaything? (Refer back to *Miss Temptation* and *The Strength of God.*)

b. Why are Blake's Daughters of Albion (Collective Womanhood or the Feminine Element of Humanity) weeping? What is the primary cause of their grief? Explain how "The Golden Nymph" is redefining the nature of Innocence and Experience when she says to Oothoon:

"Pluck thou my flower, Oothoon the mild!
Another flower shall spring, because the soul of sweet delight
Can never pass away:"

What is Oothoon's soul seeking when she plucks the flower and wears it proudly between her breasts? Contrast her state of "winged exulted swift delight" with what becomes of her in Theotormon's world, dominated by Bromion. Why does Bromion call her a harlot? What force in the world of men is Bromion? Discuss the images used to describe his world and what happens in it.

c. What imprisons Oothoon? Why can't she weep? What is it about her that invites "Theotormon's Eagles to prey upon her flesh"? What do these birds signify? Why does she call her bosom "defiled"? Who is Theotormon and what is his relationship to Oothoon? Why does he smile severely at her suffering? Why doesn't he help her? If it is his world, why does he let Bromion rule it?

d. Why is it important that Oothoon be pure for Theotormon? What is the "deadly black" in which she has been enclosed? What is wrong with her having been told that she could see only "the night & day"? What else is there to see? Is there a reality that cannot be seen or perceived with the five senses? Who or what is the "they" that limited her to five senses and removed her completely from life?

e. What is the significance of the questions that Oothoon asks about the different creatures? What is it that she wants to know? What is the question that Theotormon is raising about the nature of Thought and Memory? What does he wish that they could do? How does Bromion answer him? How does Bromion define knowledge? To what does he limit human experience?

f. What kind of person or institution is Bromion? What are "the phantoms of existence" that he would bind? In modern terms, how would he label Theotormon? What keeps Theotormon from acting? Do you agree with what Bromion says? How would you answer his rhetorical questions on the basis of your own experience?

g. Why is Urizen (Reason) called the "Creator of men" and "mistaken Demon of heaven"? What are Oothoon and her sisters crying out against in the Reason-made world? What creative force opposes Urizen's violent world and works to undo its teachings? (Discuss some of the bad things that Urizen's world teaches, as you experience it today.)

h. Why does Blake use woman to represent the creative force that opposes Urizen? According to Oothoon, what causes man to "create amorous image" of woman? (Compare "the youth shut up from/ The lustful joy" with the young man shut up with his *Playboy* magazine and the man "palely loitering on the cold hill side.") For what is "religion" being criticized? (Refer back to *Miss Temptation* and *The Strength of God*.)

i. For Oothoon, what is "Love" as opposed to "Reason"? If Oothoon understands so clearly what is wrong with the man-made, Urizen-created world, why doesn't she do something about it? Why does she need Theotormon to help her? What is *he* inside *herself?* Why does he only sit "conversing with shadows dire"? Is it bad to spend time talking with shadows? Must action in the outside world manifest itself only in the form of violence—in actors like Bromion?

17. Discuss *Winter Dreams* and *Torch Song* (from *Short Story Masterpieces*) in terms of themes raised in Part I. What kind of man is attracted to the woman in Fitzgerald's story? How is she like La Belle Dame or the "femme fatale"? What is ironic about the way she ends up? Why is the title appropriate? Can such a woman be anything but a "winter dream"—the kind of fantasy that goes with cold, desolate times and places? Compare her with Joan in Cheever's story. What force in Jack's life does Joan represent? Toward what does she lure men, and why is she so irrestible? What kind of men attract her?

PART II

The Virgin Shrouded in Snow:
The Nun Syndrome

The Virgin Shrouded in Snow: The Nun Syndrome

The feminine equivalent of the man loitering on the "cold hill side" is what William Blake calls "the virgin shrouded in snow" or the virgin "pining away with desire." Being shrouded in snow, loitering, and pining are all forms of "living death," lack of involvement in real life and in relationships with flesh-and-blood people in the outside world. Men and women who live only in their minds, with only ideas, images, and fantasies of life and of themselves, are virgins in the sense that they are untouched by reality, by real-life experience. They are protected from it by some barrier created in their minds—frequently some ideal of what life should be or a fear that life might take something away from them, that it might destroy their ideas of who they are.

The woman who has withdrawn from the world is found alone in some tower or locked away in some dungeon, rather than roaming the countryside, and her jailors, her keepers, are men—a father, husband, authoritarian masculine voices that whisper in her ear, warning her of the world beyond the castle walls. She is woman without a real man, woman with only "dream lovers." She is woman out of relationship with the outside world because she is not in relationship with her deepest self.

Poets have exalted the solitary man's loitering and pining, and have dismissed the woman's frozen sleep or dreaming with a snigger about sexual repression. The man's pining is viewed as proof of sensitivity and love of beauty, although it is just as virginal and sexually impotent as the woman's avoidance of experience. Both are out of touch with their instincts and their feelings; they live in their ideas of feelings, which is not really living at all. In both cases, flesh-and-blood reality would shatter the illusion—the image of the ideal life or love; it would mean death to that particular ego existence, but would mean life to a deeper part of the self. Instead of confronting life directly, the virgin woman discreetly withdraws to a literal or figurative convent to worship her private image of "God," while the virgin man goes wandering across the countryside like an exhibitionist, telling his melodramatic, "tragic" story to anyone humorless enough to take him seriously. He becomes the head-hanger, the breast-beater, bemoaning how unkind the world has been to him, talking often of suicide. The woman's asceticism is that of piety and purity, and the man's asceticism is that of self-pity and pruriency. They are creatures of the same ilk, living in dreams of grandeur and self-delusion. No real man can ever love such a woman as perfectly as the demon lover whispering in her ear, as her imagined "God"; and no real woman can ever love such a man as perfectly as the phantom lady, the "faery's child" who let him kiss "her wild sad eyes."

But man, seeing woman only in terms of himself, understands her problem as a need for what only he can give her. He believes that he is pursuing a real woman across that hillside, and that she really exists outside himself, even though it seems obvious to him that the solitary, palely reclining woman is living only in her ideas of life, her fantasies, and that she is suffering from "sexual repression." He does not ask what has driven her into that tower or dungeon or what keeps her there, anymore than he asks himself what keeps him loitering on that cold hillside or thumbing through a *Playboy* magazine. The problem facing both people is the human one: how to get into relationships with real people in the outside world; how to become involved in real-life experiences without losing the value of the reflective, imaginative side of one's nature; how to find one's soul within one's self so that one does not spend a lifetime seeking it in the outside world, where it exists only as an illusion; how to marry the essence of oneself so that one can marry someone in the outside world.

The problem of "split consciousness" is expressed in the mirror image that appears throughout the works included in Part II. We look in the mirror, and we see our double. Do we believe it exists as a person outside ourselves, do we love it as an ideal image of our desire (really an object of self-love), or do we realize that it is an image that we have projected, that it is a reflection of something inside us? And do we consequently incorporate it into ourselves and seek to express it in the outside world through relationships with people who are not reflected in our mirrors?

In *The Lady of Shalott,* Tennyson offers a typical simplistic, egocentric masculine response to the solitary woman, who is an enigma because she is not in relationship with a man or with the extroverted world represented by "tower'd Camelot." Men are disturbed by women who are beyond their touch and manipulation. They are compelled to explain such women's behavior in terms of their not being in contact with men and with man's world, rather than seeing in such isolation a human problem that also plagues the thinking man, imprisoned in his ideas of himself and "the way things should be." It is the problem of how to live one's life as one's self when one cannot conform to the collective images of manhood and womanhood. Why are lone men and women driven out to wander over the countryside, to shut themselves in towers, or to bury themselves underground in caves and dungeons? They are undergoing a crisis of individual identity and consciousness, which results from a deep split within the self and which may involve loss of contact with instincts and feelings. The primary problem of the man on the hillside and the woman in the tower is not that they cannot get into a relationship with a real woman and man in the outside world, but that they cannot get in touch with, and become united with, the woman and man within themselves. This is what makes is impossible for them to form relationships with real people. Their internal conflict reflects the age-old-problem of how to know and accept one's self—with all its superior and inferior qualities—so that one can know and accept equally complex persons in the outside world.

Here are some general questions to keep in mind when considering the works in this section: When fantasies replace real people, is it because there are no real people to be found in the outside world, no one to relate to? It might be said that if the outside world were not so sterile and lacking in real people, were not so bewitched by dullness and normality, then those endowed with vivid imaginations would not be forced to live only in their internal worlds, which seem richer than what the outside world can offer. What is dubious about this view? What causes a person to see the world as a sterile place? Does it look that way only through his eyes? The possibility remains that shutting oneself in a fantasy world can prevent one from experiencing whatever richness might be hidden in the external world. But that richness can be found only by those who dare to venture boldly into the outside world, like the knights in Tennyson's poem who ride out from the walls of Camelot in search of adventure.

THE LADY OF SHALOTT

Alfred, Lord Tennyson (1809–1892)

PART I

On either side the river lie
Long fields of barley and of rye,
That clothe the wold° and meet the sky;
And thro' the field the road runs by
　　To many-tower'd Camelot;°　　　　　　　　　　5
And up and down the people go,
Gazing where the lilies blow
Round an island there below,
　　The island of Shalott.

Willows whiten, aspens quiver,　　　　　　　　　　10
Little breezes dusk and shiver
Thro' the wave that runs for ever
By the island in the river
　　Flowing down to Camelot.
Four gray walls, and four gray towers,　　　　　　　15

°*wold*: open field　　°*Camelot*: city of King Arthur's Round Table

Overlook a space of flowers,
And the silent isle imbowers
  The Lady of Shalott.

By the margin, willow-veil'd,
Slide the heavy barges trail'd   20
By slow horses; and unhail'd
The shallop° flitteth silken-sail'd
  Skimming down to Camelot:
But who hath seen her wave her hand?
Or at the casement seen her stand?   25
Or is she known in all the land,
  The Lady of Shalott?

Only reapers, reaping early
In among the bearded barley,
Hear a song that echoes cheerly   30
From the river winding clearly,
  Down to tower'd Camelot;
And by the moon the reaper weary,
Piling sheaves in uplands airy,
Listening, whispers " 'T is the fairy 35
  Lady of Shalott."

PART II

There she weaves by night and day
A magic web with colors gay.
She has heard a whisper say,
A curse is on her if she stay   40
  To look down to Camelot.
She knows not what the curse may be,
And so she weaveth steadily,
And little other care hath she,
  The Lady of Shalott.   45

And moving thro' a mirror clear
That hangs before her all the year,
Shadows of the world appear.
There she sees the highway near
  Winding down to Camelot;   50
There the river eddy whirls,
And there the surly village-churls,

°*shallop*: small boat

And the red cloaks of market girls,
    Pass onward from Shalott.

Sometimes a troop of damsels glad, 55
An abbot on an ambling pad,°
Sometimes a curly shepherd-lad,
Or long-hair'd page in crimson clad,
    Goes by to tower'd Camelot;
And sometimes thro' the mirror blue 60
The knights come riding two and two:
She hath no loyal knight and true,
    The Lady of Shalott.

But in her web she still delights
To weave the mirror's magic sights, 65
For often thro' the silent nights
A funeral, with plumes and lights
    And music, went to Camelot;
Or when the moon was overhead,
Came two young lovers lately wed: 70
"I am half sick of shadows," said
    The Lady of Shalott.

PART III

A bow-shot from her bower-eaves,
He rode between the barley-sheaves.
The sun came dazzling thro' the leaves, 75
And flamed upon the brazen greaves°
    Of bold Sir Lancelot.
A red-cross knight for ever kneel'd
To a lady in his shield,
That sparkled on the yellow field, 80
    Beside remote Shalott.

The gemmy° bridle glitter'd free,
Like to some branch of stars we see
Hung in the golden Galaxy.°
The bridle bells rang merrily 85
    As he rode down to Camelot;
And from his blazon'd baldric° slung

°*pad:* horse that paces easily along   °*greaves:* armor for the legs below the knees
°*gemmy:* gem-like in brightness   °*golden galaxy:* the Milky Way   °*baldric:* a belt
worn over the shoulder to hold a sword or bugle

A mighty silver bugle hung,
And as he rode his armor rung,
  Beside remote Shalott.   90

All in the blue unclouded weather
Thick-jewell'd shone the saddle-leather,
The helmet and the helmet-feather
Burn'd like one burning flame together,
  As he rode down to Camelot;   95
As often thro' the purple night,
Below the starry clusters bright,
Some bearded meteor, trailing light,
  Moves over still Shalott.

His broad clear brow in sunlight glow'd; 100
On burnish'd hooves his war-horse trode;
From underneath his helmet flow'd
His coal-black curls as on he rode,
  As he rode down to Camelot.
From the bank and from the river   105
He flash'd into the crystal mirror,
"Tirra lirra," by the river
  Sang Sir Lancelot.

She left the web, she left the loom,
She made three paces thro' the room, 110
She saw the water-lily bloom,
She saw the helmet and the plume,
  She look'd down to Camelot.
Out flew the web and floated wide;
The mirror crack'd from side to side; 115
"The curse is come upon me," cried
  The Lady of Shalott.

PART IV

In the stormy east-wind straining,
The pale yellow woods were waning,
The broad stream in his banks complaining, 120
Heavily the low sky raining
  Over tower'd Camelot;
Down she came and found a boat
Beneath a willow left afloat,
And round about the prow she wrote 125
  The Lady of Shalott.

And down the river's dim expanse
Like some bold seër in a trance,
Seeing all his own mischance—
With a glassy countenance   130
     Did she look to Camelot.
And at the closing of the day
She loosed the chain, and down she lay;
The broad stream bore her far away,
     The Lady of Shalott.   135

Lying, robed in snowy white
That loosely flew to left and right—
The leaves upon her falling light—
Thro' the noises of the night
     She floated down to Camelot;   140
And as the boat-head wound along
The willowy hills and fields among,
They heard her singing her last song,
     The Lady of Shalott.

Heard a carol, mournful, holy,   145
Chanted loudly, chanted lowly,
Till her blood was frozen slowly,
And her eyes were darken'd wholly,
     Turn'd to tower'd Camelot.
For ere she reach'd upon the tide   150
The first house by the water-side,
Singing in her song she died,
     The Lady of Shalott.

Under tower and balcony,
By garden-wall and gallery,   155
A gleaming shape she floated by,
Dead-pale between the houses high,
     Silent into Camelot.
Out upon the wharfs they came,
Knight and burgher, lord and dame,   160
And round the prow they read her name,
     The Lady of Shalott.

Who is this? and what is here?
And in the lighted palace near
Died the sound of royal cheer;   165

And they cross'd themselves for fear,
All the knights at Camelot:
But Lancelot mused a little space;
He said, "She has a lovely face;
God in his mercy lend her grace,   170
The Lady of Shalott."

APPLE BLOSSOM IN BRITTANY°

Ernest Dowson (1867–1900)

I

IT was the feast of the Assumption° in Ploumariel, at the hottest
part of the afternoon. Benedict Campion, who had just assisted at
vespers,° in the little dove-cotted church—like everything else in Ploumariel, even vespers were said earlier than is the usage in towns—took
up his station in the market-place to watch the procession pass by. The
head of it was just then emerging into the Square: a long file of men from
the neighbouring villages, bare-headed and chaunting,° followed the
crucifer. They were all clad in the picturesque garb of the Morbihan
peasantry, and were many of them imposing, quite noble figures with
their clear-cut Breton features, and their austere type of face. After them
a troop of young girls, with white veils over their heads, carrying ban-
ners—children from the convent school of the Ursulines; and then, two
and two in motley assemblage (peasant women with their white coifs
walking with the wives and daughters of prosperous *bourgeois* in costumes
more civilised but far less pictorial) half the inhabitants of Ploumariel—
all, indeed, who had not, with Campion, preferred to be spectators, taking
refuge from a broiling sun under the grateful shadow of the chestnuts in
the market-place. Last of all a muster of clergy, four or five strong, a small
choir of bullet-headed boys, and the Curé° of the parish himself, Monsieur
Letêtre chaunting from his book, who brought up the rear.

Campion, leaning against his chestnut tree, watched them defile.°
Once a smile of recognition flashed across his face, which was answered by
a girl in the procession. She just glanced from her book, and the smile with
which she let her eyes rest upon him for a moment, before she dropped
them, did not seem to detract from her devotional air. She was very young
and slight—she might have been sixteen—and she had a singularly pretty
face; her white dress was very simple, and her little straw hat, but both
of these she wore with an air which at once set her apart from her com-

---

°*Brittany*: region in Northwest France   °*feast . . . Assumption*: church feast com-
memorating the assumption (taking into Heaven) of the Virgin Mary: observed on
August 15   °*vespers*: evening worship service   °*chaunting*: chanting   °*Curé*:
priest   °*defile*: file by

panions, with their provincial finery and their rather commonplace charms. Campion's eyes followed the little figure until it was lost in the distance, disappearing with the procession down a by-street on its return journey to the church. And after they had all passed, the singing, the last verse of the "Ave Maris Stella," was borne across to him, through the still air, the voices of children pleasantly predominating. He put on his hat at last, and moved away; every now and then he exchanged a greeting with somebody—the communal doctor, the mayor; while here and there a woman explained him to her gossip in whispers as he passed, "It is the Englishman of Mademoiselle Marie-Ursule—it is M. le Curé's guest." It was to the dwelling of M. le Curé, indeed, that Campion now made his way. Five minutes' walk brought him to it; an unpretentious white house, lying back in its large garden, away from the dusty road. It was an untidy garden, rather useful than ornamental; a very little shade was offered by one incongruous plane-tree, under which a wooden table was placed and some chairs. After *déjeuner,*° on those hot August days, Campion and the Curé took their coffee here; and in the evening it was here that they sat and talked while Mademoiselle Hortense, the Curé's sister, knitted, or appeared to knit, an interminable shawl; the young girl, Marie-Ursule, placidly completing the quartet with her silent, felicitous smile of a convent-bred child, which seemed sometimes, at least to Campion, to be after all a finer mode of conversation. He threw himself down now on the bench, wondering when his hosts would have finished their devotions, and drew a book from his pocket as if he would read. But he did not open it, but sat for a long time holding it idly in his hand, and gazing out at the village, at the expanse of dark pine-covered hills, and at the one trenchant object in the foreground, the white façade of the convent of the Ursuline nuns. Once and again he smiled, as though his thoughts, which had wandered a long way, had fallen upon extraordinarily pleasant things. He was a man of barely forty, though he looked slightly older than his age: his little, peaked beard was grizzled, and a life spent in literature, and very studiously, had given him the scholar's premature stoop. He was not handsome, but, when he smiled, his smile was so pleasant that people credited him with good looks. It brought, moreover, such a light of youth into his eyes, as to suggest that if his avocations had unjustly aged his body, that had not been without its compensations—his soul had remained remarkably young. Altogether, he looked shrewd, kindly and successful, and he was all these things, while if there was also a certain sadness in his eyes—lines of lassitude about his mouth—this was an idiosyncracy of his temperament, and hardly justified by his history, which had always been honourable and smooth. He was sitting in the same calm and pre-

---

°*déjeuner*: lunch

sumably agreeable reverie, when the garden gate opened, and a girl—the young girl of the procession, fluttered towards him.

"Are you quite alone?" she asked brightly, seating herself at his side. "Has not Aunt Hortense come back?"

Campion shook his head, and she continued speaking in English, very correctly, but with a slight accent, which gave to her pretty young voice the last charm.

"I suppose she has gone to see *la mère Guémené*. She will not live another night they say. Ah! what a pity," she cried, clasping her hands; "to die on the Assumption—that is hard."

Campion smiled softly. "Dear child, when one's time comes, when one is old as that, the day does not matter much." Then he went on: "But how is it you are back; were you not going to your nuns?"

She hesitated a moment. "It is your last day, and I wanted to make tea for you. You have had no tea this year. Do you think I have forgotten how to make it, while you have been away, as I forget my English words?"

"It's I who am forgetting such an English habit," he protested. "But run away and make it, if you like. I am sure it will be very good."

She stood for a moment looking down at him, her fingers smoothing a little bunch of palest blue ribbons on her white dress. In spite of her youth, her brightness, the expression of her face in repose was serious and thoughtful, full of unconscious wistfulness. This, together with her placid manner, the manner of a child who has lived chiefly with old people and quiet nuns, made her beauty to Campion a peculiarly touching thing. Just then her eyes fell upon Campion's wide-awake,° lying on the seat at his side, and travelled to his uncovered head. She uttered a protesting cry: "Are you not afraid of a *coup de soleil?*° See—you are not fit to be a guardian if you can be so foolish as that. It is I who have to look after you." She took up the great grey hat and set it daintily on his head; then with a little laugh she disappeared into the house.

When Campion raised his head again, his eyes were smiling, and in the light of a sudden flush which just died out of it, his face looked almost young.

II

This girl, so foreign in her education and traditions, so foreign in the grace of her movements, in everything except the shade of her dark blue eyes, was the child of an English father; and she was Benedict Campion's ward. This relation, which many persons found incongruous, had befallen naturally enough. Her father had been Campion's oldest and most familiar friend; and when Richard Heath's romantic marriage

---

°*wide-awake*: a soft felt hat °*coup de soleil*: sunstroke

had isolated him from so many others, from his family and from his native land, Campion's attachment to him had, if possible, only been increased. From his heart he had approved, had prophesied nothing but good of an alliance, which certainly, while it lasted, had been an wholly ideal relation. There had seemed no cloud on the horizon—and yet less than two years had seen the end of it. The birth of the child, Marie-Ursule, had been her mother's death; and six months later, Richard Heath, dying less from any defined malady than because he lacked any longer the necessary motive to live, was laid by the side of his wife. The helpless child remained, in the guardianship of Hortense, her mother's sister, and elder by some ten years, who had already composed herself contentedly, as some women do, to the prospect of perpetual spinsterhood, and the care of her brother's house—an ecclesiastic just appointed curé of Ploumariel. And here, ever since, in this quiet corner of Brittany, in the tranquil custody of the priest and his sister, Marie-Ursule had grown up.

Campion's share in her guardianship had not been onerous, although it was necessarily maintained; for the child had inherited, and what small property would come to her was in England, and in English funds. To Hortense Letêtre and her brother such responsibilities in an alien land were not for a moment to be entertained. And gradually, this connection, at first formal and impersonal, between Campion and the Breton presbytery, had developed into an intimacy, into a friendship singularly satisfying on both sides. Separate as their interests seemed, those of the French country-priest, and of the Englishman of letters, famous already in his own department, they had, nevertheless, much community of feeling apart from their common affection for a child. Now, for many years, he had been established in their good graces, so that it had become an habit with him to spend his holiday—it was often a very extended one—at Ploumariel; while to the Letêtres, as well as to Marie-Ursule herself, this annual sojourn of Campion's had become the occasion of the year, the one event which pleasantly relieved the monotony of life in this remote village; though that, too, was a not unpleasant routine. Insensibly Campion had come to find his chief pleasure in consideration of this child of an old friend, whose gradual growth beneath influences which seemed to him singularly exquisite and fine, he had watched so long; whose future, now that her childhood, her schooldays at the convent had come to an end, threatened to occupy him with an anxiety more intimate than any which hitherto he had known. Marie-Ursule's future! They had talked much of it that summer, the priest and the Englishman, who accompanied him in his long morning walks, through green lanes, and over white, dusty roads, and past fields perfumed with the pungently pleasant smell of the blood-red *sarrasin,* when he paid visits to the sick who lived on the outskirts of his scattered parish. Campion became aware then of an increasing difficulty in discussing this matter impersonally, in the impartial manner becoming a guardian. Odd thrills of jealousy stirred within him when he was asked to contemplate Marie-Ursule's possible suitors. And yet, it was with a very genuine surprise, at least for the moment, that he met the Curé's sudden pressing home of a more personal contingency—he took this freedom of an old friend with a shrewd twinkle in his eye, which suggested that all along this had been chiefly in his mind. *"Mon bon ami,* why should you not marry her yourself? That would please all of us so much." And he insisted, with kindly insistence, on the propriety of the thing: dwelling on Campion's established position, their long habit of friendship, his own and his sister's confidence and esteem, taking for granted, with that sure insight which is the gift of many women and of most priests, that on the ground of affection alone the justification was too obvious to be pressed. And he finished with a smile, stopping to take a pinch of snuff with a sigh of relief—the relief of a man who has at least seasonably unburdened himself.

"Surely, *mon ami,* some such possibility must have been in your mind?"

Campion hesitated for a moment; then he proffered his hand, which the other warmly grasped. "You read me aright," he said slowly, "only I hardly realised it before. Even now—no, how can I believe it possible— that she should care for me. *Non sum dignus,° non sum dignus.* Consider her youth, her inexperience; the best part of my life is behind me."

But the Curé smiled reassuringly. "The best part is before you, Campion; you have the heart of a boy. Do we not know you? And for the child—rest tranquil there! I have the word of my sister, who is a wise woman, that she is sincerely attached to you; not to speak of the evidence of my own eyes. She will be seventeen shortly, then she can speak for herself. And to whom else can we trust her?"

The shadow of these confidences hung over Campion when he next saw Marie-Ursule, and troubled him vaguely during the remainder of his visit, which this year, indeed, he considerably curtailed. Inevitably he was thrown much with the young girl, and if daily the charm which he found in her presence was sensibly increased, as he studied her from a fresh point of view, he was none the less disquieted at the part which he might be called upon to play. Diffident and scrupulous, a shy man, knowing little of women; and at least by temperament, a sad man, he trembled before felicity, as many at the palpable breath of misfortune. And his difficulty was increased by the conviction, forced upon him irresistibly, little as he could accuse himself of vanity, that the decision rested with himself. Her liking for him was genuine and deep, her confidence implicit. He had but to ask her and she would place her hand in his and go forth with him, as trustfully as a child. And when they came

---

°*Non sum dignus*: I am not worthy

to celebrate her *fête*, Marie-Ursule's seventeenth birthday— it occurred a little before the Assumption—it was almost disinterestedly that he had determined upon his course. At least it was security which he could promise her, as a younger man might not; a constant and single-minded kindness; a devotion not the less valuable, because it was mature and reticent, lacking, perhaps, the jealous ardours of youth. Nevertheless, he was going back to England without having revealed himself; there should be no unseasonable haste in the matter; he would give her another year. The Curé smiled deprecatingly at the procrastination; but on this point Campion was firm. And on this, his last evening, he spoke only of trivial things to Marie-Ursule, as they sat presently over the tea—a mild and flavourless beverage—which the young girl had prepared. Yet he noticed later, after their early supper, when she strolled up with him to the hill overlooking the village, a certain new shyness in her manner, a shadow, half timid, half expectant in her clear eyes which permitted him to believe that she was partly prepared. When they reached the summit, stood clear of the pine trees by an ancient stone Calvary, Ploumariel lay below them, very fair in the light of the setting sun; and they stopped to rest themselves, to admire.

"Ploumariel is very beautiful," said Campion after a while. "Ah! Marie-Ursule, you are fortunate to be here."

"Yes." She accepted his statement simply, then suddenly: "You should not go away." He smiled, his eyes turning from the village in the valley to rest upon her face: after all, she was the daintiest picture, and Ploumariel with its tall slate roofs, its sleeping houses, her appropriate frame.

"I shall come back, I shall come back," he murmured. She had gathered a bunch of ruddy heather as they walked, and her fingers played with it now nervously. Campion stretched out his hand for it. She gave it him without a word.

"I will take it with me to London," he said; "I will have Morbihan in my rooms."

"It will remind you—make you think of us sometimes?"

For answer he could only touch her hand lightly with his lips. "Do you think that was necessary?" And they resumed their homeward way silently, although to both of them the air seemed heavy with unspoken words.

III

When he was in London—and it was in London that for nine months out of the twelve Benedict Campion was to be found—he lived in the Temple, at the top of Hare Court, in the very same rooms in which he had installed himself, years ago, when he gave up his Oxford fellowship, electing to follow the profession of letters. Returning there from Ploumariel, he resumed at once, easily, his old avocations. He had always been a secluded man, living chiefly in books and in the past; but this year he seemed less than ever inclined to knock at the hospitable doors which were open to him. For in spite of his reserve, his diffidence, Campion's success might have been social, had he cared for it, and not purely academic. His had come to be a name in letters, in the higher paths of criticism; and he had made no enemies. To his success indeed, gradual and quiet as this was, he had never grown quite accustomed, contrasting the little he had actually achieved with all that he had desired to do. His original work was of the slightest, and a book that was in his head he had never found time to write. His name was known in other ways, as a man of ripe knowledge, of impeccable taste; as a born editor of choice reprints, of inaccessible classics: above all, as an authority—the greatest, upon the literature and the life (its flavour at once courtly, and mystical, had to him an unique charm) of the seventeenth century. His heart was in that age, and from much lingering over it, he had come to view modern life with a curious detachment, a sense of remote hostility: Democracy, the Salvation Army, the novels of M. Zola—he disliked them all impartially. A Catholic by long inheritance, he held his religion for something more than an heirloom; he exhaled it, like an intimate quality; his mind being essentially of that kind to which a mystical view of things comes easiest.

This year passed with him much as any other of the last ten years had passed; at least the routine of his daily existence admitted little outward change. And yet inwardly, he was conscious of alteration, of a certain quiet illumination which was a new thing to him.

Although at Ploumariel when the prospect of such a marriage had dawned on him, his first impression had been one of strangeness, he could reflect now that it was some such possibility as this which he had always kept vaguely in view. He had prided himself upon few things more than his patience; and now it appeared that this was to be rewarded; he was glad that he had known how to wait. This girl, Marie-Ursule, had an immense personal charm for him, but, beyond that, she was representative—her traditions were exactly those which the ideal girl of Campion's imagination would possess. She was not only personally adorable; she was also generically of the type which he admired. It was possibly because this type was, after all, so rare, that looking back, Campion in his middle age, could drag out of the recesses of his memory no spectre to compete with her. She was his first love precisely because the conditions, so choice and admirable, which rendered it inevitable for him to love her, had never occurred before. And he could watch the time of his probation gliding away with a pleased expectancy which contained no alloy of impatience. An illumination—a quite tranquil illumination: yes, it was under some such figure, without heart-burning, or adolescent fever, that love as it came to Campion was best expressed. Yet if this love was lucent rather than turbulent, that it was also deep he could remind himself, when a letter from the priest, while the spring was yet young, had sent him to Brittany, a month or two before his accustomed time, with an anxiety that was not solely due to bewilderment.

"Our child is well, mon bon," so he wrote. *"Do not alarm yourself. But it will be good for you to come, if it be only because of an idea she has, that you may remove. An idea! Call it rather a fancy—at least your coming will dispel it. Petites entêtées:° I have no patience with these mystical little girls."*

His musings on the phrase, with its interpretation varying to his mood, lengthened his long sea-passage, and the interminable leagues of railway which separated him from Pontivy, whence he had still some twenty miles to travel by the *Courrier,* before he reached his destination. But at Pontivy, the round, ruddy face of M. Letêtre greeting him on the platform dispelled any serious misgiving. Outside the post-office the familiar conveyance awaited them: its yellow inscription, "Pontivy-Plou-mariel," touched Campion electrically, as did the cheery greeting of the driver, which was that of an old friend. They shared the interior of the rusty trap—a fossil among vehicles—they chanced to be the only travellers, and to the accompaniment of jingling harness, and the clattering hoofs of the brisk little Carhaix horses, M. Letêtre explained himself.

"A vocation, *mon Dieu!* if all the little girls who fancied themselves with one, were to have their way, to whom would our poor France look for children? They are good women, *nos Ursulines,* ah, yes; but our Marie-Ursule is a good child, and blessed matrimony also is a sacrament. You shall talk to her, my Campion. It is a little fancy, you see, such as will come to young girls; a convent ague,° but when she sees you" . . . He took snuff with emphasis, and flipped his broad fingers suggestively. *"Craque!°* it is a betrothal, and a *trousseau,* and not the habit of religion, that Mademoiselle is full of. You will talk to her?"

Campion assented silently, absently, his eyes had wandered away, and looked through the little square of window at the sad-coloured Breton country, at the rows of tall poplars, which guarded the miles of dusty road like sombre sentinels. And the priest with a reassured air pulled out his breviary, and began to say his office in an imperceptible undertone. After a while he crossed himself, shut the book, and pillowing his head against the hot, shiny leather of the carriage, sought repose; very soon his regular, stertorous breathing, assured his companion that he was asleep. Campion closed his eyes also, not indeed in search of slumber, though he was travel weary; rather the better to isolate himself with the perplexity of his own thoughts. An indefinable sadness invaded him, and he could

---

°*Petites entêtées*: little fancies   °*ague*: fever   °*Craque*: a mild oath

envy the priest's simple logic, which gave such short shrift to obstacles that Campion, with his subtle melancholy, which made life to him almost morbidly an affair of fine shades and nice distinctions, might easily exaggerate.

Of the two, perhaps the priest had really the more secular mind, as it certainly excelled Campion's in that practical wisdom, or common sense, which may be of more avail than subtlety in the mere economy of life. And what to the Curé was a simple matter though, the removal of the idle fancy of a girl, might be to Campion, in his scrupulous temper, and his overweening tenderness towards just those pieties and renunciations which such a fancy implied, a task to be undertaken hardly with relish, perhaps without any real conviction, deeply as his personal wishes might be implicated in success. And the heart had gone out of his journey long before a turn of the road brought them in sight of Ploumariel.

IV

Up by the great, stone Calvary, where they had climbed nearly a year before, Campion stood, his face deliberately averted, while the young girl uttered her hesitating confidences; hesitating, yet candid, with a candour which seemed to separate him from the child by more than a measurable space of years, to set him with an appealing trustfulness in the seat of judgment—for him, for her. They had wandered there insensibly, through apple-orchards white with the promise of a bountiful harvest, and up the pine-clad hill, talking of little things—trifles to beguile their way—perhaps, in a sort of vain procrastination. Once, Marie-Ursule had plucked a branch of the snowy blossom, and he had playfully chided her that the cider would be less by a *litre* that year in Brittany. "But the blossom is so much prettier," she protested; "and there will be apples and apples—always enough apples. But I like the blossom best—and it is so soon over."

And then, emerging clear of the trees, with Ploumariel lying in its quietude in the serene sunshine below them, a sudden strenuousness had supervened, and the girl had unburdened herself, speaking tremulously, quickly, in an undertone almost passionate; and Campion, perforce, had listened. . . . A fancy? A whim? Yes, he reflected; to the normal, entirely healthy mind, any choice of exceptional conditions, any special self-consecration of withdrawal from the common lot of men and women must draw down upon it some such reproach, seeming the mere pedantry of inexperience. Yet, against his reason, and what he would fain call his better judgment, something in his heart of hearts stirred sympathetically with this notion of the girl. And it was no fixed resolution, no deliberate justification which she pleaded. She was soft, and pliable, and even her plea for renunciation contained pretty, feminine inconsequences; and it touched Campion strangely. Argument he could have met with argument; an ardent conviction he might have assailed with pleading; but that note of appeal in her pathetic young voice, for advice, for sympathy, disarmed him.

"Yet the world," he protested at last, but half-heartedly, with a sense of self-imposture: "the world, Marie-Ursule, it has its disappointments; but there are compensations."

"I am afraid, afraid," she murmured.

Their eyes alike sought instinctively the Convent of the Ursulines, white and sequestered in the valley—a visible symbol of security, of peace, perhaps of happiness.

"Even there they have their bad days: do not doubt it."

"But nothing happens," she said simply; "one day is like another. They can never be very sad, you know."

They were silent for a time: the girl, shading her eyes with one small white hand, continued to regard the convent; and Campion considered her fondly.

"What can I say?" he exclaimed at last. "What would you put on me? Your uncle—he is a priest—surely the most natural adviser—you know his wishes."

She shook her head. "With him it is different—I am one of his family—he is not a priest for me. And he considers me a little girl—and yet I am old enough to marry. Many young girls have had a vocation before my age. Ah, help me, decide for me!" she pleaded; "you are my *tuteur*."°

"And a very old friend, Marie-Ursule." He smiled rather sadly. Last year seemed so long ago, and the word, which he had almost spoken then, was no longer seasonable. A note in his voice, inexplicable, might have touched her. She took his hand impulsively, but he withdrew it quickly, as though her touch had scalded him.

"You look very tired, you are not used to our Breton rambles in this sun. See, I will run down to the cottage by the chapel and fetch you some milk. Then you shall tell me."

When he was alone the smile faded from his face and was succeeded by a look of lassitude, as he sat himself beneath the shadow of the Calvary to wrestle with his responsibility. Perhaps it was a vocation: the phrase, sounding strangely on modern ears, to him, at least, was no anachronism. Women of his race, from generation to generation, had heard some such voice and had obeyed it. That it went unheeded now was, perhaps, less a proof that it was silent, than that people had grown hard and deaf, in a world that had deteriorated. Certainly the convent had to him no vulgar, Protestant significance, to be combated for its

---

°*tuteur*: guardian

intrinsic barbarism; it suggested nothing cold nor narrow nor mean, was veritably a gracious choice, a generous effort after perfection. Then it was for his own sake, on an egoistic impulse, that he should dissuade her? And it rested with him; he had no doubt that he could mould her, even yet, to his purpose. The child! how he loved her. . . . But would it ever be quite the same with them after that morning? Or must there be henceforth a shadow between them; the knowledge of something missed, of the lower end pursued, the higher slighted? Yet, if she loved him? He let his head drop on his hands, murmured aloud at the hard chance which made him at once judge and advocate in his own cause. He was not conscious of praying, but his mind fell into that condition of aching blankness which is, perhaps, an extreme prayer. Presently he looked down again at Ploumariel, with its coronal° of faint smoke ascending in the perfectly still air, at the white convent of the Dames Ursulines, which seemed to dominate and protect it. How peaceful it was! And his thoughts wandered to London: to its bustle and noise, its squalid streets, to his life there, to its literary coteries, its politics, its society; vulgar and trivial and sordid they all seemed from this point of vantage. That was the world he had pleaded for, and it was into that he would bring the child. . . . And suddenly, with a strange reaction, he was seized with a sense of the wisdom of her choice, its pictorial fitness, its benefit for both of them. He felt at once and finally, that he acquiesced in it; that any other ending to his love had been an impossible grossness, and that to lose her in just that fashion was the only way in which he could keep her always. And his acquiescence was without bitterness, and attended only by that indefinable sadness which to a man of his temper was but the last refinement of pleasure. He had renounced, but he had triumphed; for it seemed to him that his renunciation would be an ægis° to him always against the sordid facts of life, a protest against the vulgarity of instinct, the tyranny of institutions. And he thought of the girl's life, as it should be, with a tender appreciation—as of something precious laid away in lavender. He looked up to find her waiting before him with a basin half full of milk, warm still, fresh from the cow; and she watched him in silence while he drank. Then their eyes met, and she gave a little cry.

"You will help me? Ah, I see that you will! And you think I am right?"

"I think you are right, Marie-Ursule."

"And you will persuade my uncle?"

"I will persuade him."

She took his hand in silence, and they stood so for a minute, gravely regarding each other. Then they prepared to descend.

°*coronal*: crown   °*aegis*: shield

SONNET 3

William Shakespeare (1564–1616)

Look in thy glass, and tell the face thou viewest
Now is the time that face should form another;
Whose fresh repair if now thou not renewest,
Thou dost beguile° the world, unbless some mother.
For where is she so fair whose uneared° womb   5
Disdains the tillage of thy husbandry?
Or who is he so fond° will be the tomb
Of his self-love, to stop posterity?
Thou art thy mother's glass, and she in thee
Calls back the lovely April of her prime: 10
So thou through windows of thine age shalt see,
Despite of wrinkles, this thy golden time.
    But if thou live, remembered not to be,
    Die single, and thine image dies with thee.

THE SOUL SELECTS HER OWN SOCIETY

Emily Dickinson (1830–1886)

The soul selects her own society,
Then shuts the door;
On her divine majority
Obtrude no more.

Unmoved, she notes the chariot's pausing   5
At her low gate;
Unmoved, an emperor is kneeling
Upon her mat.

I've known her from an ample nation
Choose one;   10
Then close the valves of her attention
Like stone.

°*beguile*: cheat   °*uneared*: unploughed   °*fond*: foolish

PLEAD FOR ME

Emily Brontë (1818–1848)

O thy bright eyes must answer now,
When Reason, with a scornful brow,
Is mocking at my overthrow;
O thy sweet tongue must plead for me
And tell why I have chosen thee!   5

Stern Reason is to judgment come
Arrayed in all her forms of gloom:
Wilt thou my advocate be dumb?
No, radiant angel, speak and say
Why I did cast the world away;   10

Why I have persevered to shun
The common paths that others run;
And on a strange road journeyed on
Heedless alike of Wealth and Power—
Of Glory's wreath and Pleasure's flower.   15

These once indeed seemed Beings divine,
And they perchance heard vows of mine
And saw my offerings on their shrine—
But, careless gifts are seldom prized,
And *mine* were worthily despised;   20

So with a ready heart I swore
To seek their altar-stone no more,
And gave my spirit to adore
Thee, ever present, phantom thing—
My slave, my comrade, and my King!   25

A slave because I rule thee still;
Incline thee to my changeful will
And make thy influence good or ill—
A comrade, for by day and night
Thou art my intimate delight—   30

My Darling Pain that wounds and sears
And wrings a blessing out from tears
By deadening me to earthly cares;
And yet, a king—though prudence well
Have taught thy subject to rebel.   35

And am I wrong to worship where
Faith cannot doubt nor Hope despair
Since my own soul can grant my prayer?
Speak, God of Visions, plead for me
And tell why I have chosen thee!   40

THE BOOK OF THEL

William Blake (1757–1827)

THEL'S MOTTO

Does the Eagle know what is in the pit?
Or wilt thou go ask the Mole?
Can Wisdom be put in a silver rod?
Or Love in a golden bowl?

I

The daughters of the Seraphim led round their sunny flocks,
All but the youngest: she in paleness sought the secret air,
To fade away like morning beauty from her mortal day:
Down by the river of Adona her soft voice is heard,
And thus her gentle lamentation falls like morning dew: 5

"O life of this our spring! why fades the lotus of the water,
Why fade these children of the spring, born but to smile & fall?
Ah! Thel is like a wat'ry bow, and like a parting cloud;
Like a reflection in a glass; like shadows in the water;
Like dreams of infants; like a smile upon an infant's face;   10
Like the dove's voice; like transient day; like music in the air.
Ah! gentle may I lay me down, and gentle rest my head,
And gentle sleep the sleep of death, and gentle hear the voice
Of him that walketh in the garden in the evening time."

The Lily of the valley, breathing in the humble grass,   15
Answer'd the lovely maid and said: "I am a wat'ry weed,
And I am very small and love to dwell in lowly vales;
So weak, the gilded butterfly scarce perches on my head.
Yet I am visited from heaven, and he that smiles on all
Walks in the valley and each morn over me spreads his hand,   20
Saying, 'Rejoice, thou humble grass, thou new-born lily flower,
Thou gentle maid of silent valleys and of modest brooks;
For thou shalt be clothed in light, and fed with morning
    manna,

Till summer's heat melts thee beside the fountains and the
    springs
To flourish in eternal vales.' Then why should Thel complain?   25
Why should the mistress of the vales of Har utter a sigh?"

She ceas'd & smil'd in tears, then sat down in her silver shrine.

Thel answer'd: "O thou little virgin of the peaceful valley,
Giving to those that cannot crave, the voiceless, the o'ertired;
Thy breath doth nourish the innocent lamb, he smells thy   30
    milky garments,
He crops thy flowers while thou sittest smiling in his face,
Wiping his mild and meekin mouth from all contagious taints.
Thy wine doth purify the golden honey; thy perfume,
Which thou dost scatter on every little blade of grass
    that springs,
Revives the milked cow, & tames the fire-breathing steed.   35
But Thel is like a faint cloud kindled at the rising sun:
I vanish from my pearly throne, and who shall find my place?"

"Queen of the vales," the Lily answer'd, "ask the tender cloud,
And it shall tell thee why it glitters in the morning sky,
And why it scatters its bright beauty thro' the humid air.   40
Descend, O little Cloud, & hover before the eyes of Thel."

The Cloud descended, and the Lily bow'd her modest head
And went to mind her numerous charge among the verdant grass.

II

"O little Cloud," the virgin said, "I charge thee tell to me
Why thou complainest not when in one hour thou fade away: 45
Then we shall seek thee, but not find. Ah! Thel is like to thee:
I pass away: yet I complain, and no one hears my voice."

The Cloud then shew'd his golden head & his bright form
    emerg'd,
Hovering and glittering on the air before the face of Thel.

"O virgin, know'st thou not our steeds drink of the golden   50
    springs
Where Luvah doth renew his horses? Look'st thou on my youth,
And fearest thou, because I vanish and am seen no more,
Nothing remains? O maid, I tell thee, when I pass away

THE VIRGIN SHROUDED IN SNOW   *101*

It is to tenfold life, to love, to peace and raptures holy:
Unseen descending, weigh my light wings upon balmy flowers,   55
And court the fair-eyed dew to take me to her shining tent:
The weeping virgin, trembling kneels before the risen sun,
Till we arise link'd in a golden band and never part,
But walk united, bearing food to all our tender flowers."

"Dost thou, O little Cloud? I fear that I am not like thee,   60
For I walk thro' the vales of Har, and smell the sweetest flowers,
But I feed not the little flowers; I hear the warbling birds,
But I feed not the warbling birds; they fly and seek their food:
But Thel delights in these no more, because I fade away;
And all shall say, 'Without a use this shining woman liv'd,   65
Or did she only live to be at death the food of worms?' "

The Cloud reclin'd upon his airy throne and answer'd thus:

"Then if thou art the food of worms, O virgin of the skies,
How great thy use, how great thy blessing! Every thing that
    lives
Lives not alone nor for itself. Fear not, and I will call   70
The weak worm from its lowly bed, and thou shalt hear its
    voice.
Come forth, worm of the silent valley, to thy pensive queen."

The helpless worm arose, and sat upon the Lily's leaf,
And the bright Cloud sail'd on, to find his partner in the vale.

III

Then Thel astonish'd view'd the Worm upon its dewy bed.   75

"Art thou a Worm? Image of weakness, art thou but a Worm?
I see thee like an infant wrapped in the Lily's leaf.
Ah! weep not, little voice, thou canst not speak, but thou
    canst weep.
Is this a Worm? I see thee lay helpless & naked, weeping,
And none to answer, none to cherish thee with mother's   80
    smiles."

The Clod of Clay heard the Worm's voice & rais'd her pitying
    head:
She bow'd over the weeping infant, and her life exhal'd
In milky fondness: then on Thel she fix'd her humble eyes.

"O beauty of the vales of Har! we live not for ourselves.
Thou seest me the meanest thing, and so I am indeed.   85
My bosom of itself is cold, and of itself is dark;
But he, that loves the lowly, pours his oil upon my head,
And kisses me, and binds his nuptial bands around my breast,
And says: 'Thou mother of my children, I have loved thee
And I have given thee a crown that none can take away.'   90
But how this is, sweet maid, I know not, and I cannot know;
I ponder, and I cannot ponder; yet I live and love."

The daughter of beauty wip'd her pitying tears with her white
    veil,
And said: "Alas! I knew not this, and therefore did I weep.
That God would love a Worm I knew, and punish the evil foot   95
That wilful bruis'd its helpless form; but that he cherish'd it
With milk and oil I never knew, and therefore did I weep;
And I complain'd in the mild air, because I fade away,
And lay me down in thy cold bed, and leave my shining lot."

"Queen of the vales," the matron Clay answer'd, "I heard thy   100
    sighs,
And all thy moans flew o'er my roof, but I have call'd them
    down.
Wilt thou, O Queen, enter my house? 'Tis given thee to enter
And to return: fear nothing, enter with thy virgin feet."

IV

The eternal gates' terrific porter lifted the northern bar:
Thel enter'd in & saw the secrets of the land unknown.   105
She saw the couches of the dead, & where the fibrous roots
Of every heart on earth infixes deep its restless twists:
A land of sorrows & of tears where never smile was seen.

She wander'd in the land of clouds thro' valleys dark, list'ning
Dolours & lamentations; waiting oft beside a dewy grave   110
She stood in silence, list'ning to the voices of the ground,
Till to her own grave plot she came, & there she sat down,
And heard this voice of sorrow breathed from the hollow pit.

"Why cannot the Ear be closed to its own destruction?
Or the glist'ning Eye to the poison of a smile?   115
Why are Eyelids stor'd with arrows ready drawn,
Where a thousand fighting men in ambush lie?

Or an Eye of gifts & graces show'ring fruits & coined gold?
Why a Tongue impress'd with honey from every wind?
Why an Ear, a whirlpool fierce to draw creations in?   120
Why a Nostril wide inhaling terror, trembling, & affright?
Why a tender curb upon the youthful burning boy?
Why a little curtain of flesh on the bed of our desire?"

The Virgin started from her seat, & with a shriek
Fled back unhinder'd till she came into the vales of Har.   125

THE WOMAN AT THE WASHINGTON ZOO

Randall Jarrell (1914–1965)

The saris go by me from the embassies.

Cloth from the moon. Cloth from another planet.
They look back at the leopard like the leopard.

And I. . . .
            this print of mine, that has kept its color
Alive through so many cleanings; this dull null   5
Navy I wear to work, and wear from work, and so
To my bed, so to my grave, with no
Complaints, no comment: neither from my chief,
The Deputy Chief Assistant, nor his chief—
Only I complain. . . . this serviceable   10
Body that no sunlight dyes, no hand suffuses
But, dome-shadowed, withering among columns,
Wavy beneath fountains—small, far-off, shining
In the eyes of animals, these being trapped
As I am trapped but not, themselves, the trap,   15
Aging, but without knowledge of their age,
Kept safe here, knowing not of death, for death—
Oh, bars of my own body, open, open!

The world goes by my cage and never sees me.
And there come not to me, as come to these,   20
The wild beasts, sparrows pecking the llamas' grain,
Pigeons settling on the bears' bread, buzzards
Tearing the meat the flies have clouded. . . .

When you come for the white rat that the foxes left,
Take off the red helmet of your head, the black   25
Wings that have shadowed me, and step to me as man:
The wild brother at whose feet the white wolves fawn,
To whose hand of power the great lioness
Stalks, purring. . . .
                    You know what I was,
You see what I am: change me, change me!   30

CHRISTABEL

Samuel Taylor Coleridge (1772–1834)

PART I

'Tis the middle of night by the castle clock,
And the owls have awakened the crowing cock;
Tu—whit!——Tu—whoo!
And hark, again! the crowing cock,
How drowsily it crew.   5
Sir Leoline, the Baron rich,
Hath a toothless mastiff bitch;
From her kennel beneath the rock
She maketh answer to the clock,
Four for the quarters, and twelve for the hour;   10
Ever and aye, by shine and shower,
Sixteen short howls, not over loud;
Some say, she sees my lady's shroud.

Is the night chilly and dark?
The night is chilly, but not dark.   15
The thin gray cloud is spread on high,
It covers but not hides the sky.
The moon is behind, and at the full;
And yet she looks both small and dull.
The night is chill, the cloud is gray: 20
'Tis a month before the month of May,
And the Spring comes slowly up this way.

The lovely lady, Christabel,
Whom her father loves so well,
What makes her in the wood so late,   25
A furlong from the castle gate?

She had dreams all yesternight
Of her own betrothéd knight;
And she in the midnight wood will pray
For the weal° of her lover that's far away.   30

She stole along, she nothing spoke,
The sighs she heaved were soft and low,
And naught was green upon the oak
But moss and rarest mistletoe:
She kneels beneath the huge oak tree,   35
And in silence prayeth she.

The lady sprang up suddenly,
The lovely lady, Christabel!
It moaned as near, as near can be,
But what it is she cannot tell.—   40
On the other side it seems to be,
Of the huge, broad-breasted, old oak tree.

The night is chill; the forest bare;
Is it the wind that moaneth bleak?
There is not wind enough in the air   45
To move away the ringlet curl
From the lovely lady's cheek—
There is not wind enough to twirl
The one red leaf, the last of its clan,
That dances as often as dance it can,   50
Hanging so light, and hanging so high,
On the topmost twig that looks up at the sky.

Hush, beating heart of Christabel!
Jesu, Maria, shield her well!
She folded her arms beneath her cloak,   55
And stole to the other side of the oak.
　　What sees she there?

There she sees a damsel bright,
Drest in a silken robe of white,
That shadowy in the moonlight shone: 60
The neck that made that white robe wan,
Her stately neck, and arms were bare;
Her blue-veined feet unsandal'd were,

°*weal*: well-being

And wildly glittered here and there
The gems entangled in her hair.
I guess, 'twas frightful there to see
A lady so richly clad as she—
Beautiful exceedingly!

Mary mother, save me now!
(Said Christabel,) And who art thou?

The lady strange made answer meet,
And her voice was faint and sweet:—
Have pity on my sore distress,
I scarce can speak for weariness:
Stretch forth thy hand, and have no fear!
Said Christabel, How camest thou here?
And the lady, whose voice was faint and sweet,
Did thus pursue her answer meet:—

My sire is of a noble line,
And my name is Geraldine:
Five warriors seized me yestermorn,
Me, even me, a maid forlorn:
They choked my cries with force and fright,
And tied me on a palfrey white.
The palfrey was as fleet as wind,
And they rode furiously behind.
They spurred amain,° their steeds were white:
And once we crossed the shade of night.
As sure as Heaven shall rescue me,
I have no thought what men they be;
Nor do I know how long it is
(For I have lain entranced I wis°)
Since one, the tallest of the five,
Took me from the palfrey's back,
A weary woman, scarce alive.
Some muttered words his comrades spoke:
He placed me underneath this oak;
He swore they would return with haste;
Whither they went I cannot tell—
I thought I heard, some minutes past,
Sounds as of a castle bell.
Stretch forth thy hand (thus ended she),

65

70

75

80

85

90

95

100

°*amain*: at full speed   °*wis*: know

And help a wretched maid to flee.

Then Christabel stretched forth her hand,
And comforted fair Geraldine: 105
O well, bright dame! may you command
The service of Sir Leoline;
And gladly our stout chivalry
Will he send forth and friends withal°
To guide and guard you safe and free 110
Home to your noble father's hall.

She rose: and forth with steps they passed
That strove to be, and were not, fast.
Her gracious stars the lady blest,
And thus spake on sweet Christabel: 115
All our household are at rest,
The hall as silent as the cell;
Sir Leoline is weak in health,
And may not well awakened be,
But we will move as if in stealth, 120
And I beseech your courtesy,
This night, to share your couch with me.

They crossed the moat, and Christabel
Took the key that fitted well;
A little door she opened straight, 125
All in the middle of the gate;
The gate that was ironed within and without,
Where an army in battle array had marched out.
The lady sank, belike through pain,
And Christabel with might and main 130
Lifted her up, a weary weight,
Over the threshold of the gate:
Then the lady rose again,
And moved, as she were not in pain.

So free from danger, free from fear, 135
They crossed the court: right glad they were.
And Christabel devoutly cried
To the lady by her side,
Praise we the Virgin all divine
Who hath rescued thee from thy distress! 140
Alas, alas! said Geraldine,

°*withal*: besides

I cannot speak for weariness.
So free from danger, free from fear,
They crossed the court: right glad they were.

Outside her kennel, the mastiff old   145
Lay fast asleep, in moonshine cold.
The mastiff old did not awake,
Yet she an angry moan did make!
And what can ail the mastiff bitch?
Never till now she uttered yell   150
Beneath the eye of Christabel.
Perhaps it is the owlet's scritch°:
For what can ail the mastiff bitch?

They passed the hall, that echoes still,
Pass as lightly as you will!   155
The brands were flat, the brands were dying,
Amid their own white ashes lying;
But when the lady passed, there came
A tongue of light, a fit of flame;
And Christabel saw the lady's eye,   160
And nothing else saw she thereby,
Save the boss° of the shield of Sir Leoline tall,
Which hung in a murky old niche in the wall.
O softly tread, said Christabel,
My father seldom sleepeth well.   165

Sweet Christabel her feet doth bare,
And jealous of the listening air
They steal their way from stair to stair,
Now in glimmer, and now in gloom,
And now they pass the Baron's room,   170
As still as death, with stifled breath!
And now have reached her chamber door;
And now doth Geraldine press down
The rushes of the chamber floor.

The moon shines dim in the open air,   175
And not a moonbeam enters here.
But they without its light can see
The chamber carved so curiously,
Carved with figures strange and sweet,

°*scritch*: screech   °*boss*: ornamentation

All made out of the carver's brain,   180
For a lady's chamber meet:
The lamp with twofold silver chain
Is fastened to an angel's feet.

The silver lamp burns dead and dim;
But Christabel the lamp will trim.   185
She trimmed the lamp, and made it bright,
And left it swinging to and fro,
While Geraldine, in wretched plight,
Sank down upon the floor below.

O weary lady, Geraldine,   190
I pray you, drink this cordial wine!
It is a wine of virtuous powers;
My mother made it of wild flowers.

And will your mother pity me,
Who am a maiden most forlorn?   195
Christabel answered—Woe is me!
She died the hour that I was born.
I have heard the grey-haired friar tell
How on her death-bed she did say,
That she should hear the castle-bell   200
Strike twelve upon my wedding-day.
O mother dear! that thou wert here!

I would, said Geraldine, she were!
But soon with altered voice, said she—
"Off, wandering mother! Peak and pine!   205
I have power to bid thee flee."
Alas! what ails poor Geraldine?
Why stares she with unsettled eye?
Can she the bodiless dead espy?
And why with hollow voice cries she,   210
"Off, woman, off! this hour is mine—
Though thou her guardian spirit be,
Off, woman, off! 'tis given to me."

Then Christabel knelt by the lady's side,
And raised to heaven her eyes so blue—   215
Alas! said she, this ghastly ride—
Dear lady! it hath wildered° you!

°*wildered*: bewildered

The lady wiped her moist cold brow,
And faintly said, "'tis over now!"

Again the wild-flower wine she drank: 220
Her fair large eyes 'gan glitter bright,
And from the floor whereon she sank,
The lofty lady stood upright:
She was most beautiful to see,
Like a lady of a far countrée.   225

And thus the lofty lady spake—
"All they who live in the upper sky,
Do love you, holy Christabel!
And you love them, and for their sake
And for the good which me befel,   230
Even I in my degree will try,
Fair maiden, to requite you well.
But now unrobe yourself; for I
Must pray, ere yet in bed I lie."

Quoth Christabel, So let it be!   235
And as the lady bade, did she.
Her gentle limbs did she undress,
And lay down in her loveliness.

But through her brain of weal and woe
So many thoughts moved to and fro,   240
That vain it were her lids to close;
So half-way from the bed she rose,
And on her elbow did recline
To look at the lady Geraldine.

Beneath the lamp the lady bowed,   245
And slowly rolled her eyes around;
Then drawing in her breath aloud,
Like one that shuddered, she unbound
The cincture° from beneath her breast:
Her silken robe, and inner vest,   250
Dropt to her feet, and full in view,
Behold! her bosom and half her side——
A sight to dream of, not to tell!
O shield her! shield sweet Christabel!

°*cincture*: belt, sash

Yet Geraldine nor speaks nor stirs;   255
Ah! what a stricken look was hers!
Deep from within she seems half-way
To lift some weight with sick assay,
And eyes the maid and seeks delay;
Then suddenly, as one defied,   260
Collects herself in scorn and pride,
And lay down by the Maiden's side!—
And in her arms the maid she took,
      Ah wel-a-day!
And with low voice and doleful look   265
These words did say:

"In the touch of this bosom there worketh a spell,
Which is lord of thy utterance, Christabel!
Thou knowest to-night, and wilt know to-morrow,
This mark of my shame, this seal of my sorrow;   270
      But vainly thou warrest,
        For this is alone in
      Thy power to declare,
        That in the dim forest
      Thou heard'st a low moaning,   275
And found'st a bright lady, surpassingly fair;
And didst bring her home with thee in love and in charity,
To shield her and shelter her from the damp air."

THE CONCLUSION TO PART I

It was a lovely sight to see
The lady Christabel, when she   280
Was praying at the old oak tree.
      Amid the jaggéd shadows
      Of mossy leafless boughs,
      Kneeling in the moonlight,
      To make her gentle vows;   285
Her slender palms together prest,
Heaving sometimes on her breast;
Her face resigned to bliss or bale—
Her face, oh call it fair not pale,
And both blue eyes more bright than clear,   290
Each about to have a tear.

With open eyes (ah woe is me!)
Asleep, and dreaming fearfully,

Fearfully dreaming, yet, I wis,
Dreaming that alone, which is—   295
O sorrow and shame! Can this be she,
The lady, who knelt at the old oak tree?
And lo! the worker of these harms,
That holds the maiden in her arms,
Seems to slumber still and mild,   300
As a mother with her child.

A star hath set, a star hath risen,
O Geraldine! since arms of thine
Have been the lovely lady's prison.
O Geraldine! one hour was thine—   305
Thou'st had thy will! By tairn° and rill,°
The night-birds all that hour were still.
But now they are jubilant anew,
From cliff and tower, tu—whoo! tu—whoo!
Tu—whoo! tu—whoo! from wood and fell!   310

And see! the lady Christabel
Gathers herself from out her trance;
Her limbs relax, her countenance
Grows sad and soft; the smooth thin lids
Close o'er her eyes; and tears she sheds—   315
Large tears that leave the lashes bright!
And oft the while she seems to smile
As infants at a sudden light!

Yea, she doth smile, and she doth weep,
Like a youthful hermitess,   320
Beauteous in a wilderness,
Who, praying always, prays in sleep.
And, if she move unquietly,
Perchance, 'tis but the blood so free
Comes back and tingles in her feet.   325
No doubt, she hath a vision sweet.
What if her guardian spirit 'twere,
What if she knew her mother near?
But this she knows, in joys and woes,
That saints will aid if men will call: 330
For the blue sky bends over all!

°*tairn*: tarn; mountain lake   °*rill*: small mountain brook

PART II

Each matin° bell, the Baron saith,
Knells us back to a world of death.
These words Sir Leoline first said,
When he rose and found his lady dead: 335
These words Sir Leoline will say
Many a morn to his dying day!

And hence the custom and law began
That still at dawn the sacristan,°
Who duly pulls the heavy bell,   340
Five and forty beads must tell
Between each stroke—a warning knell,
Which not a soul can choose but hear
From Bratha Head° to Wyndermere.°

Saith Bracy the bard, So let it knell!   345
And let the drowsy sacristan
Still count as slowly as he can!
There is no lack of such, I ween,°
As well fill up the space between.
In Langdale Pike° and Witch's Lair,   350
And Dungeon-ghyll so foully rent,
With ropes of rock and bells of air
Three sinful sextons' ghosts are pent,°
Who all give back, one after t'other,
The death-note to their living brother;   355
And oft too, by the knell offended,
Just as their one! two! three! is ended,
The devil mocks the doleful tale
With a merry peal from Borodale.

The air is still! through mist and cloud   360
That merry peal comes ringing loud;
And Geraldine shakes off her dread,
And rises lightly from the bed;
Puts on her silken vestments white,
And tricks her hair in lovely plight,°   365
And nothing doubting of her spell

°*matin*: early morning   °*sacristan*: sexton   °*Bratha Head, Wyndermere, Langdale Pike*, etc.: places in the English Lake District   °*ween*: suppose   °*pent*: confined
°*plight*: plait

Awakens the lady Christabel.
"Sleep you, sweet lady Christabel?
I trust that you have rested well."

And Christabel awoke and spied   370
The same who lay down by her side—
O rather say, the same whom she
Raised up beneath the old oak tree!
Nay, fairer yet! and yet more fair!
For she belike hath drunken deep   375
Of all the blessedness of sleep!
And while she spake, her looks, her air
Such gentle thankfulness declare,
That (so it seemed) her girded vests
Grew tight beneath her heaving breasts.   380
"Sure I have sinn'd!" said Christabel,
"Now heaven be praised if all be well!"
And in low faltering tones, yet sweet,
Did she the lofty lady greet
With such perplexity of mind   385
As dreams too lively leave behind.

So quickly she rose, and quickly arrayed
Her maiden limbs, and having prayed
That He, who on the cross did groan,
Might wash away her sins unknown,   390
She forthwith led fair Geraldine
To meet her sire, Sir Leoline.

The lovely maid and the lady tall
Are pacing both into the hall,
And pacing on through page and groom,   395
Enter the Baron's presence-room.

The Baron rose, and while he prest
His gentle daughter to his breast,
With cheerful wonder in his eyes
The lady Geraldine espies,   400
And gave such welcome to the same,
As might beseem so bright a dame!

But when he heard the lady's tale,
And when she told her father's name,
Why waxed Sir Leoline so pale,   405

Murmuring o'er the name again,
Lord Roland de Vaux of Tryermaine?

Alas! they had been friends in youth;
But whispering tongues can poison truth;
And constancy lives in realms above;   410
And life is thorny; and youth is vain;
And to be wroth with one we love
Doth work like madness in the brain.
And thus it chanced, as I divine,
With Roland and Sir Leoline.   415
Each spake words of high disdain
And insult to his heart's best brother:
They parted—ne'er to meet again!
But never either found another
To free the hollow heart from paining—   420
They stood aloof, the scars remaining,
Like cliffs which had been rent asunder;
A dreary sea now flows between;—
But neither heat, nor frost, nor thunder,
Shall wholly do away, I ween,   425
The marks of that which once hath been.

Sir Leoline, a moment's space,
Stood gazing on the damsel's face:
And the youthful Lord of Tryermaine
Came back upon his heart again.   430

O then the Baron forgot his age,
His noble heart swelled high with rage;
He swore by the wounds in Jesu's side
He would proclaim it far and wide,
With trump and solemn heraldry,   435
That they, who thus had wronged the dame,
Were base as spotted infamy!
"And if they dare deny the same,
My herald shall appoint a week,
And let the recreant traitors seek   440
My tourney court—that there and then
I may dislodge their reptile souls
From the bodies and forms of men!"
He spake: his eye in lightning rolls!

For the lady was ruthlessly seized; and he kenned°   445
In the beautiful lady the child of his friend!

And now the tears were on his face,
And fondly in his arms he took
Fair Geraldine, who met the embrace,
Prolonging it with joyous look.   450
Which when she viewed, a vision fell
Upon the soul of Christabel,
The vision of fear, the touch and pain!
She shrunk and shuddered, and saw again—
(Ah, woe is me! Was it for thee,   455
Thou gentle maid! such sights to see?)

Again she saw that bosom old,
Again she felt that bosom cold,
And drew in her breath with a hissing sound:
Whereat the Knight turned wildly round,   460
And nothing saw, but his own sweet maid
With eyes upraised, as one that prayed.

The touch, the sight, had passed away,
And in its stead that vision blest,
Which comforted her after-rest   465
While in the lady's arms she lay,
Had put a rapture in her breast,
And on her lips and o'er her eyes
Spread smiles like light!
                   With new surprise,
"What ails then my beloved child?"   470
The Baron said—His daughter mild
Made answer, "All will yet be well!"
I ween, she had no power to tell
Aught else: so mighty was the spell.

Yet he, who saw this Geraldine,   475
Had deemed her sure a thing divine:
Such sorrow with such grace she blended,
As if she feared she had offended
Sweet Christabel, that gentle maid!
And with such lowly tones she prayed   480
She might be sent without delay

°*kenned*: recognized

Home to her father's mansion.
                    "Nay!
Nay, by my soul!" said Leoline.
"Ho, Bracy the bard, the charge be thine!
Go thou, with music sweet and loud,   485
And take two steeds with trappings proud,
And take the youth whom thou lov'st best
To bear thy harp, and learn thy song,
And clothe you both in solemn vest,
And over the mountains haste along,   490
Lest wandering folk, that are abroad,
Detain you on the valley road.

"And when he has crossed the Irthing flood,
My merry bard! he hastes, he hastes
Up Knorren Moor, through Halegarth Wood,   495
And reaches soon that castle good
Which stands and threatens Scotland's wastes.

"Bard Bracy! bard Bracy! your horses are fleet,
Ye must ride up the hall, your music so sweet,
More loud than your horses' echoing feet!   500
And loud and loud to Lord Roland call,
Thy daughter is safe in Langdale hall!
Thy beautiful daughter is safe and free—
Sir Leoline greets thee thus through me!
He bids thee come without delay   505
With all thy numerous array
And take thy lovely daughter home:
And he will meet thee on the way
With all his numerous array
White with their panting palfreys' foam: 510
And, by mine honour! I will say,
That I repent me of the day
When I spake words of fierce disdain
To Roland de Vaux of Tryermaine!—
—For since that evil hour hath flown,   515
Many a summer's sun hath shone;
Yet ne'er found I a friend again
Like Roland de Vaux of Tryermaine."

The lady fell, and clasped his knees,
Her face upraised, her eyes o'erflowing;   520

And Bracy replied, with faltering voice,
His gracious Hail on all bestowing!—
"Thy words, thou sire of Christabel,
Are sweeter than my harp can tell;
Yet might I gain a boon of thee, 525
This day my journey should not be,
So strange a dream hath come to me,
That I had vowed with music loud
To clear yon wood from thing unblest,
Warned by a vision in my rest! 530
For in my sleep I saw that dove,
That gentle bird, whom thou dost love,
And call'st by thy own daughter's name—
Sir Leoline! I saw the same
Fluttering, and uttering fearful moan, 535
Among the green herbs in the forest alone.
Which when I saw and when I heard,
I wonder'd what might ail the bird;
For nothing near it could I see,
Save the grass and green herbs underneath the old tree. 540

"And in my dream methought I went
To search out what might there be found;
And what the sweet bird's trouble meant,
That thus lay fluttering on the ground.
I went and peered, and could descry 545
No cause for her distressful cry;
But yet for her dear lady's sake
I stooped, methought, the dove to take,
When lo! I saw a bright green snake
Coiled around its wings and neck. 550
Green as the herbs on which it couched,
Close by the dove's its head it crouched;
And with the dove it heaves and stirs,
Swelling its neck as she swelled hers!
I woke; it was the midnight hour, 555
The clock was echoing in the tower;
But though my slumber was gone by,
This dream it would not pass away—
It seems to live upon my eye!
And thence I vowed this self-same day 560
With music strong and saintly song
To wander through the forest bare,
Lest aught unholy loiter there."

Thus Bracy said: the Baron, the while,
Half-listening heard him with a smile; 565
Then turned to Lady Geraldine,
His eyes made up of wonder and love;
And said in courtly accents fine,
"Sweet maid, Lord Roland's beauteous dove,
With arms more strong than harp or song, 570
Thy sire and I will crush the snake!"
He kissed her forehead as he spake,
And Geraldine in maiden wise
Casting down her large bright eyes,
With blushing cheek and courtesy fine 575
She turned her from Sir Leoline;
Softly gathering up her train,
That o'er her right arm fell again;
And folded her arms across her chest,
And couched her head upon her breast, 580
And looked askance at Christabel——
Jesu, Maria, shield her well!

A snake's small eye blinks dull and shy;
And the lady's eyes they shrunk in her head,
Each shrunk up to a serpent's eye, 585
And with somewhat of malice, and more of dread,
At Christabel she looked askance!—
One moment—and the sight was fled!
But Christabel in dizzy trance
Stumbling on the unsteady ground 590
Shuddered aloud, with a hissing sound;
And Geraldine again turned round,
And like a thing, that sought relief,
Full of wonder and full of grief,
She rolled her large bright eyes divine 595
Wildly on Sir Leoline.

The maid, alas! her thoughts are gone,
She nothing sees—no sight but one!
The maid, devoid of guile and sin,
I know not how, in fearful wise, 600
So deeply had she drunken in
That look, those shrunken serpent eyes,
That all her features were resigned
To this sole image in her mind:
And passively did imitate 605

That look of dull and treacherous hate!
And thus she stood, in dizzy trance,
Still picturing that look askance
With forced unconscious sympathy
Full before her father's view—   610
As far as such a look could be
In eyes so innocent and blue!

And when the trance was o'er, the maid
Paused awhile, and inly prayed:
Then falling at the Baron's feet,   615
"By my mother's soul do I entreat
That thou this woman send away!"
She said: and more she could not say:
For what she knew she could not tell,
O'er-mastered by the mighty spell.   620

Why is thy cheek so wan and wild,
Sir Leoline? Thy only child
Lies at thy feet, thy joy, thy pride,
So fair, so innocent, so mild;
The same, for whom thy lady died!   625
O by the pangs of her dear mother
Think thou no evil of thy child!
For her, and thee, and for no other,
She prayed the moment ere she died:
Prayed that the babe for whom she died,   630
Might prove her dear lord's joy and pride!
    That prayer her deadly pangs beguiled,
      Sir Leoline!
    And wouldst thou wrong thy only child,
      Her child and thine?   635

Within the Baron's heart and brain
If thoughts, like these, had any share,
They only swelled his rage and pain,
And did but work confusion there.
His heart was cleft with pain and rage,   640
His cheeks they quivered, his eyes were wild,
Dishonoured thus in his old age;
Dishonoured by his only child,
And all his hospitality
To the wronged daughter of his friend   645
By more than woman's jealousy

Brought thus to a disgraceful end—
He rolled his eye with stern regard
Upon the gentle minstrel bard,
And said in tones abrupt, austere—   650
"Why, Bracy! dost thou loiter here?
I bade thee hence!" The bard obeyed;
And turning from his own sweet maid,
The agéd knight, Sir Leoline,
Led forth the lady Geraldine!   655

THE CONCLUSION TO PART II

A little child, a limber elf,
Singing, dancing to itself,
A fairy thing with red round cheeks,
That always finds, and never seeks,
Makes such a vision to the sight   660
As fills a father's eyes with light;
And pleasures flow in so thick and fast
Upon his heart, that he at last
Must needs express his love's excess
With words of unmeant bitterness.   665
Perhaps 'tis pretty to force together
Thoughts so all unlike each other;
To mutter and mock a broken charm,
To dally with wrong that does no harm.
Perhaps 'tis tender too and pretty   670
At each wild word to feel within
A sweet recoil of love and pity.
And what, if in a world of sin
(O sorrow and shame should this be true!)
Such giddiness of heart and brain   675
Comes seldom save from rage and pain,
So talks as it's most used to do.

SADIE AND MAUD

Gwendolyn Brooks (1917–   )

Maud went to college.
Sadie stayed at home.
Sadie scraped life
With a fine-tooth comb.

She didn't leave a tangle in.   5
Her comb found every strand.
Sadie was one of the livingest chits
In all the land.

Sadie bore two babies
Under her maiden name.   10
Maud and Ma and Papa
Nearly died of shame.

When Sadie said her last so-long,
Her girls struck out from home.
(Sadie had left as heritage   15
Her fine-tooth comb.)

Maud, who went to college,
Is a thin brown mouse.
She is living all alone
In this old house.   20

WORKS IN *Short Story Masterpieces*

Peter Taylor, *A Spinster's Tale*
Katherine Anne Porter, *Flowering Judas*

OTHER SUGGESTED WORKS

Virginia Woolf, *The Lady in the Looking Glass*
William Maxwell, *The Woman Who Had No Eye for Small Details*
William Faulkner, *A Rose for Emily*
Simone de Beauvoir, *The Mystic,* from *The Second Sex,*
                    Chapter XXIV
Euripides, *Electra*
William Butler Yeats, *For Anne Gregory*

QUESTIONS

1a. Compare the lady in Tennyson's poem with the woman *and* the
man in *La Belle Dame sans Merci.* Is there any similarity between
the lady's living alone in the tower and the man's "loitering on the
cold hill side"? What keeps her from being La Belle Dame or
a "femme fatale"? Why does she end up killing herself rather than
being a "man-killer"?

b. Why is she "the fairy lady"? What is the web that she is weaving? What does it signify?

c. Contrast the appearance of the tower with that of the surrounding landscape. What is the whisper that the lady has heard? Why will she be cursed if she looks down to Camelot? What does Camelot represent in contrast with her tower? Describe the kind of life this lady leads, and compare it with life in Camelot.

d. Why does the lady look at the world outside through a mirror rather than directly through her window or by going outside? Why is it significant that her mirror shows her "shadows of the world"? Why does the narrator make a point of saying that "she hath no loyal knight and true"? Why is she content to spend all of her time in her tower weaving and staring in the mirror?

e. From what in the outside world is she safe? What makes her say, "I am half sick of shadows"? What causes her discontent? What kind of figure is Lancelot? What is the impact of all that glittering metal reflecting on "the crystal mirror"? Why does it cause the lady to leave her loom? Why does the web fly away and the mirror crack?

f. What is the curse that has come upon the Lady of Shalott? Compare this curse with the one that befell the man out on "the cold hill side" when La Belle Dame had him in thrall. Is Lancelot "Le Bel Homme"?

g. What is the significance of the lady's death? What kills her? Why does she make such a big production out of her death—the boat, her name on the prow, the white robes? Why is she singing a "mournful, holy" song, and why is her blood being frozen? What is the significance of Lancelot's final remark?

2. Compare the young girl in Dowson's story with the Lady of Shalott. Do they suffer a similar predicament? Compare the man in the story with Lancelot—how are they alike; how different?

3. Consider *The Soul Selects Her Own Society* in terms of the imagery discussed in Tennyson's poem. How are the women similar? Compare and contrast the tone and attitude taken by each author towards his heroine.

4. Does Shakespeare offer a sound reason for not shutting oneself off in a tower? How is he using the mirror image?

5. What are Emily Dickinson and Emily Brontë defending? What might be their reply to Shakespeare's poem urging marriage? Whom is Emily Brontë asking to plead for her, and what does she want the plea to be? Is she talking about a real man? If not, who or what is he? Where is he to be found?

6. Why is Thel "like a reflection in a glass"? What is she bemoaning? How is her plight similar to that of the Lady of Shalott? Why is she

concerned that "all shall say, 'Without a use this shining woman liv'd, Or did she only live to be at death the food of worms?' "?

7. How does Blake describe virginity? What insight does he give into the nature of Innocence and Experience? Could the Lady of Shalott have profited from some of the observations made by the flower, the cloud, the worm, and the clod of clay? What did she need to understand? What was she afraid of?

8. What kind of prison holds Randall Jarrell's heroine? What does she want to be freed from, and for what?

9a. In *Christabel*, how does Coleridge define woman's nature? Compare Christabel and Geraldine. Are they two separate people or one? Why is it significant that Christabel finds Geraldine out in the woods at night? What is sweet Christabel doing out there in the dark all alone? Is she really going to pray for her long-gone knight?

b. Why does Christabel want to sneak back into the castle? What is the significance of their crossing the moat from the woods into the heavily fortified castle? How is the gate like a psychological threshold? Why does Geraldine need Christabel's help in order to cross it? What is Christabel really carrying into her house? Is the distress referred to in line 140 really Geraldine's?

c. What is the significance of the mastiff making an "angry moan" when Christabel passes?

d. What does Christabel's father represent? Why is he ailing? Why does his shield hang "in a murky old niche in the wall"?

e. Who is Geraldine, this "lady of a far countrée"? Why do those who "live in the upper sky" love "holy Christabel"? What does Geraldine mean when she says, "Even I in my degree will try, Fair maiden, to requite you well"? What does she reveal beneath her beautiful robe? Why is it "a sight to dream of, not to tell"?

f. Why is Geraldine "as one defied"? What is the revenge that she seeks? What split in woman's nature do Christabel and Geraldine represent? Why does Geraldine want to be united with Christabel? Why is Christabel both attracted to this side of herself and repelled by it when she sees it as it really is?

g. Why does Sir Leoline fall in love with Geraldine and rebuke Christabel? Why is it significant that Geraldine is the daughter of Sir Leoline's old friend and that the two men had quarreled and separated? Is Sir Leoline also being united with some missing part of himself through Geraldine?

10. What do Sadie and Maud share in common, although their lifestyles are different? What problem plagues them both? Is this problem unique to Black women? What do both women need? Compare Maud with Thel in Blake's poem. Is Sadie's kind of life the only

alternative to remaining "a virgin shrouded in snow" or becoming "a thin brown mouse"? Compare Maud and Sadie with Christabel and Geraldine in Coleridge's poem. What separates these women and causes them so much anguish? What is wrong with the men in their lives—the fathers and lovers (knights and bards)? Discuss the problem shared by White and Black women (fair and dark maidens). Why isn't the problem solved by these women merely changing places and roles—by Geraldine coming to live in Sir Leoline's castle or by Maud becoming a middle-class college girl?

11. Why does the girl in *A Spinster's Tale* end up being a spinster? What was she unable to accept or relate to in the real world? What aspects of life has she rejected? What does the drunken man who passes the house represent? Why is she afraid of him?

12. How is the woman in *Flowering Judas* a Judas figure? Whom or what does she betray? What does she deny in herself? Compare the ideal to which she has dedicated her life with the reality of her day-to-day existence. What is the meaning of loving humanity if you cannot love any one person? How is it possible to love someone like Braggioni? Compare Laura with the girl in Taylor's story. How is Laura also a spinster, although she appears to be an experienced woman of the world? What is wrong with trying to live up to an ideal? What has to be present in order for your ideas to be meaningful and to have an effect on real life?

PART III

The Masked World:

Martyrs, Mannequins, and Monsters

The Masked World: Martyrs, Mannequins, and Monsters

What do we find if we take a closer look at life in "tower'd Camelot," life for the woman who succumbs to Lancelot's charms and becomes a lady fulfilling the expectations of man-made society? We find that the problem of relating to the outside world is not solved by merely playing a role in that world, or by acting out the publicly accepted forms of relationships, such as marriage. By examining such so-called relationships, we see that they are not necessarily real relationships at all but frequently interactions of masks—not of people who know and accept each other as subjects.

A woman who finds herself imprisoned in a man-made role in man-made society might wish that she were back in her solitary tower, since she has merely changed her private prison for a collective one. Life is a prison for the woman who tries to live up to someone else's image of her, who tries to please some man. As soon as the lady is safely married and inside Lancelot's castle, she sees what he is really like beneath his glittering, clanking armor. He wants to make her over in his own image; he tries to change the very thing he claimed to love. The lady has just exchanged the tower of her ideas for the tower of his, which he superimposes upon her; she becomes his slave in the external world. He offers her material riches in exchange for her spiritual riches—the illusions she used to see in her mirror. He teaches her to worship her own image as reflected in his eyes. He encourages her to be a narcissist like himself: to love the outward image of herself, the physical, surface beauty. She is now his property and, through marriage, has become a public institution; her ideas, which are also his ideas, now have the authority of social sanction. The woman who revels in her married state can now enshrine herself as institutionalized "Goodness, Propriety and Moral Duty"—all the Motherly/Matronly "Virtues" of Home, Community and Country: a doll mouthing masculine platitudes. She is no longer "sin" and "temptation," because she is legally owned; now she inspires fear and hate because she puts the law before love.

The woman who gives up her individual life and identity for a life and identity chosen for her by a man, for the material rewards and security of a conventional social role, gives up her growth as a person; she is the helpless child-bride, the sweet young thing—unable to contribute anything to the world outside her husband's home. She is the virgin shrouded in Ivory Snow and household chores, or the figurine just sitting around being pretty. She gives up her role as Temptress and assumes the role of Martyr, Mannequin, or Monster—the Wife/Mother, in whom the child, the individual soul, is stifled, shut away, to be expressed only through the lives of her husband and children. She becomes obsessed with their work and their success. They must succeed to make up for her own failure.

The selections in Part III show life in the conventional, materialistic, masculine world to be a nightmare, a daily torment, which either drives the woman to despair, madness, and even suicide, or, if she learns to adapt, transforms her into that monster who imitates the worst in man: the woman who is greedy for material possessions, and who uses her will as a weapon to manipulate others. She upholds society's values and becomes man's tyrant, outdoing him at his own game; she is the victim imitating the master and then turning on him. The woman who has had to negate her own feelings and identity in order to survive becomes the "castrating bitch" who is out for blood. She is just as shallow and superficial as the man, as out of touch with her soul, her deepest self. But the problem is not that she is *"just* being a woman," as men love to say, but that she is *not* being a woman; she is being a monster like the willful monster, man, who has taught her by example what one must do to "make it" in the world. She is Yeats's "opinionated mind' without feelings, or the hollow mannequin who is obsessed with outward appearance for its own sake, believing, as she has been told over and over again, that all she is is her looks.

There is no more monstrous creature than the female who conforms to man-made ideas of womanhood. Such ideas are not flesh-and-blood reality, and women who attempt to live up to them betray their own natures. By emulating masculine ideals and spouting masculine opinions, women deny the truly feminine, the fully human, in themselves. Their actions should be dictated by Eros, by the deepest feelings inside themselves—not by the clichéd ideas of men who bind Love with Laws. Such masculine-thinking wives govern their families according to rigid moral laws which no real, Eros-governed woman would ever make up, much less obey. Women who live up to man-made ideas of womanhood claim those man-made ideas and values as their own and then use them to tyrannize men, children, and other women. They are full of what Yeats calls "intellectual hatred," which causes them "to barter Plenty's horn and all that's in it for an old bellows full of angry wind."

Woman cannot look to man for an image of her individual humanity or she will only imitate the worst in him. This is why it is important for woman to distinguish between man's ideas of her and her own awareness of herself. She must understand what is wrong with the way men live their lives, relate to her, and govern the world. She must be critical of their values and their judgments. The woman who imitates man's cold will, and brutal materialism, and his preoccupation with the surface promotes the worst in man and stifles the best in herself.

THE APPLICANT

Sylvia Plath (1932–1963)

First, are you our sort of a person?
Do you wear
A glass eye, false teeth or a crutch,
A brace or a hook,
Rubber breasts or a rubber crotch,   5

Stitches to show something's missing? No, no? Then
How can we give you a thing?
Stop crying.
Open your hand.
Empty? Empty. Here is a hand   10

To fill it and willing
To bring teacups and roll away headaches
And do whatever you tell it.
Will you marry it?
It is guaranteed   15

To thumb shut your eyes at the end
And dissolve of sorrow.
We make new stock from the salt.
I notice you are stark naked.
How about this suit—   20

Black and stiff, but not a bad fit.
Will you marry it?
It is waterproof, shatterproof, proof
Against fire and bombs through the roof.
Believe me, they'll bury you in it.   25

Now your head, excuse me, is empty.
I have the ticket for that.
Come here, sweetie, out of the closet.
Well, what do you think of *that*?
Naked as paper to start   30

But in twenty-five years she'll be silver,
In fifty, gold.
A living doll, everywhere you look.
It can sew, it can cook,
It can talk, talk, talk.   35

It works, there is nothing wrong with it.
You have a hole, it's a poultice.
You have an eye, it's an image.
My boy, it's your last resort.
Will you marry it, marry it, marry it.   40

LAPPIN AND LAPINOVA

Virginia Woolf (1882–1941)

They were married. The wedding march pealed out. The pigeons fluttered. Small boys in Eton jackets threw rice; a fox terrier sauntered across the path; and Ernest Thorburn led his bride to the car through that small inquisitive crowd of complete strangers which always collects in London to enjoy other people's happiness or unhappiness. Certainly he looked handsome and she looked shy. More rice was thrown, and the car moved off.

That was on Tuesday. Now it was Saturday. Rosalind had still to get used to the fact that she was Mrs. Ernest Thorburn. Perhaps she never would get used to the fact that she was Mrs. Ernest Anybody, she thought, as she sat in the bow window of the hotel looking over the lake to the mountains, and waited for her husband to come down to breakfast. Ernest was a difficult name to get used to. It was not the name she would have chosen. She would have preferred Timothy, Antony, or Peter. He did not look like Ernest either. The name suggested the Albert Memorial, mahogany sideboards, steel engravings of the Prince Consort with his family—her mother-in-law's dining room in Porchester Terrace in short.

But here he was. Thank goodness he did not look like Ernest—no. But what did he look like? She glanced at him sideways. Well, when he was eating toast he looked like a rabbit. Not that anyone else would have seen a likeness to a creature so diminutive and timid in this spruce, muscular young man with the straight nose, the blue eyes, and the very firm mouth. But that made it all the more amusing. His nose twitched very slightly when he ate. So did her pet rabbit's. She kept watching his nose twitch; and then she had to explain, when he caught her looking at him, why she laughed.

"It's because you're like a rabbit, Ernest," she said. "Like a wild rabbit," she added, looking at him. "A hunting rabbit; a King Rabbit; a rabbit that makes laws for all the other rabbits."

Ernest had no objection to being that kind of rabbit, and since it amused her to see him twitch his nose—he had never known that his nose twitched—he twitched it on purpose. And she laughed and laughed; and he laughed too, so that the maiden ladies and the fishing man and the Swiss waiter in his greasy black jacket all guessed right; they were very happy. But how long does such happiness last? they asked themselves; and each answered according to his own circumstances.

At lunch time, seated on a clump of heather beside the lake, "Lettuce, rabbit?" said Rosalind, holding out the lettuce that had been provided to eat with the hard-boiled eggs. "Come and take it out of my hand," she added, and he stretched out and nibbled the lettuce and twitched his nose.

"Good rabbit, nice rabbit," she said, patting him, as she used to pat her pet rabbit at home. But that was absurd. He was not a tame rabbit, whatever he was. She turned it into French. "Lapin," she called him. But whatever he was, he was not a French rabbit. He was simply and solely English—born at Porchester Terrace, educated at Rugby; now a clerk in His Majesty's Civil Service. So she tried "Bunny" next; but that was worse. "Bunny" was someone plump and soft and comic; he was thin and hard and serious. Still, his nose twitched. "Lappin," she exclaimed suddenly; and gave a little cry as if she had found the very word she looked for.

"Lappin, Lappin, King Lappin," she repeated. It seemed to suit him exactly; he was not Ernest, he was King Lappin. Why? She did not know.

When there was nothing new to talk about on their long solitary walks—and it rained, as everyone had warned them that it would rain; or when they were sitting over the fire in the evening, for it was cold, and the maiden ladies had gone and the fishing man, and the waiter only came if you rang the bell for him, she let her fancy play with the story of the Lappin tribe. Under her hands—she was sewing; he was reading—they became very real, very vivid, very amusing. Ernest put down the paper and helped her. There were the black rabbits and the red; there were the enemy rabbits and the friendly. There were the wood in which they lived and the outlying prairies and the swamp. Above all there was King Lappin, who, far from having only the one trick—that he twitched his nose—became as the days passed an animal of the greatest character; Rosalind was always finding new qualities in him. But above all he was a great hunter.

"And what," said Rosalind, on the last day of the honeymoon, "did the King do today?"

In fact they had been climbing all day; and she had worn a blister on her heel; but she did not mean that.

"Today," said Ernest, twitching his nose as he bit the end off his cigar, "he chased a hare." He paused; struck a match, and twitched again. "A woman hare," he added.

"A white hare!" Rosalind exclaimed, as if she had been expecting this. "Rather a small hare; silver grey; with big bright eyes?"

"Yes," said Ernest, looking at her as she had looked at him, "a smallish animal; with eyes popping out of her head, and two little front paws dangling." It was exactly how she sat, with her sewing dangling in her hands; and her eyes, that were so big and bright, were certainly a little prominent.

"Ah, Lapinova," Rosalind murmured.

"Is that what she's called?" said Ernest—"the real Rosalind?" He looked at her. He felt very much in love with her.

"Yes; that's what she's called," said Rosalind. "Lapinova." And before they went to bed that night it was all settled. He was King Lappin; she was Queen Lapinova. They were the opposite of each other; he was bold and determined; she wary and undependable. He ruled over the busy world of rabbits; her world was a desolate, mysterious place, which she ranged mostly by moonlight. All the same, their territories touched; they were King and Queen.

Thus when they came back from their honeymoon they possessed a private world, inhabited, save for the one white hare, entirely by rabbits. No one guessed that there was such a place, and that of course made it all the more amusing. It made them feel, more even than most young married couples, in league together against the rest of the world. Often they looked slyly at each other when people talked about rabbits and woods and traps and shooting. Or they winked furtively across the table when Aunt Mary said that she could never bear to see a hare in a dish— it looked so like a baby: or when John, Ernest's sporting brother, told them what price rabbits were fetching that autumn in Wiltshire, skins and all. Sometimes when they wanted a gamekeeper, or a poacher or a Lord of the Manor, they amused themselves by distributing the parts among their friends. Ernest's mother, Mrs. Reginald Thorburn, for example, fitted the part of the Squire to perfection. But it was all secret—that was the point of it; nobody save themselves knew that such a world existed.

Without that world, how, Rosalind wondered, that winter could she have lived at all? For instance, there was the golden-wedding party, when all the Thorburns assembled at Porchester Terrace to celebrate the fiftieth anniversary of that union which had been so blessed—had it not produced Ernest Thorburn?—and so fruitful—had it not produced nine other sons and daughters into the bargain, many themselves married and also fruitful? She dreaded that party. But it was inevitable. As she walked upstairs she felt bitterly that she was an only child and an orphan at that; a mere drop among all those Thorburns assembled in the great drawing-room with the shiny satin wallpaper and the lustrous family portraits. The living Thorburns much resembled the painted; save that instead of painted lips they had real lips; out of which came jokes; jokes about schoolrooms, and how they had pulled the chair from under the governess; jokes about frogs and how they had put them between the virgin sheets of maiden ladies. As for herself, she had never even made an apple-pie bed. Holding her present in her hand she advanced toward her mother-in-law sumptuous in yellow satin; and toward her father-in-law decorated with a rich yellow carnation. All round them on tables and chairs there were golden tributes, some nestling in cotton wool; others branching resplendent—candlesticks; cigar boxes; chains; each stamped with the goldsmith's proof that it was solid gold, hall-marked, authentic. But her present was only a little pinchbeck box pierced with holes; an old sand caster, an eighteenth-century relic, once used to sprinkle sand over wet ink. Rather a senseless present she felt—in an age of blotting paper; and as she proffered it, she saw in front of her the stubby black handwriting in which her mother-in-law when they were engaged had expressed the hope that "My son will make you happy." No, she was not happy. Not at all happy. She looked at Ernest, straight as a ramrod with a nose like all the noses in the family portraits; a nose that never twitched at all.

Then they went down to dinner. She was half hidden by the great chrysanthemums that curled their red and gold petals into large tight balls. Everything was gold. A gold-edged card with gold initials inter-twined recited the list of all the dishes that would be set one after another before them. She dipped her spoon in a plate of clear golden fluid. The raw white fog outside had been turned by the lamps into a golden mesh that blurred the edges of the plates and gave the pineapples a rough golden skin. Only she herself in her white wedding dress peering ahead of her with her prominent eyes seemed insoluble as an icicle.

As the dinner wore on, however, the room grew steamy with heat. Beads of perspiration stood out on the men's foreheads. She felt that her icicle was being turned to water. She was being melted; dispersed; dissolved into nothingness; and would soon faint. Then through the surge in her head and the din in her ears she heard a woman's voice exclaim, "But they breed so!"

The Thorburns—yes; they breed so, she echoed; looking at all the round red faces that seemed doubled in the giddiness that overcame her; and magnified in the gold mist that enhaloed them. "They breed so." Then John bawled:

"Little devils! . . . Shoot 'em! Jump on 'em with big boots! That's the only way to deal with 'em . . . rabbits!"

At that word, that magic word, she revived. Peeping between the chrysanthemums she saw Ernest's nose twitch. It rippled, it ran with successive twitches. And at that a mysterious catastrophe befell the Thorburns. The golden table became a moor with the gorse in full bloom; the din of voices turned to one peal of lark's laughter ringing down from the sky. It was a blue sky—clouds passed slowly. And they had all been changed—the Thorburns. She looked at her father-in-law, a furtive little man with dyed moustaches. His foible was collecting things—seals, enamel boxes, trifles from eighteenth-century dressing tables which he hid in the drawers of his study from his wife. Now she saw him as he was—a poacher, stealing off with his coat bulging with pheasants and partridges to drop them stealthily into a three-legged pot in his smoky little cottage. That was her real father-in-law—a poacher. And Celia, the unmarried daughter, who always nosed out other people's secrets, the little things they wished to hide—she was a white ferret with pink eyes, and a nose clotted with earth from her horrid underground nosings and pokings. Slung round men's shoulders, in a net, and thrust down a hole—it was a pitiable life—Celia's; it was none of her fault. So she saw Celia. And then she looked at her mother-in-law—whom they dubbed The Squire. Flushed, coarse, a bully—she was all that, as she stood returning thanks, but now that Rosalind—that is Lapinova—saw her, she saw behind her the decayed family mansion, the plaster peeling off the walls, and heard her, with a sob in her voice, giving thanks to her children (who hated her) for a world that had ceased to exist. There was a sudden silence. They all stood with their glasses raised; they all drank; then it was over.

"Oh, King Lappin!" she cried as they went home together in the fog, "if your nose hadn't twitched just at that moment, I should have been trapped!"

"But you're safe," said King Lappin, pressing her paw.

"Quite safe," she answered.

And they drove back through the Park, King and Queen of the marsh, of the mist, and of the gorse-scented moor.

Thus time passed; one year; two years of time. And on a winter's night, which happened by a coincidence to be the anniversary of the golden-wedding party—but Mrs. Reginald Thorburn was dead; the house was to let; and there was only a caretaker in residence—Ernest came home from the office. They had a nice little home; half a house above a saddler's shop in South Kensington, not far from the Tube station. It was cold, with fog in the air, and Rosalind was sitting over the fire, sewing.

"What d'you think happened to me today?" she began as soon as he had settled himself down with his legs stretched to the blaze. "I was crossing the stream when—"

"What stream?" Ernest interrupted her.

"The stream at the bottom, where our wood meets the black wood," she explained.

Ernest looked completely blank for a moment.

"What the deuce are you talking about?" he asked.

"My dear Ernest!" she cried in dismay. "King Lappin," she added, dangling her little front paws in the firelight. But his nose did not twitch. Her hands—they turned to hands—clutched the stuff she was holding; her eyes popped half out of her head. It took him five minutes at least to change from Ernest Thorburn to King Lappin; and while she waited she felt a load on the back of her neck, as if somebody were about to wring it. At last he changed to King Lappin; his nose twitched; and they spent the evening roaming the woods much as usual.

But she slept badly. In the middle of the night she woke, feeling as if something strange had happened to her. She was stiff and cold. At last she turned on the light and looked at Ernest lying beside her. He was sound asleep. He snored. But even though he snored, his nose remained perfectly still. It looked as if it had never twitched at all. Was it possible that he was really Ernest; and that she was really married to Ernest? A vision of her mother-in-law's dining-room came before her; and there they sat, she and Ernest, grown old, under the engravings, in front of the sideboard. . . . It was their golden-wedding day. She could not bear it.

"Lappin, King Lappin!" she whispered, and for a moment his nose seemed to twitch of its own accord. But he still slept. "Wake up, Lappin, wake up!" she cried.

Ernest woke; and seeing her sitting bolt upright beside him he asked: "What's the matter?"

"I thought my rabbit was dead!" she whimpered. Ernest was angry.

"Don't talk such rubbish, Rosalind," he said. "Lie down and go to sleep."

He turned over. In another moment he was sound asleep and snoring.

But she could not sleep. She lay curled up on her side of the bed, like a hare in its form. She had turned out the light, but the street lamp lit the ceiling faintly, and the trees outside made a lacy network over it as if there were a shadowy grove on the ceiling in which she wandered, turning, twisting, in and out, round and round, hunting, being hunted, hearing the bay of hounds and horns; flying, escaping . . . until the maid drew the blinds and brought their early tea.

Next day she could settle to nothing. She seemed to have lost something. She felt as if her body had shrunk; it had grown small, and black and hard. Her joints seemed stiff too, and when she looked in the glass, which she did several times as she wandered about the flat, her eyes seemed to burst out of her head, like currants in a bun. The rooms also seemed to have shrunk. Large pieces of furniture jutted out at odd angles and she found herself knocking against them. At last she put on her hat and went out. She walked along the Cromwell Road; and every room she passed and peered into seemed to be a dining-room where people sat eating under steel engravings, with thick yellow lace curtains, and mahogany sideboards. At last she reached the Natural History Museum; she used to like it when she was a child. But the first thing she saw when she went in was a stuffed hare standing on sham snow with pink glass eyes. Somehow it made her shiver all over. Perhaps it would be better when dusk fell. She went home and sat over the fire, without a light, and tried to imagine that she was out alone on a moor; and there was a stream rushing; and beyond the stream a dark wood. But she could get no further than the stream. At last she squatted down on the bank on the wet grass, and sat crouched in her chair, with her hands dangling empty, and her eyes glazed, like glass eyes, in the firelight. Then there was the crack of a gun.... She started as if she had been shot. It was only Ernest, turning his key in the door. She waited, trembling. He came in and switched on the light. There he stood tall, handsome, rubbing his hands that were red with cold.

"Sitting in the dark?" he said.

"Oh, Ernest, Ernest!" she cried, starting up in her chair.

"Well, what's up, now?" he asked briskly, warming his hands at the fire.

"It's Lapinova..." she faltered, glancing wildly at him out of her great startled eyes. "She's gone, Ernest. I've lost her!"

Ernest frowned. He pressed his lips tight together. "Oh, that's what's up, is it?" he said, smiling rather grimly at his wife. For ten seconds he stood there, silent; and she waited, feeling hands tightening at the back of her neck.

"Yes," he said at length. "Poor Lapinova..." He straightened his tie at the looking-glass over the mantelpiece.

"Caught in a trap," he said, "killed," and sat down and read the newspaper.

So that was the end of that marriage.

THE MASK

William Butler Yeats (1865–1939)

'Put off that mask of burning gold
With emerald eyes.'
'O no, my dear, you make so bold

To find if hearts be wild and wise,
And yet not cold.'   5
'I would but find what's there to find,
Love or deceit.'
'It was the mask engaged your mind,
And after set your heart to beat,
Not what's behind.'   10
'But lest you are my enemy,
I must enquire.'
'O no, my dear, let all that be;
What matter, so there is but fire
In you, in me?'   15

THE BIRTHMARK

Nathaniel Hawthorne (1804–1864)

In the latter part of the last century there lived a man of science, an eminent proficient in every branch of natural philosophy, who not long before our story opens had made experience of a spiritual affinity more attractive than any chemical one. He had left his laboratory to the care of an assistant, cleared his fine countenance from the furnace smoke, washed the stain of acids from his fingers, and persuaded a beautiful woman to become his wife. In those days, when the comparatively recent discovery of electricity and other kindred mysteries of Nature seemed to open paths into the region of miracle, it was not unusual for the love of science to rival the love of woman in its depth and absorbing energy. The higher intellect, the imagination, the spirit, and even the heart might all find their congenial aliment in pursuits which, as some of their ardent votaries believed, would ascend from one step of powerful intelligence to another, until the philosopher should lay his hand on the secret of creative force and perhaps make new worlds for himself. We know not whether Aylmer possessed this degree of faith in man's ultimate control over Nature. He had devoted himself, however, too unreservedly to scientific studies ever to be weaned from them by any second passion. His love for his young wife might prove the stronger of the two; but it could only be by intertwining itself with his love of science and uniting the strength of the latter to his own.

Such a union accordingly took place, and was attended with truly remarkable consequences and a deeply impressive moral. One day, very soon after their marriage, Aylmer sat gazing at his wife with a trouble in his countenance that grew stronger until he spoke.

"Georgiana," said he, "has it never occurred to you that the mark upon your cheek might be removed?"

"No, indeed," said she, smiling; but, perceiving the seriousness of his manner, she blushed deeply. "To tell you the truth, it has been so often called a charm that I was simple enough to imagine it might be so."

"Ah, upon another face perhaps it might," replied her husband; "but never on yours. No, dearest Georgiana, you came so nearly perfect from the hand of Nature that this slightest possible defect, which we hesitate whether to term a defect or a beauty, shocks me, as being the visible mark of earthly imperfection."

"Shocks you, my husband!" cried Georgiana, deeply hurt; at first reddening with momentary anger, but then bursting into tears. "Then why did you take me from my mother's side? You cannot love what shocks you!"

To explain this conversation, it must be mentioned that in the centre of Georgiana's left cheek there was a singular mark, deeply interwoven, as it were, with the texture and substance of her face. In the usual state of her complexion—a healthy though delicate bloom—the mark wore a tint of deeper crimson, which imperfectly defined its shape amid the surrounding rosiness. When she blushed it gradually became more indistinct, and finally vanished amid the triumphant rush of blood that bathed the whole cheek with its brilliant glow. But if any shifting motion caused her to turn pale there was the mark again, a crimson stain upon the snow, in what Aylmer sometimes deemed an almost fearful distinctness. Its shape bore not a little similarity to the human hand, though of the smallest pygmy size. Georgiana's lovers were wont to say that some fairy at her birth hour had laid her tiny hand upon the infant's cheek, and left this impress there in token of the magic endowments that were to give her such sway over all hearts. Many a desperate swain would have risked life for the privilege of pressing his lips to the mysterious hand. It must not be concealed, however, that the impression wrought by this fairy sign manual varied exceedingly according to the difference of temperament in the beholders. Some fastidious persons—but they were exclusively of her own sex—affirmed that the bloody hand, as they chose to call it, quite destroyed the effect of Georgiana's beauty and rendered her countenance even hideous. But it would be as reasonable to say that one of those small blue stains which sometimes occur in the purest statuary marble would convert the Eve of Powers to a monster. Masculine observers, if the birthmark did not heighten their admiration, contented themselves with wishing it away, that the world might possess one living specimen of ideal loveliness without the semblance of a flaw. After his marriage,—for he thought little or nothing of the matter before,—Aylmer discovered that this was the case with himself.

Had she been less beautiful,—if Envy's self could have found aught else to sneer at,—he might have felt his affection heightened by the prettiness of this mimic hand, now vaguely portrayed, now lost, now stealing forth again and glimmering to and fro with every pulse of emotion that throbbed within her heart; but, seeing her otherwise so perfect, he found this one defect grow more and more intolerable with every moment of their united lives. It was the fatal flaw of humanity which Nature, in one shape or another, stamps ineffaceably on all her productions, either to imply that they are temporary and finite, or that their perfection must be wrought by toil and pain. The crimson hand expressed the ineludible gripe in which mortality clutches the highest and purest of earthly mould, degrading them into kindred with the lowest, and even with the very brutes, like whom their visible frames return to dust. In this manner, selecting it as the symbol of his wife's liability to sin, sorrow, decay, and death, Aylmer's sombre imagination was not long in rendering the birthmark a frightful object, causing him more trouble and horror than ever Georgiana's beauty, whether of soul or sense, had given him delight.

At all the seasons which should have been their happiest, he invariably, and without intending it, nay, in spite of a purpose to the contrary, reverted to this one disastrous topic. Trifling as it at first appeared, it so connected itself with innumerable trains of thought and modes of feeling that it became the central point of all. With the morning twilight Aylmer opened his eyes upon his wife's face and recognized the symbol of imperfection; and when they sat together at the evening hearth his eyes wandered stealthily to her cheek, and beheld, flickering with the blaze of the wood fire, the spectral hand that wrote mortality where he would fain have worshipped. Georgiana soon learned to shudder at his gaze. It needed but a glance with the peculiar expression that his face often wore to change the roses of her cheeks into a deathlike paleness, amid which the crimson hand was brought strongly out, like a bas-relief of ruby on the whitest marble.

Late one night, when the lights were growing dim so as hardly to betray the stain on the poor wife's cheek, she herself, for the first time, voluntarily took up the subject.

"Do you remember, my dear Aylmer," said she, with a feeble attempt at a smile, "have you any recollection of a dream last night about this odious hand?"

"None! none whatever!" replied Aylmer, starting; but then he added, in a dry, cold tone, affected for the sake of concealing the real depth of his emotion, "I might well dream of it; for, before I fell asleep, it had taken a pretty firm hold of my fancy."

"And did you dream of it?" continued Georgiana, hastily; for she dreaded lest a gush of tears interrupt what she had to say. "A terrible dream! I wonder that you can forget it. Is it possible to forget this one expression?—'It is in her heart now; we must have it out!' Reflect, my husband; for by all means I would have you recall that dream."

The mind is in a sad state when Sleep, the all-involving, cannot confine her spectres within the dim region of her sway, but suffers them to break forth, affrighting this actual life with secrets that perchance belong to a deeper one. Aylmer now remembered his dream. He had fancied himself with his servant Aminadab, attempting an operation for the removal of the birthmark; but the deeper went the knife, the deeper sank the hand, until at length its tiny grasp appeared to have caught hold of Georgiana's heart; whence, however, her husband was inexorably resolved to cut or wrench it away.

When the dream had shaped itself perfectly in his memory, Aylmer sat in his wife's presence with a guilty feeling. Truth often finds its way to the mind close muffled in robes of sleep, and then speaks with uncompromising directness of matters in regard to which we practise an unconscious self-deception during our waking moments. Until now he had not been aware of the tyrannizing influence acquired by one idea over his mind, and of the lengths which he might find in his heart to go for the sake of giving himself peace.

"Aylmer," resumed Georgiana, solemnly, "I know not what may be the cost to both of us to rid me of this fatal birthmark. Perhaps its removal may cause cureless deformity; or it may be the stain goes as deep as life itself. Again: do we know that there is a possibility, on any terms, of unclasping the firm gripe of this little hand which was laid upon me before I came into the world?"

"Dearest Georgiana, I have spent much thought upon the subject," hastily interrupted Aylmer. "I am convinced of the perfect practicability of its removal."

"If there be the remotest possibility of it," continued Georgiana, "let the attempt be made, at whatever risk. Danger is nothing to me; for life, while this hateful mark makes me the object of your horror and disgust,—life is a burden which I would fling down with joy. Either remove this dreadful hand, or take my wretched life! You have deep science. All the world bears witness of it. You have achieved great wonders. Cannot you remove this little, little mark, which I cover with the tips of two small fingers? Is this beyond your power, for the sake of your own peace, and to save your poor wife from madness?"

"Noblest, dearest, tenderest wife," cried Aylmer, rapturously, "doubt not my power. I have already given this matter the deepest thought—thought which might almost have enlightened me to create a being less perfect than yourself. Georgiana, you have led me deeper than ever into the heart of science. I feel myself fully competent to render this dear cheek as faultless as its fellow; and then, most beloved, what will be my triumph when I shall have corrected what Nature left imperfect in her fairest work! Even Pygmalion, when his sculptured woman assumed life, felt not greater ecstasy than mine will be."

"It is resolved, then," said Georgiana, faintly smiling. "And, Aylmer, spare me not, though you should find the birthmark take refuge in my heart at last."

Her husband tenderly kissed her cheek—her right cheek—not that which bore the impress of the crimson hand.

The next day Aylmer apprised his wife of a plan that he had formed whereby he might have opportunity for the intense thought and constant watchfulness which the proposed operation would require; while Georgiana, likewise, would enjoy the perfect repose essential to its success. They were to seclude themselves in the extensive apartments occupied by Aylmer as a laboratory, and where, during his toilsome youth, he had made discoveries in the elemental powers of Nature that had roused the admiration of all the learned societies in Europe. Seated calmly in this laboratory, the pale philosopher had investigated the secrets of the highest cloud region and of the profoundest mines; he had satisfied himself of the causes that kindled and kept alive the fires of the volcano; and had explained the mystery of fountains, and how it is that they gush forth, some so bright and pure, and others with such rich medicinal virtues, from the dark bosom of the earth. Here, too, at an earlier period, he had studied the wonders of the human frame, and attempted to fathom the very process by which Nature assimilates all her precious influences from earth and air, and from the spiritual world, to create and foster man, her masterpiece. The latter pursuit, however, Aylmer had long laid aside in unwilling recognition of the truth—against which all seekers sooner or later stumble—that our great creative Mother, while she amuses us with apparently working in the broadest sunshine, is yet severely careful to keep her own secrets, and, in spite of her pretended openness, shows us nothing but results. She permits us, indeed, to mar, but seldom to mend, and, like a jealous patentee, on no account to make. Now, however, Aylmer resumed these half-forgotten investigations; not, of course, with such hopes or wishes as first suggested them; but because they involved much physiological truth and lay in the path of his proposed scheme for the treatment of Georgiana.

As he led her over the threshold of the laboratory, Georgiana was cold and tremulous. Aylmer looked cheerfully into her face, with intent to reassure her, but was so startled with the intense glow of the birthmark upon the whiteness of her cheek that he could not restrain a strong convulsive shudder. His wife fainted.

"Aminadab! Aminadab!" shouted Aylmer, stamping violently on the floor.

Forthwith there issued from an inner apartment a man of low stature, but bulky frame, with shaggy hair hanging about his visage, which was grimed with the vapors of the furnace. This personage had been Aylmer's underworker during his whole scientific career, and was admirably fitted for that office by his great mechanical readiness, and the skill with which, while incapable of comprehending a single principle, he executed all the details of his master's experiments. With his vast strength, his shaggy hair, his smoky aspect, and the indescribable earthiness that incrusted him, he seemed to represent man's physical nature; while Aylmer's slender figure, and pale, intellectual face, were no less apt a type of the spiritual element.

"Throw open the door of the boudoir, Aminadab," said Aylmer, "and burn a pastil."

"Yes, master," answered Aminadab, looking intently at the lifeless form of Georgiana; and then he muttered to himself, "If she were my wife, I'd never part with that birthmark."

When Georgiana recovered consciousness she found herself breathing an atmosphere of penetrating fragrance, the gentle potency of which had recalled her from her deathlike faintness. The scene around her looked like enchantment. Aylmer had converted those smoky, dingy, sombre rooms, where he had spent his brightest years in recondite pursuits, into a series of beautiful apartments not unfit to be the secluded abode of a lovely woman. The walls were hung with gorgeous curtains, which imparted the combination of grandeur and grace that no other species of adornment can achieve; and, as they fell from the ceiling to the floor, their rich and ponderous folds, concealing all angles and straight lines, appeared to shut in the scene from infinite space. For aught Georgiana knew, it might be a pavilion among the clouds. And Aylmer, excluding the sunshine, which would have interfered with his chemical processes, had supplied its place with perfumed lamps, emitting flames of various hue, but all uniting in a soft, impurpled radiance. He now knelt by his wife's side, watching her earnestly, but without alarm; for he was confident in his science, and felt that he could draw a magic circle round her within which no evil might intrude.

"Where am I? Ah, I remember," said Georgiana, faintly; and she placed her hand over her cheek to hide the terrible mark from her husband's eyes.

"Fear not, dearest!" exclaimed he. "Do not shrink from me! Believe me, Georgiana, I even rejoice in this single imperfection, since it will be such a rapture to remove it."

"O, spare me!" sadly replied his wife. "Pray do not look at it again. I never can forget that convulsive shudder."

In order to soothe Georgiana, and, as it were, to release her mind from the burden of actual things, Aylmer now put in practice some of the light and playful secrets which science had taught him among its profounder lore. Airy figures, absolutely bodiless ideas, and forms of unsubstantial beauty came and danced before her, imprinting their momentary footsteps on beams of light. Though she had some indistinct idea of the method of these optical phenomena, still the illusion was almost perfect enough to warrant the belief that her husband possessed sway over the spiritual world. Then again, when she felt a wish to look forth from her seclusion, immediately, as if her thoughts were answered, the procession of external existence flitted across a screen. The scenery and the figures of actual life were perfectly represented, but with that bewitching yet indescribable difference which always makes a picture, an image, or a shadow so much more attractive than the original. When wearied of this, Aylmer bade her cast her eyes upon a vessel containing a quantity of earth. She did so, with little interest at first; but was soon startled to perceive the germ of a plant shooting upward from the soil. Then came the slender stalk; the leaves gradually unfolded themselves; and amid them was a perfect and lovely flower.

"It is magical!" cried Georgiana. "I dare not touch it."

"Nay, pluck it," answered Aylmer,—"pluck it, and inhale its brief perfume while you may. The flower will wither in a few moments and leave nothing save its brown seed vessels; but thence may be perpetuated a race as ephemeral as itself."

But Georgiana had no sooner touched the flower than the whole plant suffered a blight, its leaves turning coal-black as if by the agency of fire.

"There was too powerful a stimulus," said Aylmer, thoughtfully.

To make up for this abortive experiment, he proposed to take her portrait by a scientific process of his own invention. It was to be effected by rays of light striking upon a polished plate of metal. Georgiana assented; but, on looking at the result, was affrighted to find the features of the portrait blurred and indefinable; while the minute figure of a hand appeared where the cheek should have been. Aylmer snatched the metallic plate and threw it into a jar of corrosive acid.

Soon, however, he forgot these mortifying failures. In the intervals of study and chemical experiment he came to her flushed and exhausted, but seemed invigorated by her presence, and spoke in glowing language of the resources of his art. He gave a history of the long dynasty of the alchemists, who spent so many ages in quest of the universal solvent by which the golden principle might be elicited from all things vile and base. Aylmer appeared to believe that, by the plainest scientific logic, it was altogether within the limits of possibility to discover this long-sought medium; "but," he added, "a philosopher who should go deep enough to acquire the power would attain too lofty a wisdom to stoop to the exercise of it." Not less singular were his opinions in regard to the elixir vitae. He more than intimated that it was at his option to concoct a liquid that should prolong life for years, perhaps interminably; but that it would produce a discord in Nature which all the world, and chiefly the quaffer of the immortal nostrum, would find cause to curse.

"Aylmer, are you in earnest?" asked Georgiana, looking at him with amazement and fear. "It is terrible to possess such power, or even to dream of possessing it."

"O, do not tremble, my love," said her husband. "I would not wrong either you or myself by working such inharmonious effects upon our lives; but I would have you consider how trifling, in comparison, is the skill requisite to remove this little hand."

At the mention of the birthmark, Georgiana, as usual, shrank as if a redhot iron had touched her cheek.

Again Aylmer applied himself to his labors. She could hear his voice in the distant furnace room giving directions to Aminadab, whose harsh, uncouth, misshapen tones were audible in response, more like the grunt or growl of a brute than human speech. After hours of absence, Aylmer reappeared and proposed that she should now examine his cabinet of chemical products and natural treasures of the earth. Among the former he showed her a small vial, in which, he remarked, was contained a gentle yet most powerful fragrance, capable of impregnating all the breezes that blow across a kingdom. They were of inestimable value, the contents of that little vial; and, as he said so, he threw some of the perfume into the air and filled the room with piercing and invigorating delight.

"And what is this?" asked Georgiana, pointing to a small crystal globe containing a gold-colored liquid. "It is so beautiful to the eye that I could imagine it the elixir of life."

"In one sense it is," replied Aylmer; "or, rather, the elixir of immortality. It is the most precious poison that ever was concocted in this world. By its aid I could apportion the lifetime of any mortal at whom you might point your finger. The strength of the dose would determine whether he were to linger out years, or drop dead in the midst of a breath. No king on his guarded throne could keep his life if I, in my private station, should deem that the welfare of millions justified me in depriving him of it."

"Why do you keep such a terrific° drug?" inquired Georgiana in horror.

"Do not mistrust me, dearest," said her husband, smiling; "its virtuous potency is yet greater than its harmful one. But see! here is a powerful cosmetic. With a few drops of this in a vase of water, freckles

---

° *terrific*: terrible

may be washed away as easily as the hands are cleansed. A stronger solution would take the blood out of the cheek, and leave the rosiest beauty a pale ghost."

"Is it with this lotion that you intend to bathe my cheek?" asked Georgiana, anxiously.

"Oh, no," hastily replied her husband; "this is merely superficial. Your case demands a remedy that shall go deeper."

In his interviews with Georgiana, Aylmer generally made minute inquiries as to her sensations, and whether the confinement of the rooms and temperature of the atmosphere agreed with her. These questions had such a particular drift that Georgiana began to conjecture that she was already subjected to certain physical influences, either breathed in with the fragrant air or taken with her food. She fancied likewise, but it might be altogether fancy, that there was a stirring up of her system—a strange, indefinite sensation creeping through her veins, and tingling, half painfully, half pleasurably, at her heart. Still, whenever she dared to look into the mirror, there she beheld herself pale as a white rose and with the crimson birthmark stamped upon her cheek. Not even Aylmer now hated it so much as she.

To dispel the tedium of the hours which her husband found it necessary to devote to the processes of combination and analysis, Georgiana turned over the volumes of his scientific library. In many dark old tomes she met with chapters full of romance and poetry. They were the works of the philosophers of the middle ages, such as Albertus Magnus, Cornelius Agrippa, Paracelsus, and the famous friar who created the prophetic Brazen Head. All these antique naturalists stood in advance of their centuries, yet were imbued with some of their credulity, and therefore were believed, and perhaps imagined themselves to have acquired from the investigation of Nature a power above Nature, and from physics a sway over the spiritual world. Hardly less curious and imaginative were the early volumes of the Transactions of the Royal Society, in which the members, knowing little of the limits of natural possibility, were continually recording wonders or proposing methods whereby wonders might be wrought.

But to Georgiana, the most engrossing volume was a large folio of her husband's own hand, in which he had recorded every experiment of his scientific career, its original aim, the methods adopted for its development, and its final success or failure, with the circumstances to which either event was attributable. The book, in truth, was both the history and emblem of his ardent, ambitious, imaginative, yet practical and laborious life. He handled physical details as if there were nothing beyond them; yet spiritualized them all and redeemed himself from materialism by his strong and eager aspiration towards the infinite. In his grasp the veriest clod of earth assumed a soul. Georgiana, as she read, reverenced

Aylmer and loved him more profoundly than ever, but with a less entire dependence on his judgment than heretofore. Much as he had accomplished, she could not but observe that his most splendid successes were almost invariably failures, if compared with the ideal at which he aimed. His brightest diamonds were the merest pebbles, and felt to be so by himself, in comparison with the inestimable gems which lay hidden beyond his reach. The volume, rich with achievements that had won renown for its author, was yet as melancholy a record as ever mortal hand had penned. It was the sad confession and continual exemplification of the shortcomings of the composite man, the spirit burdened with clay and working in matter, and of the despair that assails the higher nature at finding itself so miserably thwarted by the earthly part. Perhaps every man of genius, in whatever sphere, might recognize the image of his own experience in Aylmer's journal.

So deeply did these reflections affect Georgiana that she laid her face upon the open volume and burst into tears. In this situation she was found by her husband.

"It is dangerous to read in a sorcerer's books," said he with a smile, though his countenance was uneasy and displeased. "Georgiana, there are pages in that volume which I can scarcely glance over and keep my senses. Take heed lest it prove detrimental to you."

"It has made me worship you more than ever," said she.

"Ah, wait for this one success," rejoined he, "then worship me if you will. I shall deem myself hardly unworthy of it. But come, I have sought you for the luxury of your voice. Sing to me, dearest."

So she poured out the liquid music of her voice to quench the thirst of his spirit. He then took his leave with a boyish exuberance of gayety, assuring her that her seclusion would endure but a little longer, and that the result was already certain. Scarcely had he departed when Georgiana felt irrestibly impelled to follow him. She had forgotten to inform Aylmer of a symptom which for two or three hours past had begun to excite her attention. It was a sensation in the fatal birthmark, not painful, but which induced a restlessness throughout her system. Hastening after her husband, she intruded for the first time into the laboratory.

The first thing that struck her eye was the furnace, that hot and feverish worker, with the intense glow of its fire, which by the quantities of soot clustered above it seemed to have been burning for ages. There was a distilling apparatus in full operation. Around the room were retorts, tubes, cylinders, crucibles, and other apparatus of chemical research. An electrical machine stood ready for immediate use. The atmosphere felt oppressively close, and was tainted with gaseous odors which had been tormented forth by the processes of science. The severe and homely simplicity of the apartment, with it naked walls and brick pavement, looked strange, accustomed as Georgiana had become to the fantastic elegance of her boudoir. But what chiefly, indeed almost solely, drew her attention, was the aspect of Aylmer himself.

He was pale as death, anxious and absorbed, and hung over the furnace as if it depended upon his utmost watchfulness whether the liquid which it was distilling should be the draught of immortal happiness or misery. How different from the sanguine and joyous mien that he had assumed for Georgiana's encouragement!

"Carefully now, Aminadab; carefully, thou human machine; carefully, thou man of clay," muttered Aylmer, more to himself than his assistant. "Now, if there be a thought too much or too little, it is all over."

"Ho! ho!" mumbled Aminadad. "Look, master! look!"

Aylmer raised his eyes hastily, and at first reddened, then grew paler than ever, on beholding Georgiana. He rushed towards her and seized her arm with a grip that left the print of his fingers upon it.

"Why do you come hither? Have you no trust in your husband?" cried he, impetuously. "Would you throw the blight of that fatal birthmark over my labors? It is not well done. Go, prying woman! go!"

"Nay, Aylmer," said Georgiana with the firmness of which she possessed no stinted endowment, "it is not you that have a right to complain. You mistrust your wife; you have concealed the anxiety with which you watch the development of this experiment. Think not so unworthily of me, my husband. Tell me all the risk we run, and fear not that I shall shrink; for my share in it is far less than your own."

"No, no, Georgiana!" said Aylmer, impatiently; "it must not be."

"I submit," replied she, calmly. "And, Aylmer, I shall quaff whatever draught you bring me; but it will be on the same principle that would induce me to take a dose of poison if offered by your hand."

"My noble wife," said Aylmer, deeply moved. "I knew not the height and depth of your nature until now. Nothing shall be concealed. Know, then, that this crimson hand, superficial as it seems, has clutched its grasp into your being with a strength of which I had no previous conception. I have already administered agents powerful enough to do aught except to change your entire physical system. Only one thing remains to be tried. If that fails us we are ruined."

"Why did you hesitate to tell me this?" asked she.

"Because, Georgiana," said Aylmer, in a low voice, "there is danger."

"Danger? There is but one danger—that this horrible stigma shall be left upon my cheek!" cried Georgiana. "Remove it, remove it, whatever be the cost, or we shall both go mad!"

"Heaven knows your words are too true," said Aylmer, sadly. "And now, dearest, return to your boudoir. In a little while all will be tested."

He conducted her back and took leave of her with a solemn tenderness which spoke far more than his words how much was now at stake. After his departure Georgiana became rapt in musings. She considered the character of Aylmer and did it completer justice than at any previous moment. Her heart exulted, while it trembled, at his honorable love— so pure and lofty that it would accept nothing less than perfection nor miserably make itself contented with an earthlier nature than he had dreamed of. She felt how much more precious was such a sentiment than that meaner kind which could have borne with the imperfection for her sake, and have been guilty of treason to holy love by degrading its perfect idea to the level of the actual; and with her whole spirit she prayed that, for a single moment, she might satisfy his highest and deepest conception. Longer than one moment she well knew it could not be; for his spirit was ever on the march, ever ascending, and each instant required something that was beyond the scope of the instant before.

The sound of her husband's footsteps aroused her. He bore a crystal goblet containing a liquor colorless as water, but bright enough to be the draught of immortality. Aylmer was pale; but it seemed rather the consequence of a highly-wrought state of mind and tension of spirit than of fear or doubt.

"The concoction of the draught has been perfect," said he, in answer to Georgiana's look. "Unless all my science have deceived me, it cannot fail."

"Save on your account, my dearest Aylmer," observed his wife, "I might wish to put off this birthmark of mortality by relinquishing mortality itself in preference to any other mode. Life is but a sad possession to those who have attained precisely the degree of moral advancement at which I stand. Were I weaker and blinder, it might be happiness. Were I stronger, it might be endured hopefully. But, being what I find myself, methinks I am of all mortals the most fit to die."

"You are fit for heaven without tasting death!" replied her husband. "But why do we speak of dying? The draught cannot fail. Behold its effect upon this plant."

On the window seat there stood a geranium diseased with yellow blotches which had overspread all its leaves. Aylmer poured a small quantity of the liquid upon the soil in which it grew. In a little time, when the roots of the plant had taken up the moisture, the unsightly blotches began to be extinguished in a living verdure.

"There needed no proof," said Georgiana, quietly. "Give me the goblet. I joyfully stake all upon your word."

"Drink, then, thou lofty creature!" exclaimed Aylmer, with fervid admiration. "There is no taint of imperfection on thy spirit. Thy sensible frame, too, shall soon be all perfect."

She quaffed the liquid and returned the goblet to his hand.

"It is grateful," said she, with a placid smile. "Methinks it is like water from a heavenly fountain; for it contains I know not what of unobtrusive fragrance and deliciousness. It allays a feverish thirst that had parched me for many days. Now, dearest, let me sleep. My earthly senses are closing over my spirit like the leaves around the heart of a rose at sunset."

She spoke the last words with a gentle reluctance, as if it required almost more energy than she could command to pronounce the faint and lingering syllables. Scarcely had they loitered through her lips ere she was lost in slumber. Aylmer sat by her side, watching her aspect with the emotions proper to a man the whole value of whose existence was involved in the process now to be tested. Mingled with this mood, however, was the philosophic investigation characteristic of the man of science. Not the minutest symptom escaped him. A heightened flush of the cheek, a slight irregularity of breath, a quiver of the eyelid, a hardly perceptible tremor through the frame—such were the details which, as the moments passed, he wrote down in his folio volume. Intense thought had set its stamp upon every previous page of that volume, but the thoughts of years were all concentrated upon the last.

While thus employed, he failed not to gaze often at the fatal hand, and not without a shudder. Yet once, by a strange and unaccountable impulse, he pressed it with his lips. His spirit recoiled, however, in the very act; and Georgiana, out of the midst of her deep sleep, moved uneasily and murmured as if in remonstrance. Again Aylmer resumed his watch. Nor was it without avail. The crimson hand, which at first had been strongly visible upon the marble paleness of Georgiana's cheek, now grew more faintly outlined. She remained not less pale than ever; but the birthmark, with every breath that came and went, lost somewhat of its former distinctness. Its presence had been awful; its departure was more awful still. Watch the stain of the rainbow fading out of the sky, and you will know how that mysterious symbol passed away.

"By Heaven! it is well nigh gone!" said Aylmer to himself, in almost irrepressible ecstasy. "I can scarcely trace it now. Success! success! And now it is like the faintest rose color. The lightest flush of blood across her cheek would overcome it. But she is so pale!"

He drew aside the window curtain and suffered the light of natural day to fall into the room and rest upon her cheek. At the same time he heard a gross, hoarse chuckle, which he had long known as his servant Aminadab's expression of delight.

"Ah, clod! ah, earthly mass!" cried Aylmer, laughing in a sort of frenzy, "you have served me well! Matter and spirit—earth and heaven— have both done their part in this! Laugh, thing of the senses! You have earned the right to laugh."

These exclamations broke Georgiana's sleep. She slowly unclosed her eyes and gazed into the mirror which her husband had arranged for that purpose. A faint smile flitted over her lips when she recognized how barely perceptible was now that crimson hand which had once blazed forth with such disastrous brilliancy as to scare away all their happiness. But then her eyes sought Aylmer's face with a trouble and anxiety that he could by no means account for.

"My poor Aylmer!" murmured she.

"Poor? Nay, richest, happiest, most favored!" exclaimed he. "My peerless bride, it is successful! You are perfect!"

"My poor Aylmer," she repeated, with a more than human tenderness, "you have aimed loftily; you have done nobly. Do not repent that, with so high and pure a feeling, you have rejected the best the earth could offer. Aylmer, dearest Aylmer, I am dying!"

Alas! it was too true! The fatal hand had grappled with the mystery of life, and was the bond by which an angelic spirit kept itself in union with a mortal frame, As the last crimson tint of the birthmark—that sole token of human imperfection—faded from her cheek, the parting breath of the now perfect woman passed into the atmosphere, and her soul, lingering a moment near her husband, took its heavenward flight. Then a hoarse chuckling laugh was heard again! Thus ever does the gross fatality of earth exult in its invariable triumph over the immortal essence which, in this dim sphere of half development, demands the completeness of a higher state. Yet, had Aylmer reached a profounder wisdom, he need not thus have flung away the happiness which would have woven his mortal life of the selfsame texture with the celestial. The momentary circumstance was too strong for him; he failed to look beyond the shadowy scope of time, and, living once for all in eternity, to find the perfect future in the present.

Martyrs

NEXT DAY

Randall Jarrell (1914–1965)

Moving from Cheer to Joy, from Joy to All,
I take a box
And add it to my wild rice, my Cornish game hens.
The slacked or shorted, basketed, identical
Food-gathering flocks   5
Are selves I overlook. Wisdom, said William James,

Is learning what to overlook. And I am wise
If that is wisdom.

Yet somehow, as I buy All from these shelves
And the boy takes it to my station wagon,   10
What I've become
Troubles me even if I shut my eyes.

When I was young and miserable and pretty
And poor, I'd wish
What all girls wish: to have a husband,   15
A house and children. Now that I'm old, my wish
Is womanish:
That the boy putting groceries in my car

See me. It bewilders me he doesn't see me.
For so many years   20
I was good enough to eat: the world looked at me
And its mouth watered. How often they have undressed me,
The eyes of strangers!
And, holding their flesh within my flesh, their vile

Imaginings within my imagining,   25
I too have taken
The chance of life. Now the boy pats my dog
And we start home. Now I am good.
The last mistaken,
Ecstatic, accidental bliss, the blind   30

Happiness that, bursting, leaves upon the palm
Some soap and water——
It was so long ago, back in some Gay
Twenties, Nineties, I don't know . . . Today I miss
My lovely daughter   35
Away at school, my sons away at school,

My husband away at work—I wish for them.
The dog, the maid,
And I go through the sure unvarying days
At home in them. As I look at my life,   40
I am afraid
Only that it will change, as I am changing:

I am afraid, this morning, of my face.
It looks at me
From the rear-view mirror, with the eyes I hate,   45
The smile I hate. Its plain, lined look

Of gray discovery
Repeats to me: "You're old." That's all, I'm old.

And yet I'm afraid, as I was at the funeral
I went to yesterday.   50
My friend's cold made-up face, granite among its flowers,
Her undressed, operated-on, dressed body
Were my face and body.
As I think of her I hear her telling me

How young I seem; I *am* exceptional;   55
I think of all I have.
But really no one is exceptional,
No one has anything, I'm anybody,
I stand beside my grave
Confused with my life, that is commonplace and solitary.   60

TO AN UNEDUCATED WOMAN

Sappho (fl. ca. 600 B.C.)

When dead you will lie forever forgotten,
for you have no claim to the Pierian° roses.
Dim here, you will move more dimly in Hell,
flitting among the undistinguished dead.

MOTHER

Sherwood Anderson (1876–1941)

Elizabeth Willard, the mother of George Willard, was tall and
gaunt and her face was marked with smallpox scars. Although she was
but forty-five, some obscure disease had taken the fire out of her figure.
Listlessly she went about the disorderly old hotel looking at the faded
wall-paper and the ragged carpets and, when she was able to be about,
doing the work of a chambermaid among beds soiled by the slumbers

---

°*Pierian*: The Pierian spring, a fountain in ancient Pieria (in Macedonia), was
sacred to the Muses as the source of poetic inspiration.

of fat traveling men. Her husband, Tom Willard, a slender, graceful man with square shoulders, a quick military step, and a black mustache trained to turn sharply up at the ends, tried to put the wife out of his mind. The presence of the tall ghostly figure, moving slowly through the halls, he took as a reproach to himself. When he thought of her he grew angry and swore. The hotel was unprofitable and forever on the edge of failure and he wished himself out of it. He thought of the old house and the woman who lived there with him as things defeated and done for. The hotel in which he had begun life so hopefully was now a mere ghost of what a hotel should be. As he went spruce and business-like through the streets of Winesburg, he sometimes stopped and turned quickly about as though fearing that the spirit of the hotel and of the woman would follow him even into the streets. "Damn such a life, damn it!" he sputtered aimlessly.

Tom Willard had a passion for village politics and for years had been the leading Democrat in a strongly Republican community. Some day, he told himself, the tide of things political will turn in my favor and the years of ineffectual service count big in the bestowal of rewards. He dreamed of going to Congress and even of becoming governor. Once when a younger member of the party arose at a political conference and began to boast of his faithful service, Tom Willard grew white with fury. "Shut up, you," he roared, glaring about. "What do you know of service? What are you but a boy? Look at what I've done here! I was a Democrat here in Winesburg when it was a crime to be a Democrat. In the old days they fairly hunted us with guns."

Between Elizabeth and her one son George there was a deep unexpressed bond of sympathy, based on a girlhood dream that had long ago died. In the son's presence she was timid and reserved, but sometimes while he hurried about town intent upon his duties as a reporter, she went into his room and closing the door knelt by a little desk, made of a kitchen table, that sat near a window. In the room by the desk she went through a ceremony that was half a prayer, half a demand, addressed to the skies. In the boyish figure she yearned to see something half forgotten that had once been a part of herself re-created. The prayer concerned that. "Even though I die, I will in some way keep defeat from you," she cried, and so deep was her determination that her whole body shook. Her eyes glowed and she clenched her fists. "If I am dead and see him becoming a meaningless drab figure like myself, I will come back," she declared. "I ask God now to give me that privilege. I demand it. I will pray for it. God may beat me with his fists. I will take any blow that may befall if but this my boy be allowed to express something for us both." Pausing uncertainly, the woman stared about the boy's room. "And do not let him become smart and successful either," she added vaguely.

The communion between George Willard and his mother was outwardly a formal thing without meaning. When she was ill and sat by the window in her room he sometimes went in the evening to make her a visit. They sat by a window that looked over the roof of a small frame building into Main Street. By turning their heads they could see through another window, along an alleyway that ran behind the Main Street stores and into the back door of Abner Groff's bakery. Sometimes as they sat thus a picture of village life presented itself to them. At the back door of his shop appeared Abner Groff with a stick or an empty milk bottle in his hand. For a long time there was a feud between the baker and a grey cat that belonged to Sylvester West, the druggist. The boy and his mother saw the cat creep into the door of the bakery and presently emerge followed by the baker, who swore and waved his arms about. The baker's eyes were small and red and his black hair and beard were filled with flour dust. Sometimes he was so angry that, although the cat had disappeared, he hurled sticks, bits of broken glass, and even some of the tools of his trade about. Once he broke a window at the back of Sinning's Hardware Store. In the alley the grey cat crouched behind barrels filled with torn paper and broken bottles above which flew a black swarm of flies. Once when she was alone, and after watching a prolonged and ineffectual outburst on the part of the baker, Elizabeth Willard put her head down on her long white hands and wept. After that she did not look along the alleyway any more, but tried to forget the contest between the bearded man and the cat. It seemed like a rehearsal of her own life, terrible in its vividness.

In the evening when the son sat in the room with his mother, the silence made them both feel awkward. Darkness came on and the evening train came in at the station. In the street below feet tramped up and down upon a board sidewalk. In the station yard, after the evening train had gone, there was a heavy silence. Perhaps Skinner Leason, the express agent, moved a truck the length of the station platform. Over on Main Street sounded a man's voice, laughing. The door of the express office banged. George Willard arose and crossing the room fumbled for the doorknob. Sometimes he knocked against a chair, making it scrape along the floor. By the window sat the sick woman, perfectly still, listless. Her long hands, white and bloodless, could be seen drooping over the ends of the arms of the chair. "I think you had better be out among the boys. You are too much indoors," she said, striving to relieve the embarrassment of the departure. "I thought I would take a walk," replied George Willard, who felt awkward and confused.

One evening in July, when the transient guests who made the New Willard House their temporary home had become scarce, and the hallways, lighted only by kerosene lamps turned low, were plunged in gloom, Elizabeth Willard had an adventure. She had been ill in bed for several days and her son had not come to visit her. She was alarmed. The feeble blaze of life that remained in her body was blown into a flame by her anxiety and she crept out of bed, dressed and hurried along the hallway toward her son's room, shaking with exaggerated fears. As she went along she steadied herself with her hand, slipped along the papered walls of the hall and breathed with difficulty. The air whistled through her teeth. As she hurried forward she thought how foolish she was. "He is concerned with boyish affairs," she told herself. "Perhaps he has now begun to walk about in the evening with girls."

Elizabeth Willard had a dread of being seen by guests in the hotel that had once belonged to her father and the ownership of which still stood recorded in her name in the county courthouse. The hotel was continually losing patronage because of its shabbiness and she thought of herself as also shabby. Her own room was in an obscure corner and when she felt able to work she voluntarily worked among the beds, preferring the labor that could be done when the guests were abroad seeking trade among the merchants of Winesburg.

By the door of her son's room the mother knelt upon the floor and listened for some sound from within. When she heard the boy moving about and talking in low tones a smile came to her lips. George Willard had a habit of talking aloud to himself and to hear him doing so had always given his mother a peculiar pleasure. The habit in him, she felt, strengthened the secret bond that existed between them. A thousand times she had whispered to herself of the matter. "He is groping about, trying to find himself," she thought. "He is not a dull clod, all words and smartness. Within him there is a secret something that is striving to grow. It is the thing I let be killed in myself."

In the darkness in the hallway by the door the sick woman arose and started again toward her own room. She was afraid that the door would open and the boy come upon her. When she had reached a safe distance and was about to turn a corner into a second hallway she stopped and bracing herself with her hands waited, thinking to shake off a trembling fit of weakness that had come upon her. The presence of the boy in the room had made her happy. In her bed, during the long hours alone, the little fears that had visited her had become giants. Now they were all gone. "When I get back to my room I shall sleep," she murmured gratefully.

But Elizabeth Willard was not to return to her bed and to sleep. As she stood trembling in the darkness the door of her son's room opened and the boy's father, Tom Willard, stepped out. In the light that streamed out at the door he stood with the knob in his hand and talked. What he said infuriated the woman.

Tom Willard was ambitious for his son. He had always thought of himself as a successful man, although nothing he had ever done had turned out successfully. However, when he was out of sight of the New Willard House and had no fear of coming upon his wife, he swaggered and began to dramatize himself as one of the chief men of the town. He wanted his son to succeed. He it was who had secured for the boy the position on the *Winesburg Eagle*. Now, with a ring of earnestness in his voice, he was advising concerning some course of conduct. "I tell you what, George, you've got to wake up," he said sharply. "Will Henderson has spoken to me three times concerning the matter. He says you go along for hours not hearing when you are spoken to and acting like a gawky girl. What ails you?" Tom Willard laughed good-naturedly. "Well, I guess you'll get over it," he said. "I told Will that. You're not a fool and you're not a woman. You're Tom Willard's son and you'll wake up. I'm not afraid. What you say clears things up. If being a newspaper man had put the notion of becoming a writer into your mind that's all right. Only I guess you'll have to wake up to do that too, eh?"

Tom Willard went briskly along the hallway and down a flight of stairs to the office. The woman in the darkness could hear him laughing and talking with a guest who was striving to wear away a dull evening by dozing in a chair by the office door. She returned to the door of her son's room. The weakness had passed from her body as by a miracle and she stepped boldly along. A thousand ideas raced through her head. When she heard the scraping of a chair and the sound of a pen scratching on paper, she again turned and went back along the hallway to her own room.

A definite determination had come into the mind of the defeated wife of the Winesburg hotel keeper. The determination was the result of long years of quiet and rather ineffectual thinking. "Now," she told herself, "I will act. There is something threatening my boy and I will ward it off." The fact that the conversation between Tom Willard and his son had been rather quiet and natural, as though an understanding existed between them, maddened her. Although for years she had hated her husband, her hatred had always before been a quite impersonal thing. He had been merely a part of something else that she hated. Now, and by the few words at the door, he had become the thing personified. In the darkness of her own room she clenched her fists and glared about. Going to a cloth bag that hung on a nail by the wall she took out a long pair of sewing scissors and held them in her hand like a dagger. "I will stab him," she said aloud. "He has chosen to be the voice of evil and I will kill him. When I have killed him something will snap within myself and I will die also. It will be a release for all of us."

In her girlhood and before her marriage with Tom Willard, Elizabeth had borne a somewhat shaky reputation in Winesburg. For years she had been what is called "stage-struck" and had paraded through the streets with traveling men guests at her father's hotel, wearing loud clothes and urging them to tell her of life in the cities out of which they had come. Once she startled the town by putting on men's clothes and riding a bicycle down Main Street.

In her own mind the tall dark girl had been in those days much confused. A great restlessness was in her and it expressed itself in two ways. First there was an uneasy desire for change, for some big definite movement to her life. It was this feeling that had turned her mind to the stage. She dreamed of joining some company and wandering over the world, seeing always new faces and giving something out of herself to all people. Sometimes at night she was quite beside herself with the thought, but when she tried to talk of the matter to the members of the theatrical companies that came to Winesburg and stopped at her father's hotel, she got nowhere. They did not seem to know what she meant, or if she did get something of her passion expressed, they only laughed. "It's not like that," they said. "It's as dull and uninteresting as this here. Nothing comes of it."

With the traveling men when she walked about with them, and later with Tom Willard, it was quite different. Always they seemed to understand and sympathize with her. On the side streets of the village, in the darkness under the trees, they took hold of her hand and she thought that something unexpressed in herself came forth and became a part of an unexpressed something in them.

And then there was the second expression of her restlessness. When that came she felt for a time released and happy. She did not blame the men who walked with her and later she did not blame Tom Willard. It was always the same, beginning with kisses and ending, after strange wild emotions, with peace and then sobbing repentance. When she sobbed she put her hand upon the face of the man and had always the same thought. Even though he were large and bearded she thought he had become suddenly a little boy. She wondered why he did not sob also.

In her room, tucked away in a corner of the old Willard House, Elizabeth Willard lighted a lamp and put it on a dressing table that stood by the door. A thought had come into her mind and she went to a closet and brought out a small square box and set it on the table. The box contained material for make-up and had been left with other things by a theatrical company that had once been stranded in Winesburg. Elizabeth Willard had decided that she would be beautiful. Her hair was still black and there was a great mass of it braided and coiled about her head. The scene that was to take place in the office below began to grow in her mind. No ghostly worn-out figure should confront Tom Willard, but something quite unexpected and startling. Tall and with dusky cheeks and hair that fell in a mass from her shoulders, a figure should come striding down the stairway before the startled loungers in the hotel office. The figure would be silent—it would be swift and terrible. As a tigress whose cub had been threatened would she appear, coming out of the shadows, stealing noiselessly along and holding the long wicked scissors in her hand.

With a little broken sob in her throat, Elizabeth Willard blew out the light that stood upon the table and stood weak and trembling in the darkness. The strength that had been as a miracle in her body left and she half reeled across the floor, clutching at the back of the chair in which she had spent so many long days staring out over the tin roofs into the main street of Winesburg. In the hallway there was the sound of footsteps and George Willard came in at the door. Sitting in a chair beside his mother he began to talk. "I'm going to get out of here," he said. "I don't know where I shall go or what I shall do but I am going away."

The woman in the chair waited and trembled. An impulse came to her. "I suppose you had better wake up," she said. "You think that? You will go to the city and make money, eh? It will be better for you, you think, to be a business man, to be brisk and smart and alive?" She waited and trembled.

The son shook his head. "I suppose I can't make you understand, but oh, I wish I could," he said earnestly. "I can't even talk to father about it. I don't try. There isn't any use. I don't know what I shall do. I just want to go away and look at people and think."

Silence fell upon the room where the boy and woman sat together. Again, as on the other evenings, they were embarrassed. After a time the boy tried again to talk. "I suppose it won't be for a year or two but I've been thinking about it," he said, rising and going toward the door. "Something father said makes it sure that I shall have to go away." He fumbled with the door knob. In the room the silence became unbearable to the woman. She wanted to cry out with joy because of the words that had come from the lips of her son, but the expression of joy had become impossible to her. "I think you had better go out among the boys. You are too much indoors," she said. "I thought I would go for a little walk," replied the son stepping awkwardly out of the room and closing the door.

THE JAILOR

Sylvia Plath (1932–1963)

My night sweats grease his breakfast plate.
The same placard of blue fog is wheeled into position
With the same trees and headstones.
Is that all he can come up with,
The rattler of the keys?   5

I have been drugged and raped.
Seven hours knocked out of my right mind
Into a black sack
Where I relax, fœtus or cat,
Lever of his wet dreams.   10

Something is gone.
My sleeping capsule, my red and blue zeppelin,
Drops me from a terrible altitude.
Carapace° smashed,
I spread to the beaks of birds.   15

O little gimlets!
What holes this papery day is already full of!
He has been burning me with cigarettes,
Pretending I am a Negress with pink paws.
I am myself. That is not enough.   20

The fever trickles and stiffens in my hair.
My ribs show. What have I eaten?
Lies and smiles.
Surely the sky is not that colour,
Surely the grass should be rippling.   25

All day, gluing my church of burnt matchsticks,
I dream of someone else entirely.
And he, for this subversion,
Hurts me, he
With his armoury of fakery.   30

His high, cold masks of amnesia.
How did I get here?
Indeterminate criminal,
I die with variety—
Hung, starved, burned, hooked!   35

I imagine him
Impotent as distant thunder,
In whose shadow I have eaten my ghost ration.
I wish him dead or away.
That, it seems is the impossibility,   40

°*carapace*: a hard protective outer covering (as on a turtle)

That being free. What would the dark
Do without fevers to eat?
What would the light
Do without eyes to knife, what would he
Do, do, do without me?   45

Mannequins and Monsters

From THE FOUR ZOAS

William Blake (1757–1827)

URIZEN'S WORK

With trembling horror pale, aghast the Children of Man
Stood on the infinite Earth & saw these visions in the air,
In waters & in earth beneath; they cried to one another,
"What! are we terrors to one another? Come, O brethren, wherefore
Was this wide Earth spread all abroad? not for wild beasts to roam."   5
But many stood silent, & busied in their families.
And many said, "We see no Visions in the darksom air.
Measure the course of that sulphur orb that lights the darksom day;
Set stations on this breeding Earth & let us buy & sell."
Others arose & schools erected, forming Instruments   10
To measure out the course of heaven. Stern Urizen beheld
In woe his brethren & his sons, in dark'ning woe lamenting
Upon the winds in clouds involv'd, Uttering his voice in thunders,
Commanding all the work with care & power & severity.

Then seiz'd the Lions of Urizen their work, & heated in the forge   15
Roar the bright masses; thund'ring beat the hammers, many a pyramid
Is form'd & thrown down thund'ring into the deeps of Non Entity.
Heated red hot they, hizzing, rend their way down many a league
Till resting, each his basement finds; suspended there they stand
Casting their sparkles dire abroad into the dismal deep.   20
For, measur'd out in order'd spaces, the Sons of Urizen
With compasses divide the deep; they the strong scales erect
That Luvah rent from the faint Heart of the Fallen Man,
And weigh the massy Cubes, then fix them in their awful stations.
And all the time, in Caverns shut, the golden Looms erected   25
First spun, then wove the Atmospheres; there the Spider & Worm
Plied the wing'd shuttle, piping shrill thro' all the list'ning threads;
Beneath the Caverns roll the weights of lead & spindles of iron,
The enormous warp & woof rage direful in the affrighted deep.

While far into the vast unknown the strong wing'd Eagles bend   30
Their venturous flight in Human forms distinct; thro' darkness deep
They bear the woven draperies; on golden hooks they hang abroad
The universal curtains & spread out from Sun to Sun
The vehicles of light; they separate the furious particles
Into mild currents as the water mingles with the wine.   35

While thus the Spirits of strongest wing enlighten the dark deep,
The threads are spun & the cards twisted & drawn out; then the weak
Begin their work, & many a net is netted, many a net
Spread, & many a Spirit caught: innumerable the nets,
Innumerable the gins & traps, & many a soothing flute   40
Is form'd, & many a corded lyre outspread over the immense.
In cruel delight they trap the listeners, & in cruel delight
Bind them, condensing the strong energies into little compass.
Some became seed of every plant that shall be planted; some
The bulbous roots, thrown up together into barns & garners.   45

Then rose the Builders. First the Architect divine his plan
Unfolds. The wondrous scaffold rear'd all round the infinite,
Quadrangular the building rose, the heavens squared by a line,
Trigons & cubes divide the elements in finite bonds.
Multitudes without number work incessant: the hewn stone   50
Is plac'd in beds of mortar mingled with the ashes of Vala.
Severe the labour; female slaves the mortar trod oppressed.

Twelve halls after the names of his twelve sons compos'd
The wondrous building, & three Central Domes after the Names
Of his three daughters were encompass'd by the twelve bright halls. 55
Every hall surrounded by bright Paradises of Delight
In which were towns & Cities, Nations, Seas, Mountains & Rivers.
Each Dome open'd toward four halls, & the Three Domes Encompass'd
The Golden Hall of Urizen, whose western side glow'd bright
With ever streaming fires beaming from his awful limbs.   60
His Shadowy Feminine Semblance here repos'd on a White Couch,
Or hover'd over his starry head; & when he smil'd she brighten'd
Like a bright Cloud in harvest; but when Urizen frown'd she wept
In mists over his carved throne; & when he turned his back
Upon his Golden hall & sought the Labyrinthine porches   65
Of his wide heaven, Trembling, cold, in jealous fears she sat
A shadow of Despair; therefore toward the West, Urizen form'd
A recess in the wall for fires to glow upon the pale
Female's limbs in his absence, & her Daughters oft upon
A Golden Altar burnt perfumes: with Art Celestial form'd   70
Foursquare, sculptur'd & sweetly Engrav'd to please their shadowy mother.

Ascending into her misty garments the blue smoke roll'd to revive
Her cold limbs in the absence of her Lord. Also her sons,
With lives of Victims sacrificed upon an altar of brass
On the East side, Reviv'd her soul with lives of beasts & birds   75
Slain on the Altar, up ascending into her cloudy bosom.
Of terrible workmanship the Altar, labour of ten thousand Slaves,
One thousand Men of wondrous power spent their lives in its formation.
It stood on twelve steps nam'd after the names of her twelve sons,
And was erected at the chief entrance of Urizen's hall.   80
But infinitely beautiful the wondrous work arose
In sorrow and care, a Golden World whose porches round the heavens
And pillar'd halls & rooms receiv'd the eternal wandering stars.
A wondrous golden Building, many a window, many a door
And many a division let in & out the vast unknown.   85
Circled in infinite orb immovable, within its walls & ceilings
The heavens were clos'd, and spirits mourn'd their bondage night & day,
And the Divine Vision appear'd in Luvah's robes of blood.

Thus was the Mundane shell builded by Urizen's strong Power.

URIZEN'S BOOK OF BRASS

And Urizen Read in his book of brass in sounding tones:
"Listen, O Daughters, to my voice. Listen to the Words of Wisdom,
So shall [you] govern over all; let Moral Duty tune your tongue,
But be your hearts harder than the nether millstone.
To bring the Shadow of Enitharmon beneath our wondrous tree,   5
That Los may Evaporate like smoke & be no more,
Draw down Enitharmon to the spectre of Urthona,
And let him have dominion over Los, the terrible shade.
Compell the poor to live upon a Crust of bread, by soft mild arts.
Smile when they frown, frown when they smile; & when a man looks pale   10
With labour & abstinence, say he looks healthy & happy;
And when his children sicken, let them die; there are enough
Born, even too many, & our Earth will be overrun
Without these arts. If you would make the poor live with temper[ance],
With pomp give every crust of bread you give; with gracious cunning   15
Magnify small gifts, reduce the man to want a gift, & then give with pomp.
Say he smiles if you hear him sigh. If pale, say he is ruddy.
Preach temperance: say he is overgorg'd & drowns his wit
In strong drink, tho' you know that bread & water are all
He can afford. Flatter his wife, pity his children, till we can   20
Reduce all to our will, as spaniels are taught with art."

THE FURNITURE OF
A WOMAN'S MIND

Jonathan Swift (1667–1745)

A set of Phrases learn't by Rote;
A Passion for a Scarlet-Coat;
When at a Play to laugh, or cry,
Yet cannot tell the Reason why:
Never to hold her Tongue a Minute,   5
While all she prates has nothing in it.
Whole Hours can with a Coxcomb sit,
And take his Nonsense all for Wit:
Her Learning mounts to read a Song,
But, half the Words pronouncing wrong;   10
Has ev'ry Repartee in Store,
She spoke ten Thousand Times before.
Can ready Compliments supply
On all Occasions, cut and dry.
Such Hatred to a Parson's Gown,   15
The Sight will put her in a Swown.°
For Conversation well endu'd,
She calls it witty to be rude;
And, placing Raillery in Railing,
Will tell aloud your greatest Failing;   20
Nor makes a Scruple to expose
Your bandy Leg, or crooked Nose.
Can, at her Morning Tea, run o'er
The Scandal of the Day before.
Improving hourly in her Skill,   25
To cheat and wrangle at Quadrille.°

In choosing Lace a Critic nice,
Knows to a Groat the lowest Price;
Can in her Female Clubs dispute
What Lining best the Silk will suit;   30
What Colours each Complexion match:
And where with Art to place a Patch.°

If chance a Mouse creeps in her Sight,
Can finely counterfeit a Fright;
So, sweetly screams if it comes near her,   35
She ravishes all Hearts to hear her.
Can dext'rously her Husband tease,

°*Swown*: swoon   °*Quadrille*: a card game   °*Patch*: beauty patch

By taking Fits whene'er she please:
By frequent Practice learns the Trick
At proper Seasons to be sick;   40
Thinks nothing gives one Airs so pretty,
At once creating Love and Pity.
If *Molly* happens to be careless,
And but neglects to warm her Hair-Lace,
She gets a Cold as sure as Death;   45
And vows she scarce can fetch her Breath.
Admires how modest Women can
Be so *robustious* like a Man.

    In Party, furious to her Power;
A bitter Whig, or Tory sour;   50
Her Arguments directly tend
Against the Side she would defend:
Will prove herself a Tory plain,
From Principles the Whigs maintain;
And, to defend the Whiggist Cause,   55
Her Topics from the Tories draws.

    O yes! If any Man can find
More virtues in a Woman's Mind,
Let them be sent to Mrs. *Harding*; °
She'll pay the Charges to a Farthing: 60
Take Notice, she has my Commission
To add them in the next Edition;
They may out-sell a better Thing;
So, Holla Boys; God save the King.

SONG

John Donne (1573–1631)

Go and catch a falling star,
   Get with child a mandrake root,
Tell me where all past years are,
   Or who cleft the devil's foot,
Teach me to hear mermaids singing,   5
   Or to keep off envy's stinging,
      And find
      What wind
Serves to advance an honest mind.

°*Mrs. Harding*: Swift's printer

If thou be'st born to strange sights,   10
　　Things invisible to see,
Ride ten thousand days and nights,
　　Till Age snow white hairs on thee;
Thou, when thou return'st, wilt tell me
All strange wonders that befell thee,   15
　　　　And swear
　　　　No where
Lives a woman true and fair.

If thou find'st one, let me know;
　　Such a pilgrimage were sweet,   20
Yet do not; I would not go,
　　Though at next door we might meet.
Though she were true when you met her,
And last till you write your letter,
　　　　Yet she   25
　　　　Will be
False, ere I come, to two or three.

WOMAN'S CONSTANCY

John Donne

Now thou hast lov'd me one whole day,
Tomorrow when thou leav'st, what wilt thou say?
Wilt thou then antedate some new-made vow?
　　　　Or say that now
We are not just those persons which we were?   5
Or that oaths made in reverential fear
Of Love and his wrath, any may forswear?
Or, as true deaths true marriages untie,
So lovers' contracts, images of those,
Bind but till sleep, death's image, them unloose?   10
　　　　Or, your own end to justify,
For having purpos'd change and falsehood, you
Can have no way but falsehood to be true?
Vain lunatic, against these 'scapes I could
　　　　Dispute and conquer, if I would,   15
　　　　Which I abstain to do,
For by tomorrow I may think so too.

From JERUSALEM

William Blake (1757–1827)

THE DESOLATE WORLD

The inhabitants are sick to death: they labour to divide into
    Days
And Nights the uncertain Periods, and into Weeks & Months.
    In vain
They send the Dove & Raven & in vain the Serpent over the
    mountains
And in vain the Eagle & Lion over the four-fold wilderness:
They return not, but generate in rocky places desolate: 5
They return not, but build a habitation separate from Man.
The Sun forgets his course like a drunken man; he hesitates
Upon the Cheselden hills, thinking to sleep on the Severn.
In vain: he is hurried afar into an unknown Night:
He bleeds in torrents of blood as he rolls thro' heaven above.   10
He chokes up the paths of the sky; the Moon is leprous as snow,
Trembling & descending down, seeking to rest on high Mona,
Scattering her leprous snows in flakes of disease over Albion.
The Stars flee remote; the heaven is iron, the earth is sulphur,
And all the mountains & hills shrink up like a withering gourd   15
As the Senses of Men shrink together under the Knife of flint
In the hands of Albion's Daughters among the Druid
    Temples, . . .
And the Twelve Daughters of Albion united in Rahab &
    Tirzah,
A Double Female; and they drew out from the Rocky Stones
Fibres of Life to Weave, for every Female is a Golden Loom,   20
The Rocks are opaque hardnesses covering all Vegetated things;
And as they Wove & Cut from the Looms, in various divisions
Stretching over Europe & Asia from Ireland to Japan,
They divided into many lovely Daughters, to be counterparts
To those they Wove; for when they Wove a Male, they divided   25
Into a Female to the Woven Male: in opaque hardness
They cut the Fibres from the Rocks: groaning in pain they
    Weave,
Calling the Rocks Atomic Origins of Existence, denying
    Eternity
By the Atheistical Epicurean Philosophy of Albion's Tree.
Such are the Feminine & Masculine when separated from Man.   30
They call the Rocks Parents of Men, & adore the frowning
    Chaos,

Dancing around in howling pain, clothed in the bloody Veil,
Hiding Albion's Sons within the Veil, closing Jerusalem's
Sons without, to feed with their Souls the Spectres of Albion,
Ashamed to give Love openly to the piteous & merciful Man,   35
Counting him an imbecile mockery, but the Warrior
They adore & his revenge cherish with the blood of the
    Innocent.

THE FOOLISH VIRGIN

George Gissing (1857–1903)

Coming down to breakfast, as usual, rather late, Miss Jewell was surprised to find several persons still at table. Their conversation ceased as she entered, and all eyes were directed to her with a look in which she discerned some special meaning. For several reasons she was in an irritable humour; the significant smiles, the subdued "Good mornings," and the silence that followed, so jarred upon her nerves that, save for curiosity, she would have turned and left the room.

Mrs. Banting (generally at this hour busy in other parts of the house) inquired with a sympathetic air whether she would take porridge; the others awaited her reply as if it were a matter of general interest. Miss Jewell abruptly demanded an egg. The awkward pause was broken by a high falsetto.

"I believe you know who it is all the time, Mr. Drake," said Miss Ayres, addressing the one man present.

"I assure you I don't. Upon my word, I don't. The whole thing astonishes me."

Resolutely silent, Miss Jewell listened to a conversation the drift of which remained dark to her, until some one spoke the name "Mr. Cheeseman;" then it was with difficulty that she controlled her face and her tongue. The servant brought her an egg. She struck it clumsily with the edge of the spoon, and asked in an affected drawl:

"What are you people talking about?"

Mrs. Sleath, smiling maliciously, took it upon herself to reply.

"Mr. Drake has had a letter from Mr. Cheeseman. He writes that he's engaged, but doesn't say who to. Delicious mystery, isn't it?"

The listener tried to swallow a piece of bread-and-butter, and seemed to struggle with a constriction of the throat. Then, looking round the table, she said with contemptuous pleasantry:

"Some lodging-house servant, I shouldn't wonder."

Every one laughed. Then Mr. Drake declared he must be off and rose from the table. The ladies also moved, and in a minute or two Miss Jewell sat at her breakfast alone.

She was a tall, slim person, with unremarkable, not ill-moulded features. Nature meant her to be graceful in form and pleasantly feminine of countenance; unwholesome habit of mind and body was responsible for the defects that now appeared in her. She had no colour, no flesh; but an agreeable smile would well have become her lips, and her eyes needed only the illumination of healthy thought to be more than commonly attractive. A few months would see the close of her twenty-ninth year; but Mrs. Banting's boarders, with some excuse, judged her on the wrong side of thirty.

Her meal, a sad pretence, was soon finished. She went to the window and stood there for five minutes looking at the cabs and pedestrians in the sunny street. Then, with the languid step which had become natural to her, she ascended the stairs and turned into the drawing-room. Here, as she had expected, two ladies sat in close conversation. Without heeding them, she walked to the piano, selected a sheet of music, and sat down to play.

Presently, whilst she drummed with vigour on the keys, some one approached; she looked up and saw Mrs. Banting; the other persons had left the room.

"If it's true," murmured Mrs. Banting, with genuine kindliness on her flabby lips, "all I can say is that it's shameful—shameful!"

Miss Jewell stared at her.

"What do you mean?"

"Mr. Cheeseman—to go and——"

"I don't understand you. What is it to me?"

The words were thrown out almost fiercely, and a crash on the piano drowned whatever Mrs. Banting meant to utter in reply. Miss Jewell now had the drawing-room to herself.

She "practised" for half an hour, careering through many familiar pieces with frequent mechanical correction of time-honoured blunders. When at length she was going up to her room, a grinning servant handed her a letter which had just arrived. A glance at the envelope told her from whom it came, and in privacy she at once opened it. The writer's address was Glasgow.

"My dear Rosamund," began the letter. "I can't understand why you write in such a nasty way. For some time now your letters have been horrid. I don't show them to William because if I did he would get into a tantrum. What I have to say to you now is this, that we simply can't go on sending you the money. We haven't it to spare, and that's the plain truth. You think we're rolling in money, and it's no use telling you we are not. William said last night that you *must* find some way of supporting yourself, and I can only say the same. You are a lady and had a thorough good education, and I am sure you have only to exert yourself. William says I may promise you a five-pound note twice a year, but more than that you must not expect. Now do just think over your position——"

She threw the sheet of paper aside, and sat down to brood miserably. This little back bedroom, at no time conducive to good spirits, had seen Rosamund in many a dreary or exasperated mood; to-day it beheld her on the very verge of despair. Illuminated texts of Scripture spoke to her from the walls in vain; portraits of admired clergymen smiled vainly from the mantelpiece. She was conscious only of a dirty carpet, an ill-made bed, faded curtains, and a window that looked out on nothing. One cannot expect much for a guinea a week, when it includes board and lodging; the bedroom was at least a refuge, but even that, it seemed, would henceforth be denied her. Oh, the selfishness of people! And oh, the perfidy of man!

For eight years, since the breaking up of her home, Rosamund had lived in London boarding-houses. To begin with, she could count on a sufficient income, resulting from property in which she had a legitimate share. Owing to various causes, the value of this property had steadily diminished, until at length she became dependent upon the subsidies of kinsfolk; for more than a twelve-month now, the only person able and willing to continue such remittances had been her married sister, and Rosamund had hardly known what it was to have a shilling of pocket-money. From time to time she thought feebly and confusedly of "doing something," but her aims were so vague, her capabilities so inadequate, that she always threw aside the intention in sheer hopelessness. Whatever will she might once have possessed had evaporated in the boarding-house atmosphere. It was hard to believe that her brother-in-law would ever withhold the poor five pounds a month. And—what is the use of board-ing-houses if not to renew indefinitely the hope of marriage?

She was not of the base order of women. Conscience yet lived in her, and drew support from religion; something of modesty, of self-respect, still clad her starving soul. Ignorance and ill-luck had once or twice thrown her into such society as may be found in establishments outwardly respectable; she trembled and fled. Even in such a house as this of Mrs. Banting's, she had known sickness of disgust. Herself included, four single women abode here at the present time; and the scarcely disguised purpose of every one of them was to entrap a marriageable man. In the others, it seemed to her detestable, and she hated all three, even as they in their turn detested her. Rosamund flattered herself with the persuasion that she did not aim merely at marriage and a subsistence; she would not marry *any* one; her desire was for sympathy, true com-panionship. In year's gone by she had used to herself a more sacred word; nowadays the homely solace seemed enough. And of late a ray of hope had glimmered upon her dusty path. Mr. Cheeseman, with his plausible airs, his engaging smile, had won something more than her confidence; an acquaintance of six months, ripening at length to intimacy, justified her in regarding him with sanguine emotion. They had walked together in Kensington Gardens; they had exchanged furtive and significant glances at table and elsewhere; every one grew aware of the mutual preference. It shook her with a painful misgiving when Mr. Cheeseman went away for his holiday and spoke no word; but probably he would write. He had written—to his friend Drake; and all was over.

Her affections suffered, but that was not the worst. Her pride had never received so cruel a blow.

After a life of degradation which might well have unsexed her, Rosamund remained a woman. The practice of affectations numberless had taught her one truth, that she could never hope to charm save by reliance upon her feminine qualities. Boarding-house girls, such numbers of whom she had observed, seemed all intent upon disowning their womanhood; they cultivated masculine habits, wore as far as possible male attire, talked loud slang, threw scorn (among themselves at all events) upon domestic virtues; and not a few of them seemed to profit by the prevailing fashion. Rosamund had tried these tactics, always with conscious failure. At other times, and vastly to her relief, she aimed in precisely the opposite direction, encouraging herself in feminine extremes. She would talk with babbling *naiveté*, exaggerate the languor induced by idleness, lack of exercise, and consequent ill-health; betray timidities and pruderies, let fall a pious phrase, rise of a morning for "early celebration" and let the fact be known. These and the like extravagances had appeared to fascinate Mr. Cheeseman, who openly professed his dislike for androgynous persons. And Rosamund enjoyed the satisfaction of moderate sincerity. Thus, or very much in this way, would she be content to live. Romantic passion she felt to be beyond her scope. Long ago—ah! perhaps long ago, when she first knew Geoffrey Hunt——

The name, as it crossed her mind, suggested an escape from the insufferable *ennui* and humilation of hours till evening. It must be half a year since she called upon the Hunts, her only estimable acquaintances in or near London. They lived at Teddington, and the railway fare was always a deterrent; nor did she care much for Mrs. Hunt and her daughters, who of late years had grown reserved with her, as if uneasy about her mode of life. True, they were not at all snobbish; homely, though well-to-do people; but they had such strict views, and could not understand the existence of a woman less energetic than themselves. In her present straits, which could hardly be worse, their counsel might prove of value; though she doubted her courage when it came to making confessions.

She would do without luncheon (impossible to sit at table with those "creatures") and hope to make up for it at tea; in truth appetite was not likely to trouble her. Then for dress. Wearily she compared this garment with that, knowing beforehand that all were out of fashion and more or less shabby. Oh, what did it matter! She had come to beggary, the result that might have been foreseen long ago. Her faded costume suited fitly enough with her fortunes—nay, with her face. For just then she caught a sight of herself in the glass, and shrank. A lump choked her: looking desperately, as if for help, for pity, through gathering tears, she saw the Bible verse on the nearest wall: "Come unto me——" Her heart became that of a woful child; she put her hands before her face, and prayed in the old, simple words of childhood.

As her call must not be made before half-past three, she could not set out upon the journey forthwith; but it was a relief to get away from the house. In this bright weather, Kensington Gardens, not far away, seemed a natural place for loitering, but the alleys° would remind her too vividly of late companionship; she walked in another direction, sauntered for an hour by the shop windows of Westbourne Grove, and, when she felt tired, sat at the railway station until it was time to start. At Teddington, half a mile's walk lay before her; though she felt no hunger, long abstinence and the sun's heat taxed her strength to the point of exhaustion; on reaching her friend's door, she stood trembling with nervousness and fatigue. The door opened, and to her dismay she learnt that Mrs. Hunt was away from home. Happily, the servant added that Miss Caroline was in the garden.

"I'll go round," said Rosamund at once. "Don't trouble——"

The pathway round the pleasant little house soon brought her within view of a young lady who sat in a garden-chair, sewing. But Miss Caroline was not alone; near to her stood a man in shirt-sleeves and bare-headed, vigorously sawing a plank; he seemed to be engaged in the construction of a summer-house, and Rosamund took him at first sight for a mechanic, but when he turned round, exhibiting a ruddy face all agleam with health and good humour, she recognised the young lady's brother, Geoffrey Hunt. He, as though for the moment puzzled, looked fixedly at her.

"Oh, Miss Jewell, how glad I am to see you!"

Enlightened by his sister's words, Geoffrey dropped the saw, and stepped forward with still heartier greeting. Had civility permitted, he might easily have explained his doubts. It was some six years since his last meeting with Rosamund, and she had changed not a little; he remembered her as a graceful and rather pretty girl, with life in her, even if it ran for the most part to silliness, gaily dressed, sprightly of manner; notwithstanding the account he had received of her from his relatives, it astonished him to look upon this limp, faded woman. In Rosamund's eyes, Geoffrey was his old self; perhaps a trifle more stalwart, and if anything

---

°*alleys*: paths in the Gardens

handsomer, but with just the same light in his eyes, the same smile on his bearded face, the same cordiality of utterance. For an instant, she compared him with Mr. Cheeseman, and flushed for very shame. Unable to command her voice, she stammered incoherent nothings; only when a seat supported her weary body did she lose the dizziness which had threatened downright collapse; then she closed her eyes, and forgot everything but the sense of rest.

Geoffrey drew on his coat, and spoke jestingly of his amateur workmanship. Such employment, however, seemed not inappropriate to him, for his business was that of a timber-merchant. Of late years he had lived abroad, for the most part in Canada. Rosamund learnt that at present he was having a longish holiday.

"And you go back to Canada?"

This she asked when Miss Hunt had stepped into the house to call for tea. Geoffrey answered that it was doubtful; for various reasons he rather hoped to remain in England, but the choice did not altogether rest with him.

"At all events"—she gave a poor little laugh—"you haven't pined in exile."

"Not a bit of it. I have always had plenty of hard work—the one thing needful."

"Yes—I remember—you always used to say that. And I used to protest. You granted, I think, that it might be different with women."

"Did I?"

He wished to add something to the point, but refrained out of compassion. It was clear to him that Miss Jewell, at all events, would have been none the worse for exacting employment. Mrs. Hunt had spoken of her with the disapprobation natural in a healthy, active woman of the old school, and Geoffrey himself could not avoid a contemptuous judgment.

"You have lived in London all this time?" he asked, before she could speak.

"Yes. Where else should I live? My sister at Glasgow doesn't want me there, and—and there's nobody else, you know." She tried to laugh. "I have friends in London—well, that is to say—at all events I'm not *quite* solitary."

The man smiled, and could not allow her to suspect how profoundly he pitied such a condition. Caroline Hunt had reappeared; she began to talk of her mother and sister, who were enjoying themselves in Wales. Her own holiday would come upon their return; Geoffrey was going to take her to Switzerland.

Tea arrived just as Rosamund was again sinking into bodily faintness and desolation of spirit. It presently restored her, but she could hardly converse. She kept hoping that Caroline would offer her some invitation—

to lunch, to dine, anything; but as yet no such thought seemed to occur to the young hostess. Suddenly the aspect of things was altered by the arrival of new callers, a whole family, man, wife and three children, strangers to Rosamund. For a time it seemed as if she must go away without any kind of solace; for Geoffrey had quitted her, and she sat alone. On the spur of irrational resentment, she rose and advanced to Miss Hunt.

"Oh, but you are not going! I want you to stay and have dinner with us, if you can. Would it make you too late?"

Rosamund flushed and could scarce contain her delight. In a moment she was playing with the youngest of the children, and even laughing aloud, so that Geoffrey glanced curiously towards her. Even the opportunity of private conversation which she had not dared to count upon was granted before long; when the callers had departed Caroline excused herself, and left her brother alone with the guest for half an hour. There was no time to be lost; Rosamund broached almost immediately the subject uppermost in her mind.

"Mr. Hunt, I know how dreadful it is to have people asking for advice, but if I *might*—if you could have patience with me——"

"I haven't much wisdom to spare," he answered, with easy good-nature.

"Oh, you are very rich in it, compared with poor me.— And my position is *so* difficult. I want—I am trying to find some way of being useful in the world. I am tired of living for myself. I seem to be such a useless creature. Surely even *I* must have *some* talent, which it's my duty to put to use! Where should I turn? Could you help me with a suggestion?"

Her words, now that she had overcome the difficulty of beginning, chased each other with breathless speed, and Geoffrey was all but constrained to seriousness; he took it for granted, however, that Miss Jewell frequently used this language; doubtless it was part of her foolish, futile existence to talk of her soul's welfare, especially in *tête-à-tête* with unmarried men. The truth he did not suspect, and Rosamund could not bring herself to convey it in plain words.

"I do so envy the people who have something to live for!" Thus she panted. "I fear I have *never* had a purpose in life—I'm sure I don't know why. Of course I'm only a woman, but even women nowadays are doing so much. You don't despise their efforts, do you?"

"Not indiscriminately."

"If I could feel myself a profitable member of society!—I want to be lifted above my wretched self. Is there no great end to which I could devote myself?"

Her phrases grew only more magniloquent, and all the time she was longing for courage to say: "How can I earn money?" Geoffrey, confirmed in the suspicion that she talked only for effect, indulged his natural humour.

"I'm such a groveller, Miss Jewell. I never knew these aspirations. I see the world mainly as cubic feet of timber."

"No, no, you won't make me believe that. I *know* you have ideals!"

"That word reminds me of poor old Halliday. You remember Halliday, don't you?"

In vexed silence, Rosamund shook her head.

"But I think you must have met him, in the old days. A tall, fair man—no? He talked a great deal about ideals, and meant to move the world. We lost sight of each other when I first left England, and only met again a day or two ago. He is married, and has three children, and looks fifty years old, though he can't be much more than thirty. He took me to see his wife—they live at Forest Hill."

Rosamund was not listening, and the speaker became aware of it. Having a purpose in what he was about to say, he gently claimed her attention.

"I think Mrs. Halliday is the kind of woman who would interest you. If ever any one had a purpose in life, *she* has."

"Indeed? And what?"

"To keep house admirably, and bring up her children as well as possible, on an income which would hardly supply some women with shoe-leather."

"Oh, that's very dreadful!"

"Very fine, it seems to me. I never saw a woman for whom I could feel more respect. Halliday and she suit each other perfectly; they would be the happiest people in England if they had any money. As he walked back with me to the station he talked about their difficulties. They can't afford to engage a good servant (if one exists nowadays), and cheap sluts have driven them frantic, so that Mrs. Halliday does everything with her own hands."

"It must be awful."

"Pretty hard, no doubt. She is an educated woman—otherwise, of course, she couldn't, and wouldn't, manage it. And, by-the-bye"—he paused for quiet emphasis—"she has a sister, unmarried, who lives in the country and does nothing at all. It occurs to one—doesn't it?—that the idle sister might pretty easily find scope for *her* energies."

Rosamund stared at the ground. She was not so dull as to lose the significance of this story, and she imagined that Geoffrey reflected upon herself in relation to her own sister. She broke the long silence by saying awkwardly:

"I'm sure *I* would never allow a sister of mine to lead such a life."

"I don't think you would," replied the other. And, though he spoke genially, Rosamund felt it a very moderate declaration of his belief in her.

Overcome by strong feeling, she exclaimed:

"I would do *anything* to be of use in the world. You don't think I mean it, but I do, Mr. Hunt. I——"

Her voice faltered; the all-important word stuck in her throat. And at that moment Geoffrey rose.

"Shall we walk about? Let me show you my mother's fernery; she is very proud of it."

That was the end of intimate dialogue. Rosamund felt aggrieved, and tried to shape sarcasms, but the man's imperturbable good-humour soon made her forget everything save the pleasure of being in his company. It was a bittersweet evening, yet perhaps enjoyment predominated. Of course, Geoffrey would conduct her to the station; she never lost sight of this hope. There would be another opportunity for plain speech. But her desire was frustrated; at the time of departure, Caroline said that they might as well all go together. Rosamund could have wept for chagrin.

She returned to the detested house, the hateful little bedroom, and there let her tears have way. In dread lest the hysterical sobs should be overheard, she all but stifled herself.

Then, as if by blessed inspiration, a great thought took shape in her despairing mind. At the still hour of night she suddenly sat up in the darkness, which seemed illumined by a wondrous hope. A few minutes motionless; the mental light grew dazzling; she sprang out of bed, partly dressed herself, and by the rays of a candle sat down to write a letter:

"DEAR MR. HUNT,

"Yesterday I did not tell you the whole truth. I have nothing to live upon, and I *must* find employment or starve. My brother-in-law has been supporting me for a long time—I am ashamed to tell you, but I *will*, and he can do so no longer. I wanted to ask you for practical advice, but I did not make my meaning clear. For all that, you *did* advise me, and very well indeed. I wish to offer myself as domestic help to poor Mrs. Halliday. Do you think she would have me? I ask no wages—only food and lodging. I will work harder and better than any general servants—I *will indeed*. My health is not bad, and I am fairly strong. Don't—don't throw scorn on this! Will you recommend me to Mrs. Halliday—or ask Mrs. Hunt to do so? I beg that you will. Please write to me at once, and say yes. I shall be ever grateful to you.

"Very sincerely yours,
"Rosamund Jewell."

This she posted as early as possible. The agonies she endured in waiting for a reply served to make her heedless of boarding-house spite, and by the last post that same evening came Geoffrey's letter. He wrote that her suggestion was startling. "Your motive seems to me very praise-worthy, but whether the thing would be possible is another question. I dare not take upon myself the responsibility of counselling you to such a step. Pray, take time, and think. I am most grieved to hear of your difficulties, but is there not some better way out of them?"

Yes, there it was! Geoffrey Hunt could not believe in her power to *do* anything praiseworthy. So had it been six years ago, when she would have gone through flood and flame to win his admiration. But in those days she was a girlish simpleton; she had behaved idiotically. It should be different now; were it at the end of her life, she would prove to him that he had slighted her unjustly!

Brave words, but Rosamund attached some meaning to them. The woman in her—the ever-prevailing woman—was wrought by fears and vanities, urgencies and desires, to a strange point of exaltation. Forthwith, she wrote again: "Send me, I entreat you, Mrs. Halliday's address. I will go and see her. No, I can't do anything but work with my hands. I am no good for anything else. If Mrs. Halliday refuses me, I shall go as a servant into some other house. Don't mock at me; I don't deserve it. Write at once."

Till midnight she wept and prayed.

Geoffrey sent her the address, adding a few dry words: "If you are willing and able to carry out this project, your ambition ought to be satisfied. You will have done your part towards solving one of the gravest problems of the time." Rosamund did not at once understand; when the writer's meaning grew clear, she kept repeating the words, as though they were a new gospel. Yes! she would be working nobly, helping to show a way out of the great servant difficulty. It would be an example to poor ladies, like herself, who were ashamed of honest work. And Geoffrey Hunt was looking on. He must needs marvel; perhaps he would admire greatly; perhaps—oh, oh!

Of course, she found a difficulty in wording her letter to the lady who had never heard of her, and of whom she knew practically nothing. But zeal surmounted obstacles. She began by saying that she was in search of domestic employment, and that, through her friends at Teddington, she had heard of Mrs. Halliday as a lady who might perhaps consider her application. Then followed an account of herself, tolerably ingenuous, and an amplification of the phrases she had addressed to Geoffrey Hunt. On an afterthought, she enclosed a stamped envelope.

Whilst the outcome remained dubious, Rosamund's behaviour to her fellow-boarders was a pattern of offensiveness. She no longer shunned them—seemed, indeed, to challenge their observation for the sake of meeting it with arrogant defiance. She rudely interrupted conversations, met sneers with virulent retorts, made herself the common enemy. Mrs. Banting was appealed to; ladies declared that they could not live in a house where they were exposed to vulgar insult. When nearly a week had passed Mrs. Banting found it necessary to speak in private with Miss Jewell, and to make a plaintive remonstrance. Rosamund's flashing eye and contemptuous smile foretold the upshot.

"Spare yourself the trouble, Mrs. Banting. I leave the house tomorrow."

"Oh, but——"

"There is no need for another word. Of course, I shall pay the week in lieu of notice. I am busy, and have no time to waste."

The day before, she had been to Forest Hill, had seen Mrs. Halliday, and had entered into an engagement. At midday on the morrow she arrived at the house which was henceforth to be her home, the scene of her labours.

Sheer stress of circumstance accounted for Mrs. Halliday's decision. Geoffrey Hunt, a dispassionate observer, was not misled in forming so high an opinion of his friend's wife. Only a year or two older than Rosamund, Mrs. Halliday had the mind and the temper which enable woman to front life as a rational combatant, instead of vegetating as a more or less destructive parasite. Her voice declared her; it fell easily upon a soft, clear note; the kind of voice that expresses good-humour and reasonableness, and many other admirable qualities; womanly, but with no suggestion of the feminine gamut; a voice that was never likely to test its compass in extremes. She had enjoyed a country breeding; something of liberal education assisted her natural intelligence; thanks to a good mother, she discharged with ability and content the prime domestic duties. But physically she was not inexhaustible, and the laborious, anxious years had taxed her health. A woman of the ignorant class may keep house, and bring up a family, with her own hands; she has to deal only with the simplest demands of life; her home is a shelter, her food is primitive, her children live or die according to the law of natural selection. Infinitely more complex, more trying, is the task of the educated wife and mother; if to conscientiousness be added enduring poverty, it means not seldom an early death. Fatigue and self-denial had set upon Mrs. Halliday's features a stamp which could never be obliterated. Her husband, her children, suffered illnesses; she, the indispensable, durst not confess even to a headache. Such servants as from time to time she had engaged merely increased her toil and anxieties; she demanded, to be sure, the diligence and efficiency which in this new day can scarce be found among the menial ranks; what she obtained was sluttish stupidity, grotesque presumption, and every form of female viciousness. Rosamund Jewell, honest in her extravagant fervour, seemed at first a mocking apparition; only after a long talk, when Rosamund's ingenuousness had forcibly impressed her, would Mrs. Halliday agree to an experiment. Miss

Jewell was to live as one of the family; she did not ask this, but consented to it. She was to receive ten pounds a year, for Mrs. Halliday insisted that payment there must be.

"I can't cook," Rosamund had avowed. "I never boiled a potato in my life. If you teach me, I shall be grateful to you."

"The cooking I can do myself, and you can learn if you like."

"I should think I might wash and scrub by the light of nature?"

"Perhaps. Good will and ordinary muscles will go a long way."

"I can't sew, but I will learn."

Mrs. Halliday reflected.

"You know that you are exchanging freedom for a hard and a very dull life?"

"My life has been hard and dull enough, if you only knew. The work will seem hard at first, no doubt. But I don't think I shall be dull with you."

Mrs. Halliday held out her work-worn hand, and received a clasp of the fingers attenuated by idleness.

It was a poor little house; built—of course—with sham display of spaciousness in front, and huddling discomfort at the rear. Mrs. Halliday's servants never failed to urge the smallness of the rooms as an excuse for leaving them dirty; they had invariably been accustomed to lordly abodes, where their virtues could expand. The furniture was homely and no more than sufficient, but here and there on the walls shone a glimpse of summer landscape, done in better days by the master of the house, who knew something of various arts, but could not succeed in that of money-making. Rosamund bestowed her worldly goods in a tiny chamber which Mrs. Halliday did her best to make inviting and comfortable; she had less room here than at Mrs. Banting's, but the cleanliness of surroundings would depend upon herself, and she was not likely to spend much time by the bedside in weary discontent. Halliday, who came home each evening at half-past six, behaved to her on their first meeting with grave, even respectful, courtesy; his tone flattered Rosamund's ear, and nothing could have been more seemly than the modest gentleness of her replies.

At the close of the first day, she wrote to Geoffrey Hunt: "I do believe I have made a good beginning. Mrs. Halliday is perfect and I quite love her. Please do not answer this; I only write because I feel that I owe it to your kindness. I shall never be able to thank you enough."

When Geoffrey obeyed her and kept silence, she felt that he acted prudently; perhaps Mrs. Halliday might see the letter, and know his hand. But none the less she was disappointed.

Rosamund soon learnt the measure of her ignorance in domestic affairs. Thoroughly practical and systematic, her friend (this was to be their relation) set down a scheme of the day's and the week's work; it made a clear apportionment between them, with no preponderance of unpleasant drudgery for the new-comer's share. With astonishment, which she did not try to conceal, Rosamund awoke to the complexity and endlessness of home duties even in so small a house as this.

"Then you have *no* leisure?" she exclaimed, in sympathy, not remonstrance.

"I feel at leisure when I'm sewing—and when I take the children out. And there's Sunday."

The eldest child was about five years old, the others three and a twelvemonth, respectively. Their ailments gave a good deal of trouble, and it often happened that Mrs. Halliday was awake with one of them the greater part of the night. For children Rosamund had no natural tenderness; to endure the constant sound of their voices proved, in the beginning, her hardest trial; but the resolve to school herself in every particular soon enabled her to tend the little ones with much patience, and insensibly she grew fond of them. Until she had overcome her awkwardness in every task, it cost her no little effort to get through the day; at bedtime she ached in every joint, and morning oppressed her with a sick lassitude. Conscious however, of Mrs. Halliday's forbearance, she would not spare herself, and it soon surprised her to discover that the rigid performance of what seemed an ignoble task brought its reward. Her first success in polishing a grate gave her more delight than she had known since childhood. She summoned her friend to look, to admire, to praise.

"Haven't I done it well? Could you do it better yourself?"

"Admirable!"

Rosamund waved her black-lead brush and tasted victory.

The process of acclimatisation naturally affected her health. In a month's time she began to fear that she must break down; she suffered painful disorders, crept out of sight to moan and shed a tear. Always faint, she had no appetite for wholesome food. Tossing on her bed at night she said to herself a thousand times: "I must go on even if I die!" Her religion took the form of asceticism and bade her rejoice in her miseries; she prayed constantly and at times knew the solace of an infinite self-glorification. In such a mood she once said to Mrs. Halliday:

"Don't you think I deserve some praise for the step I took?"

"You certainly deserve both praise and thanks from me."

"But I mean—it isn't every one who could have done it? I've a right to feel myself superior to the ordinary run of girls?"

The other gave her an embarrassed look, and murmured a few satisfying words. Later in the same day she talked to Rosamund about her health and insisted on making certain changes which allowed her to take more open-air exercise. The result of this was a marked improvement; at the end of the second month Rosamund began to feel and look better than she had done for several years. Work no longer exhausted her. And the labour in itself seemed to diminish, a natural consequence of perfect co-operation between the two women. Mrs. Halliday declared that life had never been so easy for her as now; she knew the delight of rest in which there was no self-reproach. But for sufficient reasons she did not venture to express to Rosamund all the gratitude that was due.

About Christmas a letter from Forest Hill arrived at Teddington; this time it did not forbid a reply. It spoke of struggles, sufferings, achievements. "Do I not deserve a word of praise? Have I not done something, as you said, towards solving the great question? Don't you believe in me a little?" Four more weeks went by, and brought no answer. Then, one evening, in a mood of bitterness, Rosamund took a singular step; she wrote to Mr. Cheeseman. She had heard nothing of him, had utterly lost sight of the world in which they met; but his place of business was known to her, and thither she addressed the note. A few lines only: "You are a very strange person, and I really take no interest whatever in you. But I have sometimes thought you would like to ask my forgiveness. If so, write to the above address—my sister's. I am living in London, and enjoying myself, but I don't choose to let you know where." Having an opportunity on the morrow, Sunday, she posted this in a remote district.

The next day, a letter arrived for her from Canada. Here was the explanation of Geoffrey's silence. His words could hardly have been more cordial, but there were so few of them. On nourishment such as this no illusion could support itself; for the moment Rosamund renounced every hope. Well, she was no worse off than before the renewal of their friendship. But could it be called friendship? Geoffrey's mother and sisters paid no heed to her; they doubtless considered that she had finally sunk below their horizon; and Geoffrey himself, for all his fine words, most likely thought the same at heart. Of course they would never meet again. And for the rest of her life she would be nothing more than a domestic servant in genteel disguise—happy were the disguise preserved.

However, she had provided a distraction for her gloomy thoughts. With no more delay than was due to its transmission by way of Glasgow, there came a reply from Mr. Cheeseman: two sheets of notepaper. The writer prostrated himself; he had been guilty of shameful behaviour; even Miss Jewell, with all her sweet womanliness, must find it hard to think of him with charity. But let her remember what "the poets" had written about Remorse, and apply to *him* the most harrowing of their descriptions. He would be frank with her; he would "a plain, unvarnished tale unfold." Whilst away for his holiday he by chance encountered *one* with whom, in days gone by, he had held tender relations. She was a young widow; his foolish heart was touched; he sacrificed honour to the passing emotion. Their marriage would be delayed, for his affairs were just now anything but flourishing. "Dear Miss Jewell, will you not be my

friend, my sister? Alas, I am not a happy man; but it is too late to lament."
And so on to the squeezed signature at the bottom of the last page.

Rosamund allowed a fortnight to pass—not before writing, but before her letter was posted. She used a tone of condescension, mingled with airy banter. "From my heart I feel for you, but, as you say, there is no help. I am afraid you are very impulsive—yet I thought that was a fault of youth. Do not give way to despair. I really don't know whether I shall feel it right to let you hear again, but if it soothes you I don't think there would be any harm in your letting me know the cause of your troubles."

This odd correspondence, sometimes with intervals of three weeks, went on until late summer. Rosamund would soon have been a year with Mrs. Halliday. Her enthusiasm had long since burnt itself out; she was often a prey to vapours, to cheerless lassitude, even to the spirit of revolt against things in general, but on the whole she remained a thoroughly useful member of the household; the great experiment might fairly be called successful. At the end of August it was decided that the children must have sea air; their parents would take them away for a fortnight. When the project began to be talked of, Rosamund, perceiving a domestic difficulty, removed it by asking whether she would be at liberty to visit her sister in Scotland. Thus were things arranged.

Some days before that appointed for the general departure, Halliday received a letter which supplied him with a subject of conversation at breakfast.

"Hunt is going to be married," he remarked to his wife, just as Rosamund was bringing in the children's porridge.

Mrs. Halliday looked at her helper—for no more special reason than the fact of Rosamund's acquaintance with the Hunt family; she perceived a change of expression, an emotional play of feature, and at once averted her eyes.

"Where? In Canada?" she asked, off-hand.

"No, he's in England. But the lady is a Canadian.—I wonder he troubles to tell me. Hunt's a queer fellow. When we meet, once in two years, he treats me like a long-lost brother; but I don't think he'd care a bit if he never saw me or heard of me again."

"It's a family characteristic," interposed Rosamund with a dry laugh.

That day she moved about with the gait and the eyes of a somnambulist. She broke a piece of crockery, and became hysterical over it. Her afternoon leisure she spent in the bedroom, and at night she professed a headache which obliged her to retire early.

A passion of wrath inflamed her; as vehement—though so utterly unreasonable—as in the moment when she learnt the perfidy of Mr. Cheeseman. She raged at her folly in having submitted to social degradation on the mere hint of a man who uttered it in a spirit purely contemptuous. The whole hateful world had conspired against her. She banned her kinsfolk and all her acquaintances, especially the Hunts; she felt bitter even against the Hallidays—unsympathetic, selfish people, utterly indifferent to her private griefs, regarding her as a mere domestic machine. She would write to Geoffrey Hunt, and let him know very plainly what she thought of his behaviour in *urging* her to become a servant. Would such a thought have ever occurred to a *gentleman!* And her poor life was wasted, oh! oh! She would soon be thirty—thirty! The glass mocked her with savage truth. And she had not even a decent dress to put on. Self-neglect had made her appearance vulgar; her manners, her speech, doubtless, had lost their note of social superiority. Oh, it was hard! She wished for death, cried for divine justice in a better world.

On the morning of release, she travelled to London Bridge, ostensibly *en route* for the north. But, on alighting, she had her luggage taken to the cloak-room, and herself went by omnibus to the West-end. By noon she had engaged a lodging, one room in a street where she had never yet lived. And hither before night was transferred her property.

The next day she spent about half of her ready-money in the purchase of clothing—cheap, but such as the self-respect of a "lady" imperatively demands. She bought cosmetics; she set to work at removing from her hands the traces of ignoble occupation. On the day that followed—Sunday—early in the afternoon, she repaired to a certain corner of Kensington Gardens, where she came face to face with Mr. Cheeseman.

"I have come," said Rosamund, in a voice of nervous exhilaration which tried to subdue itself. "Please to consider that it is more than you could expect."

"It is! A thousand times more! You are goodness itself."

In Rosamund's eyes the man had not improved since a year ago. The growth of a beard made him look older, and he seemed in indifferent health; but his tremulous delight, his excessive homage, atoned for the defect. She, on the other hand, was so greatly changed for the better that Cheeseman beheld her with no less wonder than admiration. Her brisk step, her upright bearing, her clear eye, and pure-toned skin contrasted remarkably with the lassitude and sallowness he remembered; at this moment too, she had a pleasant rosiness of cheek which made her girlish, virginal. All was set off by the new drapery and millinery, which threw a shade upon Cheeseman's very respectable but somewhat time-honoured, Sunday costume.

They spent several hours together, Cheeseman talking of his faults, his virtues, his calamities, and his hopes, like the impulsive, well-meaning, but nerveless fellow that he was. Rosamund gathered from it all, as she had vaguely learnt from his recent correspondence, that the alluring widow no longer claimed him; but he did not enter into details on this delicate subject. They had tea at a restaurant by Notting Hill Gate; then, Miss

Jewell appearing indefatigable, they again strolled in unfrequented ways. At length was uttered the question for which Rosamund had long ago prepared her reply.

"You cannot expect me," she said sweetly, "to answer at once."

"Of course not! I shouldn't have dared to hope——"

He choked and swallowed; a few beads of perspiration shining on his troubled face.

"You have my address; most likely I shall spend a week or two there. Of course you may write. I shall probably go to my sister's in Scotland, for the autumn——"

"Oh! don't say that—don't. To lose you again—so soon——"

"I only said, 'probably'——"

"Oh, thank you!—To go so far away—And the autumn; just when I have a little freedom; the very best time—if I dared to hope such a thing——"

Rosamund graciously allowed him to bear her company as far as to the street in which she lived.

A few days later she wrote to Mrs. Halliday, heading her letter with the Glasgow address. She lamented the sudden impossibility of returning to her domestic duties. Something had happened. "In short, dear Mrs. Halliday, I am going to be married. I could not give you warning of this, it has come so unexpectedly. Do forgive me! I so earnestly hope that you will find some one to take my place, some one better and more of a help to you. I know I haven't been much use. Do write home at Glasgow and say I may still regard you as a dear friend."

This having been dispatched, she sat musing over her prospects. Mr. Cheeseman had honestly confessed the smallness of his income; he could barely count upon a hundred and fifty a year; but things *might* improve. She did not dislike him—no, she did not dislike him. He would be a very tractable husband. Compared, of course, with——

A letter was brought up to her room. She knew the flowing commercial hand, and broke the envelope without emotion. Two sheets—three sheets—and a half. But what was all this? "Despair . . . thoughts of self-destruction . . . ignoble publicity . . . practical ruin . . . impossible . . . despise . . . and forget . . . Dante's hell . . . deeper than ever plummet sounded . . .forever! . . . ." So again he had deceived her! He must have known that the widow was dangerous; his reticence was mere shuffling. His behaviour to that other woman had perhaps exceeded in baseness his treatment of herself; else, how could he be so sure that a jury would give her "ruinous damages"? Or was it all a mere illustration of a man's villainy? Why should not *she* also sue for damages? Why not? Why not?

The three months that followed were a time of graver peril, of darker crisis, than Rosamund, with all her slip-slop experiences, had ever known. An observer adequately supplied with facts, psychological and material, would more than once have felt that it depended on the mere toss of a coin whether she kept or lost her social respectability. She sounded all the depths possible to such a mind and heart—save only that from which there could have been no redemption. A saving memory lived within her, and at length, in the yellow gloom of a November morning— her tarnished, draggle-tailed finery thrown aside for the garb she had worn in lowliness—Rosamund betook herself to Forest Hill. The house of the Hallidays looked just as usual. She slunk up to the door, rang the bell, and waited in fear of a strange face. There appeared Mrs. Halliday herself. The surprised but friendly smile at once proved her forgiveness of Rosamund's desertion. She had written, indeed, with calm good sense, hoping only that all would be well.

"Let me see you alone, Mrs. Halliday.—How glad I am to sit in this room again! Who is helping you now?"

"No one. Help such as I want is not easy to find."

"Oh, let me comeback!—I am *not* married.—No, no, there is nothing to be ashamed of. I am no worse than I ever was. I'll tell you everything— the whole silly, wretched story."

She told it, blurring only her existence of the past three months.

"I would have come before, but I was so bitterly ashamed. I ran away so disgracefully. Now I'm penniless—all but suffering hunger. Will you have me again, Mrs. Halliday? I've been a horrid fool, but—I do believe— for the last time in my life. Try me again, dear Mrs. Halliday!"

There was no need of the miserable tears, the impassioned pleading. Her home received her as though she had been absent but for an hour. That night she knelt again by her bedside in the little room, and at seven o'clock next morning she was lighting fires, sweeping floors, mute in thankfulness.

Halliday heard the story from his wife, and shook a dreamy, compassionate head.

"For goodness' sake," urged the practical woman, "don't let her think she's a martyr."

"No, no; but the poor girl should have her taste of happiness."

"Of course I'm sorry for her, but there are plenty of people more to be pitied. Work she must, and there's only one kind of work she's fit for. It's no small thing to find your vocation—is it? Thousands of such women—all meant by nature to scrub and cook—live and die miserably because they think themselves too good for it."

"The whole social structure is rotten!"

"It'll last our time," rejoined Mrs. Halliday, as she gave a little laugh and stretched her weary arms.

A PRAYER FOR MY DAUGHTER°

William Butler Yeats (1865–1939)

Once more the storm is howling, and half hid
Under this cradle-hood and coverlid
My child sleeps on. There is no obstacle
But Gregory's wood° and one bare hill
Whereby the haystack- and roof-levelling wind,   5
Bred on the Atlantic, can be stayed;
And for an hour I have walked and prayed
Because of the great gloom that is in my mind.

I have walked and prayed for this young child an hour
And heard the sea-wind scream upon the tower,   10
And under the arches of the bridge, and scream
In the elms above the flooded stream;
Imagining in excited reverie
That the future years had come,
Dancing to a frenzied drum,   15
Out of the murderous innocence of the sea.

May she be granted beauty and yet not
Beauty to make a stranger's eye distraught,
Or hers before a looking-glass, for such,
Being made beautiful overmuch,   20
Consider beauty a sufficient end,
Lose natural kindness and maybe
The heart-revealing intimacy
That chooses right, and never find a friend.

Helen being chosen found life flat and dull   25
And later had much trouble from a fool,°
While that great Queen,° that rose out of the spray,
Being fatherless could have her way

°*Daughter*: Anne Butler Yeats, born February 24, 1919
°*Gregory's wood*: In 1917, Yeats bought some land on Lady Gregory's estate; his
study was in an old Norman tower on the property.
°*Helen . . . fool*: Helen and Paris   °*Queen*: Aphrodite (Venus), born of sea-foam

Yet chose a bandy-leggèd smith ° for man.
It's certain that fine women eat 30
A crazy salad with their meat
Whereby the Horn of Plenty is undone.

In courtesy I'd have her chiefly learned;
Hearts are not had as a gift but hearts are earned
By those that are not entirely beautiful; 35
Yet many, that have played the fool
For beauty's very self, has charm made wise,
And many a poor man that has roved,
Loved and thought himself beloved,
From a glad kindness cannot take his eyes. 40

May she become a flourishing hidden tree
That all her thoughts may like the linnet° be,
And have no business but dispensing round
Their magnanimities of sound,
Nor but in merriment begin a chase, 45
Nor but in merriment a quarrel.
O may she live like some green laurel
Rooted in one dear perpetual place.

My mind, because the minds that I have loved,
The sort of beauty that I have approved, 50
Prosper but little, has dried up of late,
Yet knows that to be choked with hate
May well be of all evil chances chief.
If there's no hatred in a mind
Assault and battery of the wind 55
Can never tear the linnet from the leaf.

An intellectual hatred is the worst,
So let her think opinions are accursed.
Have I not seen the loveliest woman° born
Out of the mouth of Plenty's horn, 60
Because of her opinionated mind
Barter that horn and every good
By quiet natures understood
For an old bellows full of angry wind?

°*bandy-legged smith*: Hephaestus (Vulcan), Aphrodite's husband
°*linnet*: a small finch, known for its sweet song
°*woman*: Maud Gonne, a beautiful Irish revolutionary whom Yeats had once loved;
lines 59–64 refer to her activities in the struggle for Irish independence.

Considering that, all hatred driven hence,   65
The soul recovers radical° innocence
And learns at last that it is self-delighting,
Self-appeasing, self-affrighting,
And that its own sweet will is Heaven's will;
She can, though every face should scowl   70
And every windy quarter howl
Or every bellows burst, be happy still.

And may her bridegroom bring her to a house
Where all's accustomed, ceremonious;
For arrogance and hatred are the wares   75
Peddled in the thoroughfares.
How but in custom and in ceremony
Are innocence and beauty born?
Ceremony's a name for the rich horn,
And custom for the spreading laurel tree.   80

WORKS IN *Short Story Masterpieces*

J. D. Salinger, *Uncle Wiggily in Connecticut*
Sinclair Lewis, *Virga Vay & Allan Cedar*
Mary McCarthy, *Cruel and Barbarous Treatment*
Katherine Mansfield, *Marriage à la Mode*
James Joyce, *The Boarding House*
J. F. Powers, *The Valiant Woman*

OTHER SUGGESTED WORKS

Nathaniel Hawthorne, *The Scarlet Letter*
Elizabeth Bowen, *Death of the Heart*
Doris Lessing, *A Proper Marriage*
Virginia Woolf, *The New Dress*
              Mrs. Dalloway
              A Room of One's Own, Chapter Three
William Shakespeare, *Macbeth*
Henrik Ibsen, *Hedda Gabler*
Simon de Beauvoir, *The Narcissist*, from *The Second Sex*,
              Chapter XXII

° *radical*: rooted; also fundamental

QUESTIONS

1. In *The Applicant,* how does Sylvia Plath define conventional marriage? What does she consider woman's function?

2. What is the purpose of the rabbit fantasy for the couple in Woolf's story, *Lappin and Lapinova*? What is it a reaction to in their lives? Why does Ernest stop taking part in the fantasy? Why does the death of Lapinova put an end to the marriage? What is the trap in which she is caught?

3. What insight does *The Mask* offer into the nature of love relationships, into the reasons people are attracted to one another? Is the first speaker right to want to know what is behind the mask? What happens when the fire burns out and the mask no longer engages the mind? Is a marriage of masks enough? Refer back to the marriage in Woolf's story.

4a. How is Hawthorne's story also about a marriage of masks? What is Aylmer seeking in his wife? Why does he want to remove the birthmark from her face? Why does it bother him? What is the danger of spiritualizing the physical, particularly when you believe that there is nothing beyond the external appearance? (Refer back to *Visions of the Daughters of Albion.* Compare Aylmer with Theotormon and Bromion.)

b. What does Aylmer reject in his own nature that is embodied in the figure of his assistant? What kind of approach to life and human relationships is Hawthorne criticizing? What is wrong with Aylmer's idea of perfection? Why does Aylmer's wife allow herself to be manipulated, to be made a guinea pig? Why doesn't she fight back? Is this the plight of the lady who leaves her tower to go live with some glittering knight in "tower'd Camelot"? What does she sacrifice?

5. *Next Day* describes a typical day in the life of a modern married woman. Unlike the woman in Sappho's poem, Jarrell's woman is educated, but what has her education done for her? Why is she troubled by what she has become? What is she afraid of? Why does she hate herself?

6. Why does Sappho place so much importance on geing educated? Is she referring to formal education only? The woman in Jarrell's poem appears to be well-educated in a formal sense, but is her plight any better than that of Sappho's uneducated woman? What is Sappho really asking of woman as an individual? What causes a life to become "commonplace and solitary"? What kind of self-education is needed to prevent that kind of life?

7. Anderson's story also describes an "uneducated woman." What did the mother give up in order to be a wife and mother? What does

her son mean to her? Compare her with the woman in *Next Day*. Why isn't being a wife/mother enough?

8. Describe the nature of the prison in Plath's poem, *The Jailor*. Is the jailor just a flesh-and-blood husband? What kind of freedom does the woman want? Why is it impossible? Why did the woman get herself into such a destructive situation in the first place? Compare her with Oothoon and the wife in Hawthorne's story. Does she have any choice? What has to happen inside herself before she can be free of the external tyrant?

9a. Describe the world created in *Urizen's Work*. Contrast it with the natural Earth. What keeps the people in Urizen's world from seeing "Visions in the darksom air"? What have they been taught to see and do? Why aren't they happy obeying Urizen?

b. What do the nets represent? Why do "the weak" want to trap and bind "the Spirits"? What are these Spirits? Why must Urizen's world be built on Vala's ashes?

c. Why must females be slaves in this concrete world? Why is Urizen's female counterpart a "Shadowy Feminine Semblance . . . reposed on a White Couch"? (Compare her with the women in the works in Part I—particularly in *The Crystal Cabinet* and *Ligeia*.) Why does this kind of woman spend most of her time reclining? How is she like the man "palely loitering"? What does she lack? Discuss the images used to describe her appearance and behavior.

d. Why is this woman Reason's perfect mate? Why does she sit "Trembling, cold, in jealous fears" when Urizen is away from her? Why is she revived "with lives of Victims sacrificed upon an altar of brass" by her sons? What is the significance of "the Altar," and why is it appropriate that its steps be named after her sons? Why the emphasis on twelve steps and twelve sons?

e. Contrast this man-made "Golden World" with the natural world outside, with "the eternal wandering stars" and "the vast unknown." What is the bondage that the spirits are mourning? Why is Urizen's world closed? Discuss what it shuts out and what it closes in.

f. What is the "Divine Vision" that "appeared in Luvah's robes of blood"? Why "robes of blood"? What is meant by "Mundane shell"? Discuss woman's position in this closed world. What is the only role that she can play?

10a. What message is Urizen preaching from "his book of brass"? Why is it appropriate that this book is brass? What is the nature of Urizen's so-called wisdom? What does he mean by "Moral Duty"? Why does he want the women's hearts to be "harder than the nether millstone"? Why do hard hearts go with "Moral Duty"?

b. Why does Urizen want to capture Enitharmon and destroy Los? Why does he call Los "the terrible shade"?

c. What is Imagination compared with Urizen's almighty Reason? What "wondrous tree" is Urizen referring to? If Urthona is Creativity and Poetic Energy embodied as Los, what is "the spectre of Urthona" (the disembodied, dead or abstract form of Urthona) that serves Urizen? What does Urizen want to use Art for?

d. How is Urizen's counsel destructive to life? How does it deceive and manipulate people, making them its slaves? How are women affected by this masculine will that dominates the world and replaces Real Art with Artifice? Is the problem Reason in itself or Reason isolated from Imagination? Why is Urizen so threatened by Los?

e. Discuss the distinction that Blake makes between "Artifice" and "Art." What insight does he offer into the nature of masks, of the games people play in order to have their way? Why is it so easy for women to become victims of artifice, concerned with outward appearance, flattering, following the rules, "doing their duty"? Why is Urizen's voice so compelling? Why are women so willing to imitate the worst in man as embodied in Urizen (Cold Reason concerned with the materialistic world)? Discuss why Reason is so seductive to women, why they are easily talked into things contrary to their real feelings. What must women deny in their own natures in order to obey Urizen's Law?

11. What is the quality that Swift is attacking in *The Furniture of a Woman's Mind*? Do all women have such "furniture" in their minds or only a particular kind of woman? What does the woman being satirized lack? What produces and nurtures such an insubstantial, artificial creature? Is this what woman becomes when she is not educated?

12. What is Donne's narrator's complaint against women? What is the point of all the exaggerated imagery in *Song*? Why is woman's fickleness so offensive to man? Discuss the nature of "woman's constancy." On what does woman base her actions? Why does the speaker call her "vain lunatic"? How could he "dispute, and conquer"? Why does he place so much importance on vows? What does he expect her to obey? What is his view of love? What does the comment at the end of *Woman's Constancy* reveal?

13a. What makes the world desolate in Blake's poem *The Desolate World*? What does it lack? Why are the women weaving life out of rocks? What is the "Eternity" that they are denying? What is "the Atheistical Epicurian Philosophy of Albion's Tree"? What is Blake saying about the nature of "the Feminine and Masculine when separated from Man"? What is "Man" (meaning the fully human) in comparison with "the Rocks" and "the frowning Chaos"? What are the feminine and masculine qualities that are essential to human life?

b. If "Jerusalem" represents reality seen spiritually, what is being closed out of the world of collective humanity? What are "the Spectres of Albion"? What is monstrous about these women of Urizen's World? Why are they "ashamed to give Love openly"? Why do they adore "the Warrior" and delight in "the blood of the Innocent"? How are they phantoms, ideas of womanhood, but not real women? Compare them with La Belle Dame.

14. Why is the world of the woman in Gissing's story so desolate? Why is she a "foolish virgin"? Compare her with the women in Blake's poem. What does she worship? What is she separated from in her own nature? How is she a product of Urizen's world? What is the solution to her problem? Compare her condition with that of the woman in *Urizen's Work*.

15a. Discuss how the women in the works in Part III could profit from the qualities that Yeats would give his daughter. What kind of woman is he afraid his daughter might become unless his prayer is answered? What kind of beauty does he want for her? How is it different from the beauty that attracts him in *Adam's Curse*? Why isn't physical beauty "a sufficient end"? What does he mean by "natural kindness" and "the heart-revealing intimacy"? What are these qualities essential for in life?

b. What does Yeats mean by the last three lines in Stanza 4? What is "a crazy salad" compared with meat? What is "the Horn of Plenty"? Why is it undone by this "crazy salad"?

c. Why would Yeats have his daughter educated? What does real education involve? Why does he want her to "become a flourishing hidden tree"? What does he mean by "hidden"? Why are a tree and a bird appropriate images? What does the interaction of the two represent in human life? What purpose should "thinking" serve in woman?

d. Why does Yeats want her "rooted in one dear perpetual place"? What kind of stability is he describing? How is it different from the stability of Urizen's desolate world of rocks?

e. Why has Yeats's mind "dried up of late"? What function do women serve in his life? What is evil about hate? How is it like Urizen's spectres? What does it negate? What does the wind signify and how is it served by hate? Why does the absence of hate allow thoughts (the linnet) to remain connected with the body (the earth, the natural)?

f. What is it about "an intellectual hatred" that separates the mind from the body, ideas from feelings? What is wrong with "opinions"? How are they different from linnet-like thoughts? Discuss the nature of an "opinionated mind." How is it like "an old bellows full of angry wind"? What does it deny? What kind of good is understood "by quiet natures"?

g. What does Yeats mean by "radical innocence"? How is it different from early, childhood innocence (or "the murderous innocence of the sea")? How is it something that "the soul recovers" once hatred is removed?

h. What does the soul need to learn about itself? What do the women in Part III need to learn about who they are and what it means to be fully human? What is the nature of the soul's "own sweet will" compared with Urizen's will? Why is the soul's will also "Heaven's will"? How is Yeats's definition of "heavenly" like Blake's? What attitude do both take towards Reason isolated from the natural world? Would Yeats's daughter not be dependent upon what enslaves the women in Part III?

i. Discuss the significance of the last three lines of Stanza 9. What does Yeats mean by "custom" and "ceremony"? Why are "arrogance and hatred" present "in the thoroughfares" but not inside the couple's house? Why can't "innocence and beauty" be born without "the rich horn" and "the spreading laurel tree"? Why can't they be born in Urizen's world? What is the cause of the "arrogance and hatred" that opposes "innocence and beauty"? Compare and contrast these qualities. (Refer back to the conflict between Urizen and Los. What change must take place in Urizen's world before Los and Enitharmon can be united there?) How is woman's "opinionated mind" like a spectre of Urizen?

16. Discuss how the women in the stories in *Short Story Masterpieces* are counterparts of Urizen rather than of The Real Man. What is lacking in their lives? Which of the women are mannequins and which are monsters? What masks do they wear? How do they use people (particularly men)? Discuss the nature of the society that produces such creatures.

17. Discuss Macbeth and Lady Macbeth in terms of the masculine and feminine elements within the human psyche. How are they split and warring within themselves? How does Macbeth separate himself from the feminine side of his nature? How does Lady Macbeth weave him into a rock? Compare her early in the play with Macbeth at the end. Discuss how they change roles and become more like each other as the play progresses. How are they both tempted and seduced by Urizen's world? What form do the tempters take? Why is it significant that they are supernatural (or unnatural) figures? (Compare them with the spectres of Blake's poems.) What are they inside every person? Compare what the tempters tell Macbeth with "the Words of Wisdom" spoken by Urizen from his "Book of Brass."

How is Macbeth's and Lady Macbeth's world like *The Desolate World*? What kind of man does Lady Macbeth admire? What does she scorn in Macbeth's nature? Discuss the passages in which she describes Macbeth's nature and her own. What are the values by which she judges him, on which she bases her actions? What drives Lady Macbeth insane? What turns Macbeth into a monster. Discuss their marriage in terms of an interaction of masks.

PART IV

The Androgynous Mind:
The Marriage of Self and Soul

The Androgynous Mind: The Marriage of Self and Soul

No real marriage (or union of opposites, of masculine and feminine) can take place in the outside world until it has first taken place inside the individuals involved. A man cannot be united with a flesh-and-blood woman until he is united with the spiritual woman inside himself—the feminine element of his own nature, which might be called his soul. People who marry other people before they have "married" themselves are like some of those men and women seen in the works of Part III: they are masks playing roles.

The selections in Part IV present some images of the androgynous mind—of men and women who are in touch with the feminine and masculine elements of their natures. Is there any noticeable difference in the way these men and woman talk about each other? Compare the dialogues with some of the monologues in Part I. What quality is present in these selections that is missing in Parts I, II, and III? What quality of Logos and Eros is manifested? Is any particular feeling evoked by the union of the two? Do you find humor in the selections in Part IV?

The selections in Part IV are concerned with woman as seen by herself and by men who are in touch with the feminine parts of their natures. Woman here is not at all the same insubstantial creature presented in Part I. She is not shut away from experience in the outside world like the women in Part II, and she is far from being one of the suffering martyrs, mannequins, or monsters of Part III. What sets her apart from them? How does she transcend them? How is her passion different from the sentimentality of the man-made world? How is her anger different from "intellectual hatred" and cynicism? How does the masculine element inside her serve Eros rather than enslave it?

SONNET 130

William Shakespeare (1564–1616)

My mistress' eyes are nothing like the sun;
Coral is far more red than her lips' red;
If snow be white, why then her breasts are dun;
If hairs be wires, black wires grow on her head.
I have seen roses damask'd, red and white,   5
But no such roses see I in her cheeks;
And in some perfumes is there more delight
Than in the breath that from my mistress reeks.
I love to hear her speak, yet well I know
That music hath a far more pleasing sound;   10

I grant I never saw a goddess go;
My mistress, when she walks, treads on the ground:
And yet, by heaven, I think my love as rare
As any she belied with false compare.

WOMAN

Randall Jarrell (1914–1965)

"All things become thee, being thine," I think sometimes
As I think of you. I think: "How many faults
In thee have seemed a virtue!" While your taste is on my
   tongue
The years return, blessings innumerable
As the breaths that you have quickened, gild my flesh.   5
Lie there in majesty!
               When, like Disraeli,° I murmur
That you are more like a mistress than a wife,
More like an angel than a mistress; when, like Satan,
I hiss in your ear some vile suggestion,
Some delectable abomination,   10
You smile at me indulgently: "Men, men!"

You smile at mankind, recognizing in it
The absurd occasion of your fall.
For men—as your soap operas, as your *Home Journals,*
As your hearts whisper—men are only children.   15
And you believe them. Truly, you are children.

Should I love you so dearly if you weren't?
If I weren't?
         O morning star,
Each morning my dull heart goes out to you
And rises with the sun, but with the sun   20
Sets not, but all the long night nests within your eyes.

Men's share of grace, of all that can make bearable,
Lovable almost, the apparition, Man,
Has fallen to you. Erect, extraordinary
As a polar bear on roller skates, he passes   25

°*Disraeli*: British politician and writer; Prime Minister (1868, 1874–80)

From *The Lost World* by Randall Jarrell. Copyright © 1964, 1965, by Randall Jarrell. Reprinted with permission of The Macmillan Company.

On into the Eternal . . .

                   From your pedestal, you watch
Admiringly, when you remember to.

Let us form, as Freud has said, "a group of two."
You are the best thing that this world can offer—
He said so. Or I remember that he said so;   30
If I am mistaken it's a Freudian error,
An error nothing but a man would make.
Women can't bear women. Cunningly engraved
On many an old wife's dead heart is "Women,
Beware women!" And yet it was a man°   35
Sick of too much sweetness—of a life
Rich with a mother, wife, three daughters, a wife's sister,
An abyss of analysands°—who wrote: "I cannot
Escape the notion (though I hesitate
To give it expression) that for women   40
The level of what is ethically normal
Is different from what it is in men.
Their superego"—he goes on without hesitation—
"Is never so inexorable, so impersonal,
So independent of its emotional   45
Origins as we require it in a man."

Did not the angel say to Abraham
That he would spare the cities of the plain
If there were found in them ten unjust women?
—That is to say, merciful; that is to say,   50
Extravagant; that is to say, unjust as judges
Who look past judgment, always, to the eyes
(Long-lashed, a scapegoat's, yearning sheepishly)
Under the curly-yarned and finger-tickling locks
Of that dear-wooled, inconsequential head.   55

You save him and knit an afghan from his hair.
And in the cold tomb, save for you, and afghanless,
He leaves you to wage wars, build bridges, visit women
Who like to run their fingers through his hair.
He complains of you to them, describing you   60
As "the great love of my life." What pains it took
To win you, a mere woman!—"worst of all,"
He ends, "a woman who was not my type."

°*man*: Freud   °*analysands*: people undergoing psychoanalysis

But then, a woman never is a man's type.
Possessed by that prehistoric unforgettable   65
Other One, who never again is equaled
By anyone, he searches for his ideal,
The Good Whore who reminds him of his mother.
The realities are too much one or the other,
Too much like Mother or too bad . . . Too bad!   70
He resigns himself to them—as "they are, after all,
The best things that are offered in that line";
And should he not spare Nineveh, that city
Wherein are more than sixscore thousand women
Who cannot tell their left hand from their right,°   75
But smile up hopefully at the policeman?

Are you as mercenary as the surveys show?
What a way to put it! Let us write instead
That you are realists; or as a realist might say,
Naturalists. It's in man's nature—woman's nature   80
To want the best, and to be careless how it comes.
And what have we all to sell except ourselves?
Poor medlar, no sooner ripe than rotten!
You must be seized today, or stale tomorrow
Into a wife, a mother, a homemaker,   85
An Elector of the League of Women Voters.
Simply by your persistence, you betray
Yourselves and all that was yours, you momentary
And starry instances; are falling, falling
Into the sagging prison of your flesh,   90
Residuary legatees of earth, grandmothers
And legal guardians of the tribes of men.
If all Being showered down on you in gold
Would you not murmur, with averted breasts: "Not now"?

When he looks upon your nakedness he is blinded.   95
Your breasts and belly are one incandescence
Like the belly of an idol: how can a man go in that fire
And come out living? "The burnt child dreads the fire,"°
He says later, warming his hands before the fire.
Last—last of all—he says that there are three things sure: 100
"That the Dog returns to his Vomit and the Sow returns to
    her Mire,

°*should he . . . right*: see the Biblical story of Jonah   °*The . . . fire*: from John
Lyly's "Euphues" (1579)

And the burnt Fool's bandaged finger goes wabbling back to
    the Fire."

Part of himself is shocked at part of himself
As, beside the remnants of a horrible
Steak, a little champagne, he confesses 105
Candidly to you: "In the beginning
There was a baby boy that loved its mother,
There was a baby girl that loved its mother.
The boy grew up and got to love a woman,
The girl grew up and had to love a man. 110
Because isn't that what's wrong with women? Men?
Isn't that the reason you're the way you are?
Why *are* you the way you are?"
                        You say: "Because."

When you float with me through the Tunnel of Love
Or Chamber of Horrors—one of those concessions— 115
And a great hand, dripping, daggered, reaches out for you
And you scream, and it misses, and another hand,
Soiled, hairy, lustful, reaches out for you
And you faint, and it misses: when you come to,
You say, looking up weakly: "Did you notice? 120
The second one had on a wedding ring."

May the Devil fly away with the roof of the house
That you and I aren't happy in, you angel!
And yet, how quickly the bride's veils evaporate!
A girl hesitates a moment in mid-air 125
And settles to the ground a wife, a mother.
Each evening a tired spirit visits
Her full house; wiping his feet upon a mat
Marked *Women and Children First,* the husband looks
At this grown woman. She stands there in slacks 130
Among the real world's appliances,
Women, and children; kisses him hello
Just as, that morning, she kissed him goodbye,
And he sits down, till dinner, with the paper.
This home of theirs is haunted by a girl's 135
Ghost. At sunset a woodpecker knocks
At a tree by the window, asking their opinion
Of life. The husband answers, "Life is life,"
And when his wife calls to him from the kitchen
He tells her who it was, and what he wanted. 140
Beating the whites of seven eggs, the beater

Asks her her own opinion; she says, "Life
Is life." "See how it sounds to say it isn't,"
The beater tempts her. "Life is not life,"
She says. It sounds the same. Putting her cake   145
Into the oven, she is satisfied
Or else dissatisfied: it sounds the same.
With knitted brows, with care's swift furrows nightly
Smoothed out with slow care, and come again with care
Each morning, she lives out her gracious life.   150

But you should gush out over being like a spring
The drinker sighs to lift his mouth from: a dark source
That brims over, with its shining, every cup
That is brought to it in shadow, filled there, broken there.
You look at us out of sunlight and of shade,   155
Dappled, inexorable, the last human power.
All earth is the labyrinth along whose ways
You walk mirrored: rosy-fingered, many-breasted
As Diana of the Ephesians, strewing garments
Before the world's eyes narrowed in desire.   160
Now, naked on my doorstep, in the sun
Gold-armed, white-breasted, pink-cheeked, and black-furred,
You call to me, "Come"; and when I come say, "Go,"
Smiling your soft contrary smile . . .
                                        He who has these
Is secure from the other sorrows of the world.   165
While you are how am I alone? Your voice
Soothes me to sleep, and finds fault with my dreams,
Till I murmur in my sleep: "Man is the animal
That finds fault."
                        And you say: "Who said that?"

But be, as you have been, my happiness;   170
Let me sleep beside you, each night, like a spoon;
When, starting from my dreams, I groan to you,
May your *I love you* send me back to sleep.
At morning bring me, grayer for its mirroring,
The heavens' sun perfected in your eyes.   175

THE MENTAL TRAVELLER

William Blake (1757–1827)

I travel'd thro' a Land of Men,
A Land of Men & Women too,

And heard & saw such dreadful things
As cold Earth wanderers never knew.

For there the Babe is born in joy 5
That was begotten in dire woe;
Just as we Reap in joy the fruit
Which we in bitter tears did sow.

And if the Babe is born a Boy
He's given to a Woman Old, 10
Who nails him down upon a rock,
Catches his shrieks in cups of gold.

She binds iron thorns around his head,
She pierces both his hands & feet,
She cuts his heart out at his side 15
To make it feel both cold & heat.

Her fingers number every Nerve,
Just as a Miser counts his gold;
She lives upon his shrieks & cries,
And she grows young as he grows old. 20

Till he becomes a bleeding youth,
And she becomes a Virgin bright;
Then he rends up his Manacles
And binds her down for his delight.

He plants himself in all her Nerves, 25
Just as a Husbandman his mould;
And she becomes his dwelling place
And Garden fruitful seventy fold.

An aged Shadow, soon he fades,
Wand'ring round an Earthly Cot, 30
Full filled all with gems & gold
Which he by industry had got.

And these are the gems of the Human Soul,
The rubies & pearls of a lovesick eye,
The countless gold of the aching heart, 35
The martyr's groan & the lover's sigh.

They are his meat, they are his drink;
He feeds the Beggar & the Poor

And the wayfaring Traveller:
For ever open is his door. 40

His grief is their eternal joy;
They make the roofs & walls to ring;
Till from the fire on the hearth
A little Female Babe does spring.

And she is all of solid fire 45
And gems & gold, that none his hand
Dares stretch to touch her Baby form,
Or wrap her in his swaddling-band.

But She comes to the Man she loves,
If young or old, or rich or poor; 50
They soon drive out the aged Host,
A Beggar at another's door.

He wanders weeping far away,
Until some other take him in;
Oft blind & age-bent, sore distrest, 55
Until he can a Maiden win.

And to allay his freezing Age
The Poor Man takes her in his arms;
The Cottage fades before his sight,
The Garden & its lovely Charms. 60

The Guests are scatter'd thro' the land,
For the Eye altering alters all;
The Senses roll themselves in fear,
And the flat Earth becomes a Ball;

The stars, sun, Moon, all shrink away, 65
A desert vast without a bound,
And nothing left to eat or drink,
And a dark desert all around.

The honey of her Infant lips,
The bread & wine of her sweet smile, 70
The wild game of her roving Eye,
Does him to Infancy beguile;

For as he eats & drinks he grows
Younger & younger every day;

And on the desert wild they both   75
Wander in terror & dismay.

Like the wild Stag she flees away,
Her fear plants many a thicket wild;
While he pursues her night & day,
By various arts of Love beguil'd,   80

By various arts of Love & Hate,
Till the wide desert planted o'er
With Labyrinths of wayward Love,
Where roam the Lion, Wolf & Boar,

Till he becomes a wayward Babe,   85
And she a weeping Woman Old.
Then many a Lover wanders here;
The Sun & Stars are nearer roll'd.

The trees bring forth sweet Ecstasy
To all who in the desert roam;   90
Till many a City there is Built,
And many a pleasant Shepherd's home.

But when they find the frowning Babe,
Terror strikes thro' the region wide:
They cry "The Babe! the Babe is Born!"   95
And flee away on every side.

For who dare touch the frowning form,
His arm is wither'd to its root;
Lions, Boars, Wolves, all howling flee,
And every Tree does shed its fruit.   100

And none can touch that frowning form,
Except it be a Woman Old;
She nails him down upon the Rock,
And all is done as I have told.

A WOMAN WAITS FOR ME

Walt Whitman (1819–1892)

A woman waits for me, she contains all, nothing is lacking,
Yet all were lacking if sex were lacking, or if the moisture of
   the right man were lacking.

Sex contains all, bodies, souls,
Meanings, proofs, purities, delicacies, results, promulgations,
Songs, commands, health, pride, the maternal mystery, the   5
    seminal milk,
All hopes, benefactions, bestowals, all the passions, loves,
    beauties, delights of the earth,
All the governments, judges, gods, follow'd persons of the earth,
These are contain'd in sex as parts of itself and justifications
    of itself.

Without shame the man I like knows and avows the
    deliciousness of his sex,
Without shame the woman I like knows and avows hers.   10

Now I will dimiss myself from impassive women,
I will go stay with her who waits for me, and with those
    women that are warm-blooded and sufficient for me,
I see that they understand me and do not deny me,
I see that they are worthy of me, I will be the robust husband
    of those women.

They are not one jot less than I am,   15
They are tann'd in the face by shining suns and blowing winds,
Their flesh has the old divine suppleness and strength,
They know how to swim, row, ride, wrestle, shoot, run, strike,
    retreat, advance, resist, defend themselves,
They are ultimate in their own right—they are calm, clear,
    well-possess'd of themselves.

I draw you close to me, you women,   20
I cannot let you go, I would do you good,
I am for you, and you are for me, not only for our own sake,
    but for others' sakes,
Envelop'd in you sleep greater heroes and bards,
They refuse to awake at the touch of any man but me.

It is I, you women, I make my way,   25
I am stern, acrid, large, undissuadable, but I love you,
I do not hurt you any more than is necessary for you,
I pour the stuff to start sons and daughters fit for these States,
    I press with slow rude muscle,
I brace myself effectually, I listen to no entreaties,
I dare not withdraw till I deposit what has so long accumulated   30
    within me.

Through you I drain the pent-up rivers of myself,
In you I wrap a thousand onward years,
On you I graft the grafts of the best-beloved of me and
    America,
The drops I distil upon you shall grow fierce and athletic girls,
    new artists, musicians, and singers,
The babes I beget upon you are to beget babes in their turn,   35
I shall demand perfect men and women out of my love-
    spendings,
I shall expect them to interpenetrate with others, as I and you
    interpenetrate now,
I shall count on the fruits of the gushing showers of them, as
    I count on the fruits of the gushing showers I give now,
I shall look for loving crops from the birth, life, death,
    immortality, I plant so lovingly now.

THE QUESTION ANSWERED

William Blake (1757–1827)

What is it men in women do require?
The lineaments of Gratified Desire.
What is it women do in men require?
The lineaments of Gratified Desire.

TO EROS

Sappho (fl. ca. 600 B.C.)

You burn me.

TO EROS

Sappho

From all the offspring
of the earth and heaven
love is the most precious.

From *Greek Lyric Poetry* by Willis Barnstone. Copyright © 1962, 1967, by Willis Barnstone. Reprinted by permission of Schocken Books Inc.

US

Anne Sexton (1928–

I was wrapped in black
fur and white fur and
you undid me and then
you placed me in gold light
and then you crowned me,   5
while snow fell outside
the door in diagonal darts.
While a ten-inch snow
came down like stars
in small calcium fragments,   10
we were in our own bodies
(that room that will bury us)
and you were in my body
(that room that will outlive us)
and at first I rubbed your   15
feet dry with a towel
because I was your slave
and then you called me princess.
Princess!

Oh, then   20
I stood up in my gold skin
and I beat down the psalms
and I beat down the clothes
and you undid the bridle
and you undid the reins   25
and I undid the buttons,
the bones, the confusions,
the New England postcards,
the January ten-o'clock night,
and we rose up like wheat,   30
acre after acre of gold,
and we harvested,
we harvested.

SONNET 116

William Shakespeare (1564–1616)

Let me not to the marriage of true minds
Admit impediments.° Love is not love
Which alters when it alteration finds,
Or bends with the remover° to remove:
O, no! it is an ever-fixèd mark,°   5
That looks on tempests and is never shaken;
It is the star to every wand'ring bark,
Whose worth's unknown, although his height be taken.°
Love's not Time's fool,° though rosy lips and cheeks
Within his bending sickle's compass° come;   10
Love alters not with his brief hours and weeks,
But bears it out even to the edge of doom:—
If this be error and upon me proved,
I never writ, nor no man ever loved.

WEDDING PROCESSION FROM A WINDOW

James A. Emanuel (1921–   )

Together, we looked down
When the young horns blared.
We saw glassed-in grins,
Flippant ribbons,
Tough tin cans,   5
The bridal pair.

We looked down
The corridor of the years
And saw the wreckage,
Tough little monuments   10
To the Paradise that seldom was.
(Yet our fingers lightly touched.)

°*Let . . . impediments*: recalls the marriage service in the Book of Common Prayer:
"If any of you know cause or just impediment"   °*remover*: the inconstant one
°*mark*: sea-mark   °*whose . . . taken*: i.e., the make-up of a star is unknown, but
its distance (*height*) can be determined °*fool*: dupe °*within . . . compass*: i.e.,
within the range the sickle can cut

From *The Treehouse and Other Poems* by James Emanuel. Copyright © 1968 by
James Emanuel. Reprinted by permission of Broadside Press.

The Two looked up.
As if from Eden
They waved. Our hands remembered.   15
And the tough, young horns
Blared flippantly
Farewell.

MOST LIKE AN ARCH
THIS MARRIAGE

John Ciardi (1916–   )

Most like an arch—an entrance which upholds
and shores the stone-crush up the air like lace.
Mass made idea, and idea held in place.
A lock in time. Inside half-heaven unfolds.

Most like an arch—two weaknesses that lean   5
into a strength. Two fallings become firm.
Two joined abeyances become a term
naming the fact that teaches fact to mean.

Not quite that? Not much less. World as it is,
what's strong and separate falters. All I do   10
at piling stone on stone apart from you
is roofless around nothing. Till we kiss

I am no more than upright and unset.
It is by falling in and in we make
the all-bearing point, for one another's sake,   15
in faultless failing, raised by our own weight.

THE DAUGHTERS OF LOS

William Blake (1757–1827)

And in the North Gate, in the West of the North, toward
    Beulah,
Cathedron's Looms are builded, and Los's Furnaces in the
    South.
A wondrous golden Building immense with ornaments sublime
Is bright Cathedron's golden Hall, its Courts, Towers &
    Pinnacles.

From *I Marry You* by John Ciardi. Copyright 1958 by Rutgers, the State University.
Reprinted by permission of the author.

And one Daughter of Los sat at the fiery Reel, & another   5
Sat at the shining Loom with her Sisters attending round,
Terrible their distress, & their sorrow cannot be utter'd;
And another Daughter of Los sat at the Spinning Wheel,
Endless their labour, with bitter food, void of sleep;
Tho' hungry, they labour: they rouse themselves anxious   10
Hour after hour labouring at the whirling Wheel,
Many Wheels & as many lovely Daughters sit weeping.

Yet the intoxicating delight that they take in their work
Obliterates every other evil; none pities their tears,
Yet they regard not pity & they expect no one to pity,   15
For they labour for life & love regardless of any one
But the poor Spectres that they work for always, incessantly.

They are mock'd by every one that passes by; they regard not,
They labour, & when their Wheels are broken by scorn & malice
They mend them sorrowing with many tears & afflictions.   20

Other Daughters Weave on the Cushion & Pillow Network fine
That Rahab & Tirzah may exist & live & breathe & love.
Ah, that it could be as the Daughters of Beulah wish!

Other Daughters of Los, labouring at Looms less fine,
Create the Silk-worm & the Spider & the Catterpiller   25
To asist in their most grievous work of pity & compassion;
And others Create the wooly Lamb & the downy Fowl
To assist in the work; the Lamb bleats, the Sea-fowl cries:
Men understand not the distress & the labour & sorrow
That in the Interior Worlds is carried on in fear & trembling,   30
Weaving the shudd'ring fears & loves of Albion's Families.
Thunderous rage the Spindles of iron, & the iron Distaff
Maddens in the fury of their hands, weaving in bitter tears
The Veil of Goats-hair & Purple & Scarlet & fine twined Linen.

MICHAEL ROBARTES AND THE DANCER

William Butler Yeats (1865–1939)

He.   Opinion is not worth a rush;
         In this altar-piece the knight,

Who grips his long spear so to push
That dragon through the fading light,
Loved the lady; and it's plain   5
The half-dead dragon was her thought,
That every morning rose again
And dug its claws and shrieked and fought.
Could the impossible come to pass
She would have time to turn her eyes,   10
Her lover thought, upon the glass
And on the instant would grow wise.

She.   You mean they argued.

He.   Put it so;
But bear in mind your lover's wage
Is what your looking-glass can show,   15
And that he will turn green with rage
At all that is not pictured there.

She.   May I not put myself to college?

He.   Go pluck Athene by the hair;
For what mere book can grant a knowledge   20
With an impassioned gravity
Appropriate to that beating breast,
That vigorous thigh, that dreaming eye?
And may the Devil take the rest.

She.   And must no beautiful woman be   25
Learned like a man?

He.   Paul Veronese°
And all his sacred company
Imagined bodies all their days
By the lagoon you love so much,
For proud, soft, ceremonious proof   30
That all must come to sight and touch;
While Michael Angelo's Sistine roof,
His 'Morning' and his 'Night' disclose

° *Veronese*: Venetian painter (1528-1588); the point Yeats is making is that Michael-
angelo and Veronese and "all his sacred company"/"Imagined bodies all their days,"
i.e., were concerned with flesh-and-blood reality and not with the kind of "education" that comes from books.

How sinew that has been pulled tight,
Or it may be loosened in repose,   35
Can rule by supernatural right
Yet be but sinew.

She.   I have heard said
There is great danger in the body.

He.   Did God in portioning wine and bread
Give man His thought or His mere body?   40

She.   My wretched dragon is perplexed.

He.   I have principles to prove me right.
It follows from this Latin text
That blest souls are not composite,
And that all beautiful women may   45
Live in uncomposite blessedness,
And lead us to the like—if they
Will banish every thought, unless
The lineaments that please their view
When the long looking-glass is full,   50
Even from the foot-sole think it too.

She.   They say such different things at school.

A DIALOGUE OF ELF AND MOLE

(For Yeats's Unmirrored Daughter)

Barbara Warren (1947–   )

MOLE: You must accept my world and all that's in it.
When will you cease your childish rage
and be the linnet?

ELF: Stay locked in Logos worlds of Sin!
Knock on my door some drunken night,   5
you'll not get in.

MOLE: I'll answer all your doubts, just talk to me.
I'll root you yet in that Eternal Tree.

ELF: A woman's thoughts remind all men of Age.
They clutch their crutch and fear The End.   10

MOLE: Why won't you rest within my mind?
       I love you for your earth, not sky.

ELF: I'll uproot trees, hurl down your Prince's star,
       because I am my 'I' and not your 'She.'

MOLE: Why rave that tongueless beauty is a lie?   15
       You're but a slave to your idea of free.

ELF: Your very words entangle you
       and hang you from that tree.
       As long as you believe your will,
       you can't grow real with me.   20

MOLE: But you're mere body with a heart,
       while I'm a heart with mind.
       You do not need to understand,
       just kiss me and be kind.

ELF: Kiss your own Mother's lips and sigh!   25
       My Self transfigures Earth and Sky.

MOLE: Why doubt your body is sublime?

ELF: Why judge complexity a crime?
       You'd have me just inspire the verse,
       but I will write the rhyme.   30

FOR WITCHES

Susan Sutheim

today
i lost my temper.

temper, when one talks of metal
means make strong,
perfect.   5

temper, for humans, means angry
irrational
bad.

From *Women: A Journal of Liberation* (Fall, 1969). Reprinted with permission.

today i found my temper.
i said,   10
you step on my head
for 27 years you step on my head
and though i have been trained
to excuse you for your inevitable
clumsiness   15
today i think
i prefer my head to your clumsiness.

today i began
to find
myself.   20

tomorrow
perhaps
i will begin
to find
you.   25

"IN TROUBLE"

Jane Harriman (1940–   )

There was a cold heaviness reeling inside me. If it was an illness, it would be fatal because it was stronger and more powerful than I could ever be. When sleep was less urgent, I would face it. Two weeks later, it was worse. I could no longer eat. The floor was bubbling, sometimes buckling dangerously. And I was scared, terribly scared, until one morning I dreamt a formless sort of warmth, a love without fear or sadness. When I awoke, I was reassured enough to go to a doctor. On the way to his office I prepared a list of symptoms. However, when I began to speak to him and stared at the desk-top photograph of his pig-tailed daughters, I diagnosed what I was only simultaneously ready to face: "I'm pregnant."

He questioned and considered: "Nonsense. Highly unlikely." He prodded and peered: "Possible." He tested: "Yes, about nine weeks. Where's the father? No chance of marriage? What are you going to do?"

"Have a baby. Become a mother, I suppose."

"You should think about abortion, adoption. There are alternatives."

But actually, there were no alternatives for me. After years of thinking that I believed in abortion, I was mortally afraid when it was more than a word to me. I felt that what was inside me was not an embryo or a fetus but the essence of life itself. The spark of human existence was demanding that my body clothe it in tissue that it might be born. If I fought that spark, or allowed anyone to put it out, I would be destroyed in a most complete and terrifying way.

So I was going to become an unwed mother. But surely not in the traditional sense of the young, helpless girl cast away in the blizzard, "in trouble." I was twenty-seven years old, and had worked for a metropolitan newspaper for six years. Although my father was dead and there was no money in the immediate family, I was earning $10,000 a year and was dependent on no one. Of course, it would be embarrassing, and it would perhaps be emotionally difficult, but I was too well schooled in the Christian ethic—all worthwhile things are difficult, you must stand up to life's challenges—to let that faze me.

Gradually, I became more and more excited about the idea of having a baby. As I thought about it I realized it was the one thing I'd always wanted. My reservations had been about marriage. And unless I came to view marriage with less fear, my child would have only one parent. This was a handicap, but a fairly common one. I had always had lots of men in my life, and there was no reason to expect this to change. The child would have male role models.

The child would be illegitimate (the father was neither available, nor on the evidence, likely to be), but what did that mean? It meant the parents had done something illegal, not the child. I would say to it: "Most women are married when they have a baby, most, but not all. I was not married when I had you. And I had to decide whether to give you away to a married couple or to keep you myself. Some people thought it would be better for you if I gave you away so you could have a mother *and* a father. But I just loved you too much. I wanted you to live with me, your real mother, and I hoped we would have a good life together until you grew up."

At the end of my fourth month, the only people who knew I was pregnant were the baby's father, my physician, my obstetrician, my sister, and a psychiatrist I had consulted to make sure I was doing the right thing. Soon I would look pregnant, and so when opportunities arose, I would begin to tell people. I was confident and optimistic. And naive. I had no idea of how vulnerable I had made myself by following the course I had to.

A great many people assumed that I hoped they would refer me to an abortionist. "But I'm four months pregnant!" "OK. Good-bye." An hour later the telephone would ring and yet another name and *modus operandi* would be presented: a doctor in San Juan; a chiropractor in New Jersey; a med school dropout who made house calls in Cambridge.

I began to think of going away to a place where I could gestate in peace, a place where there would be no negative vibrations toward the baby, where I would be free to work things out inside myself without embarrassing or endangering anyone. If I could get a leave of absence from my job, I would go to England on my vacation and stay on for a while. When I came back with a giant belly or a baby, no one could nag me about abortion.

I asked one of the executives if I could have a leave of absence, saying, I wanted to do some free-lance work from England and I would need the money. I wanted very much to come back to work in four or five months. He thought this was possible, although they'd regret losing me for that long a time. Yes, of course. What was I planning to do?

"Have a baby, actually."

This, he said, changed the picture somewhat. He would have to talk it over with one of the other executives.

That night he telephoned me at home. I was not going to get married? Would I consider having an abortion?—a friend of theirs had gone to Sweden. Would I consider giving the baby up for adoption? No? In that case, he was sorry but I was fired. I could have my vacation pay, and I could probably collect unemployment insurance. I offered to announce a phony marriage to a Vietnam serviceman. No. I was still fired.

Unfortunately, there was no newspaper guild to which I could appeal. White-collar employees were covered by an employees' association whose principal function was to sponsor annual picnics and bowling leagues. The contract it had agreed to allowed employees to be fired without cause and specified that severance pay did not have to be given in the case of "gross personal misconduct" (that was me). Apparently, I had been too quick to laugh when people had said, "You won't be able to support a baby without a husband."

When I hired a lawyer, the newspaper agreed to let me resign and to give me about as much severance pay as I would have received from several months of unemployment conpensation. It also arranged a partial compensation for the medical expenses I found would not be covered by my health insurance plan. (I'd have been protected if injured robbing a bank, or driving while drunk, but unwed mothers, manifestly, fall into a forbidden category.)

The State Division of Employment Security suggested that I try temporary office work until my seventh month, when, as I recall, I could no longer work legally. With my two-fingered typing, I was unlikely to realize a financial windfall through that, so I set about relearning to type. But it was ridiculous. I could not possibly earn enough money to stay in my apartment, or even pay for another one in the Boston area. Life in England was less costly. I would certainly earn enough money there to support myself. My severance pay would cover the time between delivery and re-employment.

Before I risked the cost of a round-trip ticket to England, however, I thought I should protect myself against unforeseen disaster. My only male relative was an uncle to whom I had felt very close before he had retired to live in the Caribbean. When he flew into town for a week, I told him about my pregnancy and asked if he would, in the case of an emergency, be willing to lend me some money. He was amazingly supportive. He was proud of the way I was handling a difficult situation. Of course he'd help. He was a man of considerable means. He wanted to write me a check then and there.

"No, thank you," I said, "I'm taking on a responsibility, and I think I should prove myself capable of it."

The next day he had changed his mind. He'd talked it over with his wife and the best course for me was to have a Caesarean abortion. Their old friend, a Boston gynecologist, had agreed, patient unseen, to perform it.

I refused.

"Well, I think you're making a mistake, but that doesn't change anything. I'll still help you in any way you want," he said.

The day I was to leave the country, he telephoned long distance. I hadn't been to see his friend, the gynecologist.

"'You won't take the mature and reasonable course. I am afraid I have nothing more to say to you, and you can forget about asking me for help, ever."

"Tell her you won't support the baby, either," his wife urged in the background.

I hung up, and my mind snapped off. I was tired down to my bone marrow. The new tenants and their furniture would fill my empty apartment at any minute. I was going thousands of miles away to a strange land, where I knew two people. But I was leaving nothing, as it had turned out. I pressed my hands into the dusty linoleum of the floor until I was very quiet, and then I called the baby's father.

"You're being very weak, chickening out," he said: "I think going is the best thing for you. I'll write to you; I've already arranged to send you money."

I believed him. For the first time in two years, I trusted him completely. He was good and strong and he'd never abandon me. I felt quite happy as I dragged my suitcase down the subway steps toward the airport.

Eight months later he stood up in a crowded courtroom, glanced nervously in my direction, and pleaded "not guilty" in my paternity suit.

I came back six weeks before the baby was due. London had been humane but grim. Earning 5 shillings an hour as a typist, I had just enough money to cover my living expenses. There would be a few weeks following the baby's birth when I could not go out to work every day, and it seemed best to find a way to live for free then.

My sister had a one-room apartment, and I shared her single bed while I looked for a situation where I could earn my room and board. No employment agency could help, and the Massachusetts Bay United Fund referred me to the Florence Crittenton League's shelter for "girls in trouble."

The Crittenton assured me that it encouraged girls to make their own decisions about what they would do with their babies. But that decision is almost always to give them up for adoption. In fact, girls who are fairly sure they will keep their babies are discouraged from entering the home. They are judged to be too emotionally disturbed, or too much of a threat to the smooth group proccesses.

A social worker spent several hours telling me why I could not keep my baby. I would never find a baby-sitter. I was being selfish: I wanted the baby to make up for my lonely, empty life (no husband). If I had normal, healthy maternal feelings, I would come to want what was best for the baby—adoption. She then got down to practicalities: the Crittenton rate was $100 a week (as I recall), plus $500 for the delivery. No matter what I claimed, the health insurance policy would not cover the medical expenses, she said, and she would have to have the $500 in advance. She figured, I guess, that the type of client she attracted might flee while the sheets were still warm.

A stay in the Crittenton would not leave me penniless; it would leave me in debt, and out of work, with an infant to support.

"Well," she said, "you may decide that the responsible thing to do is to give up your baby. It takes some courage, but most of our girls find it."

When I decided not to enter the Crittenton, its social worker referred me to a nurse who would give me room and board in exchange for helping her get dressed and bathed. She had a broken leg.

In addition to helping her, the invalid explained, I would be expected to keep the seven-room house clean, atttend to her husband's laundry, and prepare three meals a day. I didn't have to wear a maid's uniform, a plain, dark dress and apron would be enough, and I would please wear a hairnet (over my Joan of Arc hairdo). She understood, she told me, that girls like me weren't bad, they had made a bad mistake. And usually, she found, it didn't show in the children. Her son and his wife had been forced to adopt "two of them," infant girls, and honestly, to look at them today you'd never suspect there was anything wrong or unusual about them.

I next visited a university professor who was looking for cook-typist. Just supper, and four or five hours of typing a day. A nice room for me, with a desk and books. I was leaving to get my suitcase, when he grabbed me: "Why not? You are already pregnant."

I finally found much more acceptable arrangements, which were generous enough to leave my days pretty much free. A minister also got me a typing job in an office in Boston, and I worked until the day the baby was born.

But I was not yet through with the Crittenton social worker. She gave me the name of a community service organization in Cambridge which would make day-care arrangements for me. The social worker there sang the old adoption song. A slightly new ending was that she'd take care of everything to do with the adoption for only $125.

When she was apparently convinced that I was going to keep my baby, she discussed my psychological responsibilities. It would be very harmful to the baby to go home from the hospital with me and stay with me for several weeks before beginning a day-care routine. Trust would be established and then broken at the tender age of one month. It would be much better for me not to see the baby until I was completely settled in a new job, and could send for it, if I still wanted to. (Apparently the trust which would be established between the "wonderfully warm" foster-home mother and my baby could be broken with no ill effects, or with less harm than would be caused by the disruption of *my* full-time presence.)

For an hour or so I answered questions about my family, life, and health record. When I could not tell her a great deal about the baby's paternal grandparents, she asked to interview the father. I really thought that was unnecessary. It seems amazing that I did not wonder why such detailed information was necessary to find good day care. But I did not. I suppose I still believed that helping agencies were in business only to help those in need.

A week later she telephoned me to say she was sorry, but she'd "forgotten"—her agency had not been making any day-care arrangements for years; in fact, it was philosophically opposed to the idea. She didn't want to leave me in the lurch, though. She had found an excellent adoptive home, if I'd reconsider. I hung up, and fortunately my fury and panic were soon interrupted by the sudden onset of labor.

My baby was born at the Boston Lying-In. I watched in overhead mirrors as the intern (who had told me I was too whimsical to be a mother) guided a tiny head, bleating like a lamb, into the world. It was healthy. It was a boy. It was really all right. It squinted its dark eyes and glared at me. What was it? Where had it come from? That wasn't the thing that had been tapping out messages inside me for so long. Where was my baby? I hoped I didn't have to hold that thing, I was too tired.

About seventy-two hours later, a nurse woke me up, as usual, at one in the morning. She had the shrieking, thrashing, furious red lizard in her arms. "He's really hungry this morning," she said.

I took hold of it, and it sunk its gums ravenously into my breast. I screamed, and then burst into tears of joy. He was a separate human being, strong, savage, completely untamed. He was ruthlessly taking what he had to have to survive. He was unafraid and unawed by me or anyone. Oh, little baby, how glad I am to meet you.

In the fall, I accepted a writing job at a research and consulting firm which prides itself on its liberalism. I made no mention of marital status or child when I applied for work, and when the company discovered, after several months, that I had a child, the question seemed academic.

While the unwed mother has to assume almost complete responsibility for her child, society does not really consider her a responsible adult. To give an example, in order to get life insurance, I was told by the salesman that I had to lie and call myself "divorced." Also, the first diaper service I called asked my husband's name, and then, after I said "unmarried," would not accept me as a customer. When I called a second service, I said, with a catch in my voice, "Wid-dowed." The diapers were delivered that day.

Contrary to the social workers' predictions, I had no trouble whatsoever finding a marvelous, intelligent, affectionate baby-sitter who genuinely loves and respects children. She is part of a large, closely knit, happy family. David spends his days in her house with grandparents, parents, aunts, uncles, brothers, and sisters. He gets sunshine and fresh air and home-grown fruits and vegetables. He also has a natural mother who is very happy to be with him every morning and evening.

This day-care situation is expensive, however. It costs a quarter of my income, and I am always just making ends meet. I cannot remember the last time I bought red meat or owned more than one pair of shoes.

When I first began to look for child care, I called the State and was transferred from one agency to another. Finally a man in the Welfare Department explained to me that there was no day care available in Massachusetts for children under two. In fact, until very recently, it had been illegal. The General Court had finally seen its way to legalizing it, and calling for the establishment of licensing procedures. In its wisdom, however, the legislature had consistently failed to appropriate even the minimal funds required to inspect privately financed centers. In this situation, it was illegal for a woman to take in a baby for the day without having a license, and a license was unobtainable. He suggested that I come on the welfare rolls.

I had hoped that when I went back to work as a writer, when summer was over and David was settled down, my social life would improve. It grew worse. There is not much room in society for a single woman, particularly one with a child.

Before, I had had lots of friends, but they were men. A few men seemed willing to accept me, but I did not want them. I had a full-time job, a small household to run, and a baby to care for. David and I continually traded respiratory infections. I was simply too tired to play games with men, to sit, drink in hand, eyelashes fluttering, listening, far into the night. I needed friendship and exchange, not an additional demand. I had, in conventional terms, nothing to give a man.

I absorbed everyone's feelings and reactions toward unmarried mothers. At best, these feelings were ones of curiosity and timid identification: "What was it like, all alone? Dreadful? You know my husband never really shared . . ."

The more liberal and the more compassionate reacted, after reflection, "You're so brave." Such comments did not in any way boost my spirits; rather they affirmed the existence of the opposition and condemnation I already felt. I didn't want to be brave. I simply wanted to be—without comment or judgment.

When I began to suffer crying fits of unknown origin, I sought professional help. Because I could not afford psychotherapy, I went to a Family Service agency. I was referred to a social worker who specialized in unmarried mothers. Her orientation was strongly toward adoption. (I couldn't believe it—my baby was more than a year old!) Yes, she did counsel a few women who kept their babies. I asked if her agency would sponsor a group of unmarried mothers in therapy or at least regular discussions. I felt we could lend one another support and begin to work out solutions to mutual problems. She discussed the idea with her supervisors: no, the agency did not think it was a good idea.

But I did. I wrote an advertisement: "UNWED MOTHERS. Same wants to meet you. Object, mutual support and aid." None of the above-ground newspapers would carry it.

Parents Without Partners mailed me material which asked if the recipient were divorced, widowed, or separated: I telephoned and asked if unmarried parents were eligible. "I wouldn't think so, would you?" a woman said. I didn't pursue the question any further because the organization was so blatantly dedicated to remarriage. (Its pamphlet was decorated with a waltzing couple. Several dozen events were listed for the month, only one of which was of a nonsocial nature—a lecture on "Your Teen-ager," or something along that line. The first meeting I could have attended was a "happy hour" in the cocktail lounge of Sammy White's Brighton Bowl.) I note, with interest, that PWP's current literature welcomes as members parents who have "never married."

My needs—to talk about my experiences with someone who would listen, to regain a sense of self-respect and a sense of my worthiness as a human being, to feel myself an accepted member of some segment of society—would not be met by any kind of mating game with which I was familiar.

A friend gave me some literature on Women's Liberation. I read a few paragraphs and tossed it aside: "Lesbian anarchists." Several hours later, I fished it out of the trash. The language was extreme, but the message was true and not entirely new to me.

(I had read *The Golden Notebook* and *The Second Sex* and *A Room of One's Own*. I had searched for five years to find a psychiatrist who would not urge me to get married at the end of the initial interview, but would yell at me, "You're a woman, sure, but goddamnit, you're a human being. Why don't you act like one?")

I went to a Women's Liberation meeting. It was run along the lines of Alcoholics Anonymous—everyone told something about her own life. After I spoke, a woman next to me murmured, "You kept the baby! Good for you." But that was the only reaction I perceived.

I joined a group of a dozen women, and for almost a year we have met once a week to discuss our lives, past and present, and our future role as women in the world, as well as in the home. None of us hates men, none of us wants to live a life without men. We feel that we have been oppressed by society and by our own attitudes. We recognize that men are often as oppressed as women, if not more so. And children are the most oppressed of all. In a technological society, there is no need for strongly defined sexual roles—in fact to say that a man must be aggressive and competitive, and a woman must stay at home and cook frozen foods, is more than arbitrary, it is barbarous.

I hope that someday I will meet a man who is sure enough of his own identity and his own sex to love me as an equal human being, and participate in all facets of the life we build within the community. I hope to find a man who feels, as I do, that children are not extensions of your body and soul, but individual human beings lent you for a few years to cherish and enjoy, while you are guiding them toward an early liberation.

I think of David and the delight people take in him: "I've never seen such a happy child, so loving and outgoing. I can't get over it; he has some strange power."

I look at him, and of course he wears a halo because he and I have shared much laughter and love and anger and tears.

But why does he look special to other people? Do they expect a "bastard" to be ugly and miserable? Perhaps. I like to think, however, that they unconsciously expect something unusual of a child born in ancient symbolism, outside of wed*lock,* a happy, healthy child, conceived and carried and born in independence and freedom from the constraints of society. A child whose existence and whose nature have today—as at all times—the power to begin to change the world once more.

From A ROOM OF ONE'S OWN

Virginia Woolf (1882–1941)

CHAPTER SIX

Next day the light of the October morning was falling in dusty shafts through the uncurtained windows, and the hum of traffic rose from the street. London then was winding itself up again; the factory was astir; the machines were beginning. It was tempting, after all this reading, to look out of the window and see what London was doing on the morning of the twenty-sixth of October 1928. And what was London doing? Nobody, it seemed, was reading *Antony and Cleopatra*. London was wholly indifferent, it appeared, to Shakespeare's plays. Nobody cared a straw—and I do not blame them—for the future of fiction, the death of poetry or the development by the average woman of a prose style completely expressive of her mind. If opinions upon any of these matters had been chalked on the pavement, nobody would have stooped to read them. The nonchalance of the hurrying feet would have rubbed them out in half an hour. Here came an errand-boy; here a woman with a dog on a lead. The fascination of the London street is that no two people are ever alike; each seems bound on some private affair of his own. There were the business-like, with their little bags; there were the drifters rattling sticks upon area railings; there were affable characters to whom the streets serve for clubroom, hailing men in carts and giving information without being asked for it. Also there were funerals to which men, thus suddenly reminded of the passing of their own bodies, lifted their hats. And then a very distinguished gentleman came slowly down a doorstep and paused to avoid collision with a bustling lady who had, by some means or other, acquired a splendid fur coat and a bunch of Parma violets. They all seemed separate, self-absorbed, on business of their own.

At this moment, as so often happens in London, there was a complete lull and suspension of traffic. Nothing came down the street; nobody passed. A single leaf detached itself from the plane tree at the end of the street, and in that pause and suspension fell. Somehow it was like a signal falling, a signal pointing to a force in things which one had overlooked. It seemed to point to a river, which flowed past, invisibly, round the corner, down the street, and took people and eddied them along, as the stream at Oxbridge had taken the undergraduate in his boat and the dead leaves. Now it was bringing from one side of the street to the other diagonally a girl in patent leather boots, and then a young man in a maroon overcoat; it was also bringing a taxi-cab; and it brought all three together at a point directly beneath my window; where the taxi stopped; and the girl and the young man stopped; and they got into the taxi; and then the cab glided off as if it were swept on by the current elsewhere.

The sight was ordinary enough; what was strange was the rhythmical order with which my imagination had invested it; and the fact that the ordinary sight of two people getting into a cab had the power to communicate something of their own seeming satisfaction. The sight of two people coming down the street and meeting at the corner seems to ease the mind of some strain, I thought, watching the taxi turn and make off. Perhaps to think, as I had been thinking these two days, of one sex as distinct from the other is an effort. It interferes with the unity of the mind. Now that effort had ceased and that unity had been restored by seeing two people come together and get into a taxi-cab. The mind is certainly a very mysterious organ, I reflected, drawing my head in from the window, about which nothing whatever is known, though we depend upon it so completely. Why do I feel that there are severances and oppositions in the mind, as there are strains from obvious causes on the body? What does one mean by "the unity of the mind," I pondered, for clearly the mind has so great a power of concentrating at any point at any moment that it seems to have no single state of being. It can separate itself from the people in the street, for example, and think of itself as apart from them, at an upper window looking down on them. Or it can think with other people spontaneously, as, for instance, in a crowd waiting to hear some piece of news read out. It can think back through its fathers or through its mothers, as I have said that a woman writing thinks back through her mothers. Again if one is a woman one is often surprised by a sudden splitting off of consciousness, say in walking down Whitehall, when from being the natural inheritor of that civilisation, she becomes, on the contrary, outside of it, alien and critical. Clearly the mind is always altering its focus, and bringing the world into different perspectives. But some of these states of mind seem, even if adopted spontaneously, to be less comfortable than others. In order to keep oneself continuing in them one is unconsciously holding something back, and gradually the repression becomes an effort. But there may be some state of mind in which one could continue without effort because nothing is required to be held back. And this perhaps, I thought, coming in from the window, is one of them. For certainly when I saw the couple get into the taxi-cab the mind felt as if, after being divided, it had come together again in a natural fusion. The obvious reason would be that it is natural for the sexes to co-operate. One has a profound, if irrational, instinct in favour of the theory that the union of man and woman makes for the greatest satisfaction, the most complete happiness. But the sight of the two people getting into the taxi and the satisfaction it gave me made me also ask whether there are two sexes in the mind corresponding to the two sexes in the body, and whether they also require to be united in order to get complete satisfaction and happiness. And I went on amateurishly to sketch a plan of the soul so that in each of us two powers preside, one male, one female; and in the man's brain, the man predominates over the woman, and in the woman's brain, the woman predominates over the man. The normal and comfortable state of being is that when the two live in harmony together, spiritually cooperating. If one is a man, still the woman part of the brain must have effect; and a woman also must have intercourse with the man in her. Coleridge perhaps meant this when he said that a great mind is androgynous. It is when this fusion takes place that the mind is fully fertilised and uses all its faculties. Perhaps a mind that is purely masculine cannot create, any more than a mind that is purely feminine, I thought. But it would be well to test what one meant by man-womanly, and conversely by woman-manly, by pausing and looking at a book or two.

Coleridge certainly did not mean, when he said that a great mind is androgynous, that it is a mind that has any special sympathy with women; a mind that takes up their cause or devotes itself to their interpretation. Perhaps the androgynous mind is less apt to make these distinctions than the single-sexed mind. He meant, perhaps, that the androgynous mind is resonant and porous; that it transmits emotion without impediment; that it is naturally creative, incandesecnt and undivided. In fact one goes back to Shakespeare's mind as the type of the androgynous, of the man-womanly mind, though it would be impossible to say what Shakespeare thought of women. And if it be true that it is one of the tokens of the fully developed mind that it does not think specially or separately of sex, how much harder it is to attain that condition now than ever before. Here I came to the books by living writers, and there paused and wondered if this fact were not at the root of something that had long puzzled me. No age can ever have been as stridently sex-conscious as our own; those innumerable books by men about women in the British Museum are a proof of it. The Suffrage campaign was no doubt to blame. It must have roused in men an extraordinary desire for self-assertion; it must have made them lay an emphasis upon their own sex and its characteristics which they would not have troubled to think about had they not been challenged. And when one is challenged, even by a few women in black bonnets, one retaliates, if one has never been challenged before, rather excessively. That perhaps accounts for some of the characteristics that I remember to have found here, I thought, taking down a new novel by Mr. A, who is in the prime of life and very well thought of, apparently, by the reviewers. I opened it. Indeed, it was delightful to read a man's writing again. It was so direct, so straightforward after the writing of women. It indicated such freedom of mind, such liberty of person, such confidence in himself. One had a sense of physical well-being in the presence of this well-nourished, well-educated, free mind, which had never been thwarted or opposed, but had had full liberty from birth to stretch itself in whatever way it liked. All this was admirable. But after reading a chapter or two a shadow seemed to lie across the page. It was a straight dark bar, a shadow shaped something like the letter "I." One began dodging this way and that to catch a glimpse of the landscape behind it. Whether that was indeed a tree or a woman walking I was not quite sure. Back one was always hailed to the letter "I." One began to be tired of "I." Not but what this "I" was a most respectable "I"; honest and logical; as hard as a nut, and polished for centuries by good teaching and good feeding. I respect and admire that "I" from the bottom of my heart. But—here I turned a page or two, looking for something or other—the worst of it is that in the shadow of the letter "I" all is shapeless as mist. Is that a tree? No, it is a woman. But . . . she has not a bone in her body, I thought, watching Phoebe, for that was her name, coming across the beach. Then Alan got up and the shadow of Alan at once obliterated Phoebe. For Alan had views and Phoebe was quenched in the flood of his views. And then Alan, I thought, has passions; and here I turned page after page very fast, feeling that the crisis was approaching, and so it was. It took place on the beach under the sun. It was done very openly. It was done very vigorously. Nothing could have been more indecent. But . . . I had said "but" too often. One cannot go on saying "but." One must finish the sentence somehow, I rebuked myself. Shall I finish it, "But—I am bored!" But why was I bored? Partly because of the dominance of the letter "I" and the aridity, which, like the giant beech tree, it casts within its shade. Nothing will grow there. And partly for some more obscure reason. There seemed to be some obstacle, some impediment of Mr. A's mind which blocked the fountain of creative energy and shored it within narrow limits. And remembering the lunch party at Oxbridge, and the cigarette ash and the Manx cat and Tennyson and Christina Rossetti all in a bunch, it seemed possible that the impediment lay there. As he no longer hums under his breath, "There has fallen a splended tear from the passion-flower at the gate," when Phoebe crosses the beach, and she no longer replies, "My heart is like a singing bird whose nest is in a water'd shoot," when Alan approaches what can he do? Being honest as the day and logical as the sun, there is only one thing he can do. And that he does, to do him justice, over and over (I said, turning the pages) and over again. And that, I added, aware of the awful nature of the confession, seems somehow dull. Shakespeare's indecency uproots a thousand other things in one's mind, and is far from being dull. But Shakespeare does it for pleasure; Mr. A, as the nurses say, does it on purpose. He does it in protest. He is protesting against the equality of the other sex by asserting his own superiority. He is therefore impeded and inhibited and self-conscious as Shakespeare might have been if he too had known Miss Clough and Miss Davies. Doubtless Elizabethan literature would have been very different from what it is if the woman's movement had begun in the sixteenth century and not in the nineteenth.

What, then, it amounts to, if this theory of the two sides of the mind holds good, is that virility has now become self-conscious—men, that is to say, are now writing only with the male side of their brains. It is a mistake for a woman to read them, for she will inevitably look for something that she will not find. It is the power of suggestion that one most misses, I thought, taking Mr. B the critic in my hand and reading, very carefully and very dutifully, his remarks upon the art of poetry. Very able they were, acute and full of learning; but the trouble was, that his feelings no longer communicated; his mind seemed separated into different chambers; not a sound carried from one to the other. Thus, when one takes a sentence of Mr. B into the mind it falls plump to the ground—dead; but when one takes a sentence of Coleridge into the mind, it explodes and gives birth to all kinds of other ideas, and that is the only sort of writing of which one can say that it has the secret of perpetual life.

But whatever the reason may be, it is a fact that one must deplore. For it means—here I had come to rows of books by Mr. Galsworthy and Mr. Kipling—that some of the finest works of our greatest living writers fall upon deaf ears. Do what she will a woman cannot find in them that fountain of perpetual life which the critics assure her is there. It is not only that they celebrate male virtues, enforce male values and describe the world of men; it is that the emotion with which these books are permeated is to a woman incomprehensible. It is coming, it is gathering, it is about to burst on one's head, one begins saying long before the end. That picture will fall on old Jolyon's head; he will die of the shock; the old clerk will speak over him two or three obituary words; and all the swans on the Thames will simultaneously burst out singing. But one will rush away before that happens and hide in the gooseberry bushes, for the emotion which is so deep, so subtle, so symbolical to a man moves a woman to wonder. So with Mr. Kipling's officers who turn their backs; and his Sowers who sow the Seed; and his Men who are alone with their Work; and the Flag—one blushes at all these capital letters as if one had been caught eavesdropping at some purely masculine orgy. The fact is that neither Mr. Galsworthy nor Mr. Kipling has a spark of the woman in him. Thus all their qualities seem to a woman, if one may generalise, crude and immature. They lack suggestive power. And when a book lacks suggestive power, however hard it hits the surface of the mind it cannot penetrate within.

And in that restless mood in which one takes books out and puts them back again without looking at them I began to envisage an age to come of pure, of self-assertive virility, such as the letters of professors (take Sir Walter Raleigh's letters, for instance) seem to forebode, and the rulers of Italy have already brought into being. For one can hardly fail to be impressed in Rome by the sense of unmitigated masculinity; and whatever the value of unmitigated masculinity upon the state, one may question the effect of it upon the art of poetry. At any rate, according to the newspapers, there is a certain anxiety about fiction in Italy. There has been a meeting of academicians whose object it is "to develop the Italian novel." "Men famous by birth, or in finance, industry or the Fascist corporations" came together the other day and discussed the matter, and a telegram was sent to the Duce expressing the hope "that the Fascist era would soon give birth to a poet worthy of it." We may all join in that pious hope, but it is doubtful whether poetry can come out of an incubator. Poetry ought to have a mother as well as a father. The Fascist poem, one may fear, will be a horrid little abortion such as one sees in a glass jar in the museum of some county town. Such monsters never live long, it is said; one has never seen a prodigy of that sort cropping grass in a field. Two heads on one body do not make for length of life.

However, the blame for all this, if one is anxious to lay blame, rests no more upon one sex than upon the other. All seducers and reformers are responsible, Lady Bessborough when she lied to Lord Granville; Miss Davies when she told the truth to Mr. Greg. All who have brought about a state of sex-consciousness are to blame, and it is they who drive me, when I want to stretch my faculties on a book, to seek it in that happy age, before Miss Davies and Miss Clough were born, when the writer used both sides of his mind equally. One must turn back to Shakespeare then, for Shakespeare was androgynous; and so was Keats and Sterne and Cowper and Lamb and Coleridge. Shelley perhaps was sexless. Milton and Ben Jonson had a dash too much of the male in them. So had Wordsworth and Tolstoi. In our time Proust was wholly androgynous, if not perhaps a little too much of a woman. But that failing is too rare for one to complain of it, since without some mixture of the kind the intellect seems to predominate and the other faculties of the mind harden and become barren. However, I consoled myself with the reflection that this is perhaps a passing phase; much of what I have said in obedience to my promise to give you the course of my thoughts will seem out of date; much of what flames in my eyes will seem dubious to you who have not yet come of age.

Even so, the very first sentence that I would write here, I said, crossing over to the writing-table and taking up the page headed Women and Fiction, is that it is fatal for any one who writes to think of their sex. It is fatal to be a man or woman pure and simple; one must be woman-manly or man-womanly. It is fatal for a woman to lay the least stress on any grievance; to plead even with justice any cause; in any way to speak consciously as a woman. And fatal is no figure of speech; for anything written with that conscious bias is doomed to death. It ceases to be fertilised. Brilliant and effective, powerful and masterly, as it may appear for a day or two, it must wither at nightfall; it cannot grow in the minds of others. Some collaboration has to take place in the mind between the woman and the man before the act of creation can be accomplished. Some marriage of opposites has to be consummated. The whole of the mind must lie wide open if we are to get the sense that the writer is communicating his experience with perfect fullness. There must be freedom and there must be peace. Not a wheel must grate, not a light glimmer. The curtains must be close drawn. The writer, I thought, once his experience is over, must lie back and let his mind celebrate its nuptials in darkness. He must not look or question what is being done. Rather, he must pluck the petals from a rose or watch the swans float calmly down the river. And I saw again the current which took the boat and the undergraduate and the dead leaves; and the taxi took the man and the woman, I thought, seeing them come together across the street, and the current swept them away, I thought, hearing far off the roar of London's traffic, into that tremendous stream.

Here, then, Mary Beton ceases to speak. She has told you how she reached the conclusion—the prosaic conclusion—that it is necessary to have five hundred a year and a room with a lock on the door if you are to write fiction or poetry. She has tried to lay bare the thoughts and impressions that led her to think this. She has asked you to follow her flying into the arms of a Beadle, lunching here, dining there, drawing pictures in the British Museum, taking books from the shelf, looking out of the window. While she has been doing all these things, you no doubt have been observing her failings and foibles and deciding what effect they have had on her opinions. You have ben contradicting her and making whatever additions and deductions seem good to you. That is all as it should be, for in a question like this truth is only to be had by laying together many varieties of error. And I will end now in my own person by anticipating two criticisms, so obvious that you can hardly fail to make them.

No opinion has been expressed, you may say, upon the comparative merits of the sexes even as writers. That was done purposely, because, even if the time had come for such a valuation—and it is far more important at the moment to know how much money women had and how many rooms than to theorise about their capacities—even if the time had come I do not believe that gifts, whether of mind or character, can be weighed like sugar and butter, not even in Cambridge, where they are so adept at putting people into classes and fixing caps on their heads and letters after their names. I do not believe that even the Table of Precedency which you will find in Whitaker's *Almanac* represents a final order of values, or that there is any sound reason to suppose that a Commander of the Bath will ultimately walk in to dinner behind a Master in Lunacy. All this pitting of sex against sex, of quality against quality; all this claiming of superiority and imputing of inferiority, belong to the private-school stage of human existence where there are "sides," and it is necessary for one side to beat another side, and of the utmost importance to walk up to a platform and receive from the hands of the Headmaster himself a highly ornamental pot. As people mature they cease to believe in sides or in Headmasters or in highly ornamental pots. At any rate, where books are concerned, it is notoriously difficult to fix labels of merit in such a way that they do not come off. Are not reviews of current literature a perpetual illustration of the difficulty of judgment? "This great book," "this worthless book," the same book is called by both names. Praise and blame alike mean nothing. No, delightful as the pastime of measuring may be, it is the most futile of all occupations, and to submit to the decrees of the measurers the most servile of attitudes. So long as you write what you wish to write, that is all that matters; and whether it matters for ages or only for hours, nobody can say. But to sacrifice a hair of the head of your vision, a shade of its colour, in deference to some Headmaster with a silver pot in his hand or to some professor with a measuring-rod up his sleeve, is the most abject treachery, and the sacrifice of wealth and chastity which used to be said to be the greatest of human disasters, a mere flea-bite in comparison.

Next I think that you may object that in all this I have made too much of the importance of material things. Even allowing a generous margin for symbolism, that five hundred a year stands for the power to contemplate, that a lock on the door means the power to think for oneself; still you may say that the mind should rise above such things; and that great poets have often been poor men. Let me then quote to you the words of your own Professor of Literature, who knows better than I do what goes to the making of a poet. Sir Arthur Quiller-Couch writes:[*]

"What are the great poetical names of the last hundred years or so? Coleridge, Wordsworth, Byron, Shelley, Landor, Keats, Tennyson,

---

[*] *The Art of Writing*, by Sir Arthur Quiller-Couch.

Browning, Arnold, Morris, Rossetti, Swinburne—we may stop there. Of these, all but Keats, Browning, Rossetti were University men; and of these three, Keats, who died young, cut off in his prime, was the only one not fairly well to do. It may seem a brutal thing to say, and it is a sad thing to say: but, as a matter of hard fact, the theory that poetical genius bloweth where it listeth, and equally in poor and rich, holds little truth. As a matter of hard fact, nine out of those twelve were University men: which means that somehow or other they procured the means to get the best education England can give. As a matter of hard fact, of the remaining three you know that Browning was well to do, and I challenge you that, if he had not been well to do, he would no more have attained to write *Saul* or *The Ring and the Book* than Ruskin would have attained to writing *Modern Painters* if his father had not dealt prosperously in business. Rossetti had a small private income; and, moreover, he painted. There remains but Keats; whom Atropos slew young, as she slew John Clare in a mad-house, and James Thomson by the laudanum he took to drug disappointment. These are dreadful facts, but let us face them. It is—however dishonouring to us as a nation— certain that, by some fault in our commonwealth, the poor poet has not in these days, nor has had for two hundred years, a dog's chance. Believe me—and I have spent a great part of ten years in watching some three hundred and twenty elementary schools—we may prate of democracy, but actually, a poor child in England has little more hope than had the son of an Athenian slave to be emancipated into that intellectual freedom of which great writings are born."

Nobody could put the point more plainly. "The poor poet has not in these days, nor has had for two hundred years, a dog's chance . . . a poor child in England has little more hope than had the son of an Athenian slave to be emancipated into that intellectual freedom of which great writings are born." That is it. Intellectual freedom depends upon material things. Poetry depends upon intellectual freedom. And women have always been poor, not for two hundred years merely, but from the beginning of time. Women have had less intellectual freedom than the sons of Athenian slaves. Women, then, have not had a dog's chance of writing poetry. That is why I have laid so much stress on money and a room of one's own. However, thanks to the toils of those obscure women in the past, of whom I wish we knew more, thanks, curiously enough, to two wars, the Crimean which let Florence Nightingale out of her drawing-room, and the European War which opened the doors to the average woman some sixty years later, these evils are in the way to be bettered. Otherwise you would not be here tonight, and your chance of earning five hundred pounds a year, precarious as I am afraid that it still is, would be minute in the extreme.

Still, you may object, why do you attach so much importance to this writing of books by women when, according to you, it requires so much effort, leads perhaps to the murder of one's aunts, will make one almost certainly late for luncheon, and may bring one into very grave disputes with certain very good fellows? My motives, let me admit, are partly selfish. Like most uneducated Englishwomen, I like reading—I like reading books in the bulk. Lately my diet has become a trifle monotonous; history is too much about wars; biography too much about great men; poetry has shown, I think, a tendency to sterility, and fiction—but I have sufficiently exposed my disabilities as a critic of modern fiction and will say no more about it. Therefore I would ask you to write all kinds of books, hesitating at no subject however trivial or however vast. By hook or by crook, I hope that you will possess yourselves of money enough to travel and to idle, to contemplate the future or the past of the world, to dream over books and loiter at street corners and let the line of thought dip deep into the stream. For I am by no means confining you to fiction. If you would please me—and there are thousands like me—you would write books of travel and adventure, and research and scholarship, and history and biography, and criticism and philosophy and science. By so doing you will certainly profit the art of fiction. For books have a way of influencing each other. Fiction will be much the better for standing cheek by jowl with poetry and philosophy. Moreover, if you consider any great figure of the past, like Sappho, like the Lady Murasaki, like Emily Brontë, you will find that she is an inheritor as well as an originator, and has come into existence because women have come to have the habit of writing naturally; so that even as a prelude to poetry such activity on your part would be invaluable.

But when I look back through these notes and criticise my own train of thought as I made them, I find that my motives were not altogether selfish. There runs through these comments and discursions the conviction—or is it the instinct?—that good books are desirable and that good writers, even if they show every variety of human depravity, are still good human beings. Thus when I ask you to write more books I am urging you to do what will be for your good and for the good of the world at large. How to justify this instinct or belief I do not know, for philosophic words, if one has not been educated at a university, are apt to play one false. What is meant by "reality"? It would seem to be something very erratic, very undependable—now to be found in a dusty road, now in a scrap of newspaper in the street, now in a daffodil in the sun. It lights up a group in a room and stamps some casual saying. It overwhelms one walking home beneath the stars and makes the silent world more real than the world of speech—and then there it is again in an omnibus in the uproar of Piccadilly. Sometimes, too, it seems to dwell in shapes too far away for us to discern what their nature is. But whatever it touches, it fixes and makes permanent. That is what remains over when the skin of the day has been cast into the hedge; that is what is left of past time and of our loves and hates. Now the writer, as I think, has the chance to live more than other people in the presence of this reality. It is his business to find it and collect it and communicate it to the rest of us. So at least I infer from reading *Lear* or *Emma* or *La Recherche du Temps Perdu*. For the reading of these books seems to perform a curious couching operation on the senses; one sees more intensely afterwards; the world seems bared of its covering and given an intenser life. Those are the enviable people who live at enmity with unreality; and those are the pitiable who are knocked on the head by the thing done without knowing or caring. So that when I ask you to earn money and have a room of your own, I am asking you to live in the presence of reality, an invigorating life, it would appear, whether one can impart it or not.

Here I would stop, but the pressure of convention decrees that every speech must end with a peroration. And a peroration addressed to women should have something, you will agree, particularly exalting and ennobling about it. I should implore you to remember your responsibilities, to be higher, more spiritual; I should remind you how much depends upon you, and what an influence you can exert upon the future. But those exhortations can safely, I think, be left to the other sex, who will put them, and indeed have put them, with far greater eloquence than I can compass. When I rummage in my own mind I find no noble sentiments about being companions and equals and influencing the world to higher ends. I find myself saying briefly and prosaically that it is much more important to be oneself than anything else. Do not dream of influencing other people, I would say, if I knew how to make it sound exalted. Think of things in themselves.

And again I am reminded by dipping into newspapers and novels and biographies that when a woman speaks to women she should have something very unpleasant up her sleeve. Women are hard on women. Women dislike women. Women—but are you not sick to death of the word? I can assure you that I am. Let us agree, then, that a paper read by a woman to women should end with something particularly disagreeable.

But how does it go? What can I think of? The truth is, I often like women. I like their unconventionality. I like their subtlety. I like their anonymity. I like—but I must not run on this way. That cupboard there—you say it holds clean table-napkins only; but what if Sir Archibald Bodkin were concealed among them? Let me then adopt a sterner tone. Have I, in the preceding words, conveyed to you sufficiently the warnings and reprobation of mankind? I have told you the very low opinion in which you were held by Mr. Oscar Browning. I have indicated what Napoleon once thought of you and what Mussolini thinks now. Then, in case any of you aspire to fiction, I have copied out for your benefit the advice of the critic about courageously acknowledging the limitations of your sex. I have referred to Professor X and given prominence to his statement that women are intellectually, morally and physically inferior to men. I have handed on all that has come my way without going in search of it, and here is a final warning—from Mr. John Langdon Davies.° Mr. John Langdon Davies warns women "that when children cease to be altogether desirable, women cease to be altogether necessary." I hope you will make a note of it.

How can I further encourage you to go about the business of life? Young women, I would say, and please attend, for the peroration is beginning, you are, in my opinion, disgracefully ignorant. You have never made a discovery of any sort of importance. You have never shaken an empire or led an army into battle. The plays of Shakespeare are not by you, and you have never introduced a barbarous race to the blessings of civilisation. What is your excuse? It is all very well for you to say, pointing to the streets and squares and forests of the globe swarming with black and white and coffee-coloured inhabitants, all busily engaged in traffic and enterprise and love-making, we have had other work on our hands. Without our doing, those seas would be unsailed and those fertile lands a desert. We have borne and bred and washed and taught, perhaps to the age of six or seven years, the one thousand six hundred and twenty-three million human beings who are, according to statistics, at present in existence, and that, allowing that some had help, takes time.

There is truth in what you say—I will not deny it. But at the same time may I remind you that there have been at least two colleges for women in existence in England since the year 1866; that after the year 1880 a married woman was allowed by law to possess her own property; and that in 1919—which is a whole nine years ago—she was given a vote? May I also remind you that the most of the professions have been open to you for close on ten years now? When you reflect upon these immense privileges and the length of time during which they have been enjoyed, and the fact that there must be at this moment some two thousand women capable of earning over five hundred a year in one way or another, you will agree that the excuse of lack of opportunity, training, encouragement, leisure and money no longer holds good. Moreover, the economists are telling us that Mrs. Seton has had too many children. You must, of course, go on bearing children, but, so they say, in twos and threes, not in tens and twelves.

Thus, with some time on your hands and with some book learning in your brains—you have had enough of the other kind, and are sent to

---

° *A Short History of Women,* by John Langdon Davies.

college partly, I suspect, to be uneducated—surely you should embark upon another stage of your very long, very laborious and highly obscure career. A thousand pens are ready to suggest what you should do and what effect you will have. My own suggestion is a little fantastic, I admit; I prefer, therefore, to put it in the form of fiction.

I told you in the course of this paper that Shakespeare had a sister; but do not look for her in Sir Sidney Lee's life of the poet. She died young—alas, she never wrote a word. She lies buried where the omnibuses now stop, opposite the Elephant and Castle. Now my belief is that this poet who never wrote a word and was buried at the crossroads still lives. She lives in you and in me, and in many other women who are not here tonight, for they are washing up the dishes and putting the children to bed. But she lives; for great poets do not die; they are continuing presences; they need only the opportunity to walk among us in the flesh. This opportunity, as I think, it is now coming within your power to give her. For my belief is that if we live another century or so—I am talking of the common life which is the real life and not of the little separate lives which we live as individuals—and have five hundred a year each of us and rooms of our own; if we have the habit of freedom and the courage to write exactly what we think; if we escape a little from the common sitting-room and see human beings not always in their relation to each other but in relation to reality; and the sky, too, and the trees or whatever it may be in themselves; if we look past Milton's bogey, for no human being should shut out the view; if we face the fact, for it is a fact, that there is no arm to cling to, but that we go alone and that our relation is to the world of reality and not only to the world of men and women, then the opportunity will come and the dead poet who was Shakespeare's sister will put on the body which she has so often laid down. Drawing her life from the lives of the unknown who were her forerunners, as her brother did before her, she will be born. As for her coming without that preparation, without that effort on our part, without that determination that when she is born again she shall find it possible to live and write her poetry, that we cannot expect, for that would be impossible. But I maintain that she would come if we worked for her, and that so to work, even in poverty and obscurity, is worth while.

From THE SECOND SEX

Simone de Beauvoir (1908–   )

CONCLUSION

"No, woman is not our brother; through indolence and depravity we have made of her a being apart, unknown, having no weapon other than her sex, which not only means constant strife but is moreover an unfair weapon of the eternal little slave's mistrust—adoring or hating, but never our frank companion, a being set apart as if in *esprit de corps* and freemasonry."

Many men would still subscribe to these words of Laforgue;° many think that there will always be "strife and dispute," as Montaigne put it, and that fraternity will never be possible. The fact is that today neither men nor women are satisfied with each other. But the question is to know whether there is an original curse that condemns them to rend each other or whether the conflicts in which they are opposed merely mark a transitional moment in human history.

We have seen that in spite of legends no physiological destiny imposes an eternal hostility upon Male and Female as such; even the famous praying mantis devours her male only for want of other food and for the good of the species: it is to this, the species, that all individuals are subordinated, from the top to the bottom of the scale of animal life. Moreover, humanity is something more than a mere species: it is a historical development; it is to be defined by the manner in which it deals with its natural, fixed characteristics, its *facticité*. Indeed, even with the most extreme bad faith in the world, it is impossible to demonstrate the existence of a rivalry between the human male and female of a truly physiological nature. Further, their hostility may be allocated rather to that intermediate terrain between biology and psychology: psychoanalysis. Woman, we are told, envies man his penis and wishes to castrate him; but the childish desire for the penis is important in the life of the adult woman only if she feels her femininity as a mutilation; and then it is as a symbol of all the privileges of manhood that she wishes to appropriate the male organ. We may readily agree that her dream of castration has this symbolic significance: she wishes, it is thought, to deprive the male of his transcendence.°

From *The Second Sex* by Simone de Beauvoir. Translated and edited by H. M. Parshley. Copyright, 1952, by Alfred A. Knopf, Inc. Reprinted by permission of the publisher.

°*Laforgue* (Jules): French poet (1860–1887)

°*transcendence:* The state of being separate from, independent of, the material universe (the physical environment and social circumstances) and being able to act as subject in this world because no longer bound and manipulated by it (and, by fact of birth, no longer in a state of natural oneness with it). It is the state of individual sovereignty desired by every essential being who strives to be more than

But her desire, as we have seen, is much more ambiguous: she wishes, in a contradictory fashion, *to have* this transcendence, which is to suppose that she at once respects it and denies it, that she intends at once to throw herself into it and keep it within herself. This is to say that the drama does not unfold on a sexual level; further, sexuality has never seemed to us to define a destiny, to furnish in itself the key to human behavior, but to express the totality of a situation that it only helps to define. The battle of the sexes is not immediately implied in the anatomy of man and woman. The truth is that when one evokes it, one takes for granted that in the timeless realm of Ideas a battle is being waged between those vague essences the Eternal Feminine and the Eternal Masculine; and one neglects the fact that this titanic combat assumes on earth two totally different forms, corresponding with two different moments of history.

The woman who is shut up in immanence° endeavors to hold man in that prison also; thus the prison will be confused with the world, and woman will no longer suffer from being confined there: mother, wife, sweetheart are the jailers. Society, being codified by man, decrees that woman is inferior: she can do away with this inferiority only by destroying the male's superiority. She sets about mutilating, dominating man, she contradicts him, she denies his truth and his values. But in doing this she is only defending herself; it was neither a changeless essence nor a mistaken choice that doomed her to immanence, to inferiority. They were imposed upon her. All oppression creates a state of war. And this is no exception. The existent° who is regarded as inessential cannot fail to demand the re-establishment of her sovereignty.

Today the combat takes a different shape; instead of wishing to put man in a prison, woman endeavors to escape from one; she no longer

---

inanimate object; it is being outside oneself, able to "engage in freely chosen projects"; it is the state of "being for itself," subject viewing itself as object and acting in its own behalf.

°*immanence*: The state of being dependent upon and controlled by the material world into which one is born. It is a state of passivity, stagnation—a materialistic prison, a life defined and limited by external circumstances. The person in such a state is incapable of getting outside himself; everything takes place within his mind but has no effect outside it. Such a person's identity is dependent totally on what he is in himself, on what he thinks of himself, rather than on what he does, on his actions in the outside world. It is the state of "being in itself"—"the brutish life of subjection to given conditions," to being a motionless mass, an inessential thing, a subject who experiences itself only as subject and thus becomes an object for other people to possess, to control.

°*existent*: One who is torn from immanence, from oneness with the material universe, who is aware that he is more than a given, an already inherently defined essence, or an unconscious, passive thing. Such a person is able to stand off and view himself as object as well as subject; he is able to define himself in relation to others in the outside world through actions; he is an essential being who longs to act, to strive towards transcendence; his identity is realized in what he does.

seeks to drag him into the realms of immanence but to emerge, herself, into the light of transcendence. Now the attitude of the males creates a new conflict: it is with a bad grace that the man lets her go. He is very well pleased to remain the sovereign subject, the absolute superior, the essential being; he refuses to accept his companion as an equal in any concrete way. She replies to his lack of confidence in her by assuming an aggressive attitude. It is no longer a question of a war between individuals each shut up in his or her sphere: a caste claiming its rights goes over the top and it is resisted by the privileged caste. Here two transcendences are face to face; instead of displaying mutual recognition, each free being wishes to dominate the other.

This difference of attitude is manifest on the sexual plane as on the spiritual plane. The "feminine" woman in making herself prey tries to reduce man, also, to her carnal passivity; she occupies herself in catching him in her trap, in enchaining him by means of the desire she arouses in him in submissively making herself a thing. The emancipated woman, on the contrary, wants to be active, a taker, and refuses the passivity man means to impose on her. Thus Elise and her emulators deny the values of the activities of virile type; they put the flesh above the spirit, contingence above liberty, their routine wisdom above creative audacity. But the "modern" woman accepts masculine values: she prides herself on thinking, taking action, working, creating, on the same terms as men; instead of seeking to disparage them, she declares herself their equal.

In so far as she expresses herself in definite action, this claim is legitimate, and male insolence must then bear the blame. But in men's defense it must be said that women are wont to confuse the issue. A Mabel Dodge Luhan intended to subjugate D. H. Lawrence by her feminine charms so as to dominate him spiritually thereafter; many women, in order to show by their successes their equivalence to men, try to secure male support by sexual means; they play on both sides, demanding old-fashioned respect and modern esteem, banking on their old magic and their new rights. It is understandable that a man becomes irritated and puts himself on the defensive; but he is also double-dealing when he requires woman to play the game fairly while he denies them the indispensable trump cards through distrust and hostility. Indeed, the struggle cannot be clearly drawn between them, since woman is opaque in her very being; she stands before man not as a subject but as an object paradoxically endued with subjectivity; she takes herself simultaneously as *self* and as *other*, a contradiction that entails baffling consequences. When she makes weapons at once of her weakness and of her strength, it is not a matter of designing calculation: she seeks salvation spontaneously in the way that has been imposed on her, that of passivity, at the same time when she is actively demanding her sovereignty; and no doubt this procedure is unfair tactics, but it is dictated to her by the ambiguous situation assigned her. Man, however, becomes indignant when he treats her as a free and independent being and then realizes that she is still a trap for him; if he gratifies and satisfies her in her posture as prey, he finds her claims to autonomy irritating; whatever he does, he feels tricked and she feels wronged.

The quarrel will go on as long as men and women fail to recognize each other as peers; that is to say, as long as femininity is perpetuated as such. Which sex is the more eager to maintain it? Woman, who is being emancipated from it, wishes none the less to retain its privileges; and man, in that case, wants her to assume its limitations. "It is easier to accuse one sex than to excuse the other," says Montaigne. It is vain to apportion praise and blame. The truth is that if the vicious circle is so hard to break, it is because the two sexes are each the victim at once of the other and of itself. Between two adversaries confronting each other in their pure liberty, an agreement could be easily reached: the more so as the war profits neither. But the complexity of the whole affair derives from the fact that each camp is giving aid and comfort to the enemy; woman is pursuing a dream of submission, man a dream of identification. Want of authenticity does not pay: each blames the other for the unhappiness he or she has incurred in yielding to the temptations of the easy way; what man and woman loathe in each other is the shattering frustration of each one's own bad faith and baseness.

We have seen why men enslaved women in the first place; the devaluation of femininity has been a necessary step in human evolution, but it might have led to collaboration between the two sexes; oppression is to be explained by the tendency of the existent to flee from himself by means of identification with the other, whom he oppresses to that end. In each individual man that tendency exists today; and the vast majority yield to it. The husband wants to find himself in his wife, the lover in his mistress, in the form of a stone image; he is seeking in her the myth of his virility, of his sovereignty, of his immediate reality. "My husband never goes to the movies," says his wife, and the dubious masculine opinion is graved in the marble of eternity. But he is himself the slave of his double: what an effort to build up an image in which he is always in danger! In spite of everything his success in this depends upon the capricious freedom of women: he must constantly try to keep this propitious to him. Man is concerned with the effort to appear male, important, superior; he pretends so as to get pretense in return; he, too, is aggressive, uneasy; he feels hostility for women because he is afraid of them, he is afraid of them because he is afraid of the personage, the image, with which he identifies himself. What time and strength he squanders in liquidating, sublimating, transferring complexes, in talking about women, in seducing them, in fearing them! He would be liberated himself in their liberation. But this is precisely what he dreads. And so he obstinately persists in the mystifications intended to keep woman in her chains.

That she is being tricked, many men have realized. "What a misfortune to be a woman! And yet the misfortune, when one is a woman, is at bottom not to comprehend that it is one," says Kirkegaard.° For a long time there have been efforts to disguise this misfortune. For example, guardianship has been done away with: women have been given "protectors," and if they are invested with the rights of the old-time guardians, it is in woman's own interest. To forbid her working, to keep her at home, is to defend her against herself and to assure her happiness. We have seen what poetic veils are thrown over her monotonous burdens of housekeeping and maternity: in exchange for her liberty she has received the false treasures of her "femininity." Balzac illustrates this maneuver very well in counseling man to treat her as a slave while persuading her that she is a queen. Less cynical, many men try to convince themselves that she is really privileged. There are American sociologists who seriously teach today the theory of "low-class gain." In France, also, it has often been proclaimed—although in a less scientific manner—that the workers are very fortunate in not being obliged to "keep up appearances" and still more so the bums who can dress in rags and sleep on the sidewalks, pleasures forbidden to the Count de Beaumont and the Wendels. Like the carefree wretches gaily scratching at their vermin, like the merry Negroes laughing under the lash and those joyous Tunisian Arabs burying their starved children with a smile, woman enjoys that incomparable privilege: irresponsibility. Free from troublesome burdens and cares, she obviously has "the better part." But it is disturbing that with an obstinate perversity—connected no doubt with original sin—down through the centuries and in all countries, the people who have the better part are always crying to their benefactors: "It is too much! I will be satisfied with yours!" But the munificent capitalists, the generous colonists, the superb males, stick to their guns: "Keep the better part, hold on to it!"

It must be admitted that the males find in woman more complicity than the oppressor usually finds in the oppressed. And in bad faith they take authorization from this to declare that she has *desired* the destiny they have imposed on her. We have seen that all the main features of her training combine to bar her from the roads of revolt and adventure.

°*In Vino Veritas.* He says further: "Politeness is pleasing—essentially—to woman, and the fact that she accepts it without hesitation is explained by nature's care for the weaker, for the unfavored being, and for one to whom an illusion means more than a material compensation. But this illusion, precisely, is fatal to her. ... To feel oneself freed from distress thanks to something imaginary, to be the dupe of something imaginary, is that not a still deeper mockery? ... Woman is very far from being *verwahrlost* (neglected), but in another sense she is, since she can never free herself from the illusion that nature has used to console her." [Author's note.]

Society in general—beginning with her respected parents—lies to her by praising the lofty values of love, devotion, the gift of herself, and then concealing from her the fact that neither lover nor husband nor yet her children will be inclined to accept the burdensome charge of all that. She cheerfully believes these lies because they invite her to follow the easy slope: in this others commit their worst crime against her; throughout her life from childhood on, they damage and corrupt her by designating as her true vocation this submission, which is the temptation of every existent in the anxiety of liberty. If a child is taught idleness by being amused all day long and never being led to study, or shown its usefulness, it will hardly be said, when he grows up, that he chose to be incapable and ignorant; yet this is how woman is brought up, without ever being impressed with the necessity of taking charge of her own existence. So she readily lets herself come to count on the protection, love, assistance, and supervision of others, she lets herself be fascinated with the hope of self-realization without *doing* anything. She does wrong in yielding to the temptation; but man is in no position to blame her, since he has led her into the temptation. When conflict arises between them, each will hold the other responsible for the situation; she will reproach him with having made her what she is: "No one taught me to reason or to earn my own living"; he will reproach her with having accepted the consequences: "You don't know anything, you are an incompetent," and so on. Each sex thinks it can justify itself by taking the offensive; but the wrongs done by one do not make the other innocent.

The innumerable conflicts that set men and women against one another come from the fact that neither is prepared to assume all the consequences of this situation which the one has offered and the other accepted. The doubtful concept of "equality in inequality," which the one uses to mask his despotism and the other to mask her cowardice, does not stand the test of experience: in their exchanges, woman appeals to the theoretical equality she has been guaranteed, and man the concrete inequality that exists. The result is that in every association an endless debate goes on concerning the ambiguous meaning of the words *give* and *take*: she complains of giving her all, he protests that she takes his all. Woman has to learn that exchanges—it is a fundamental law of political economy—are based on the value the merchandise offered has for the buyer, and not for the seller: she has been deceived in being persuaded that her worth is priceless. The truth is that for man she is an amusement, a pleasure, company, an inessential boon; he is for her the meaning, the justification of her existence. The exchange, therefore, is not of two items of equal value.

This inequality will be especially brought out in the fact that the time they spend together—which fallaciously seems to be the same time— does not have the same value for both partners. During the evening the lover spends with his mistress he could be doing something of advantage to his career, seeing friends, cultivating business relationships, seeking recreation; for a man normally integrated in society, time is a positive value: money, reputation, pleasure. For the idle, bored woman, on the contrary, it is a burden she wishes to get rid of; when she succeeds in killing time, it is a benefit to her: the man's presence is pure profit. In a liaison what most clearly interests the man, in many cases, is the sexual benefit he gets from it: if need be, he can be content to spend no more time with his mistress than is required for the sexual act; but—with exceptions—what she, on her part, wants is to kill all the excess time she has on her hands; and—like the storekeeper who will not sell potatoes unless the customer will take turnips also—she will not yield her body unless her lover will take hours of conversation and "going out" into the bargain. A balance is reached if, on the whole, the cost does not seem too high to the man, and this depends, of course, on the strength of his desire and the importance he gives to what is to be sacrificed. But if the woman demands—offers—too much time, she becomes wholly intrusive, like the river overflowing its banks, and the man will prefer to have nothing rather than too much. Then she reduces her demands; but very often the balance is reached at the cost of a double tension: she feels that the man has "had" her at a bargain, and he thinks her price is too high. This analysis, of course, is put in somewhat humorous terms; but— except for those affairs of jealous and exclusive passion in which the man wants total possession of the woman—this conflict constantly appears in cases of affection, desire, and even love. He always has "other things to do" with his time; whereas she has time to burn; and he considers much of the time she gives him not as a gift but as a burden.

As a rule he consents to assume the burden because he knows very well that he is on the privileged side, he has a bad conscience; and if he is of reasonable good will he tries to compensate for the inequality by being generous. He prides himself on his compassion, however, and at the first clash he treats the woman as ungrateful and thinks, with some irritation: "I'm too good to her." She feels she is behaving like a beggar when she is convinced of the high value of her gifts, and that humiliates her.

Here we find the explanation of the cruelty that woman often shows she is capable of practicing; she has a good conscience because she is on the unprivileged side; she feels she is under no obligation to deal gently with the favored caste, and her only thought is to defend herself. She will even be very happy if she has occasion to show her resentment to a lover who has not been able to satisfy all her demands: since he does not give her enough, she takes savage delight in taking back everything from him. At this point the wounded lover suddenly discovers the value *in toto* of a liaison each moment of which he held more or less in contempt: he is ready to promise her everything, even though he will feel exploited again when he has to make good. He accuses his mistress of blackmailing him: she calls him stingy; both feel wronged.

Once again it is useless to apportion blame and excuses: justice can never be done in the midst of injustice. A colonial administrator has no possibility of acting rightly toward the natives, nor a general toward his soldiers; the only solution is to be neither colonist nor military chief; but a man could not prevent himself from being a man. So there he is, culpable in spite of himself and laboring under the effects of a fault he did not himself commit; and here she is, victim and shrew in spite of herself. Sometimes he rebels and becomes cruel, but then he makes himself an accomplice of the injustice, and the fault becomes really his. Sometimes he lets himself be annihilated, devoured, by his demanding victim; but in that case he feels duped. Often he stops at a compromise that at once belittles him and leaves him ill at ease. A well-disposed man will be more tortured by the situation than the woman herself: in a sense it is always better to be on the side of the vanquished; but if she is well-disposed also, incapable of self-sufficiency, reluctant to crush the man with the weight of her destiny, she struggles in hopeless confusion.

In daily life we meet with an abundance of these cases which are incapable of satisfactory solution because they are determined by unsatisfactory conditions. A man who is compelled to go on materially and morally supporting a woman whom he no longer loves feels he is victimized; but if he abandons without resources the woman who has pledged her whole life to him, she will be quite as unjustly victimized. The evil originates not in the perversity of individuals—and bad faith first appears when each blames the other—it originates rather in a situation against which all individual action is powerless. Women are "clinging," they are a dead weight, and they suffer for it; the point is that their situation is like that of a parasite sucking out the living strength of another organism. Let them be provided with living strength of their own, let them have the means to attack the world and wrest from it their own subsistence, and their dependence will be abolished—that of man also. There is no doubt that both men and women will profit greatly from the new situation.

A world where men and women would be equal is easy to visualize, for that precisely is what the Soviet Revolution *promised:* women raised and trained exactly like men were to work under the same conditions° and for the same wages. Erotic liberty was to be recognized by custom, but the sexual act was not to be considered a "service" to be paid for; woman was to be *obliged* to provide herself with other ways of earning

---

°That certain too laborious occupations were to be closed to women is not in contradiction to this project. Even among men there is an increasing effort to obtain adaptation to profession; their varying physical and mental capacities limit their possibilities of choice; what is asked is that, in any case, no line of sex or caste be drawn. [Author's note.]

a living; marriage was to be based on a free agreement that the spouses could break at will; maternity was to be voluntary, which meant that contraception and abortion were to be authorized and that, on the other hand, all mothers and their children were to have exactly the same rights, in or out of marriage; pregnancy leaves were to be paid for by the State, which would assume charge of the children, signifying not that they would be *taken away* from their parents, but that they would not be *abandoned* to them.

But is it enough to change laws, institutions, customs, public opinion, and the whole social context, for men and women to become truly equal? "Women will always be women," say the skeptics. Other seers prophesy that in casting off their femininity they will not succeed in changing themselves into men and they will become monsters. This would be to admit that the woman of today is a creation of nature; it must be repeated once more that in human society nothing is natural and that woman, like much else, is a product elaborated by civilization. The intervention of others in her destiny is fundamental: if this action took a different direction, it would produce a quite different result. Woman is determined not by her hormones or by mysterious instincts, but by the manner in which her body and her relation to the world are modified through the action of others than herself. The abyss that separates the adolescent boy and girl has been deliberately opened out between them since earliest childhood; later on, woman could not be other than what she *was made,* and that past was bound to shadow her for life. If we appreciate its influence, we see clearly that her destiny is not predetermined for all eternity.

We must not believe, certainly, that a change in woman's economic condition alone is enough to transform her, though this factor has been and remains the basic factor in her evolution; but until it has brought about the moral, social, cultural, and other consequences that it promises and requires, the new woman cannot appear. At this moment they have been realized nowhere, in Russia no more than in France or the United States; and this explains why the woman of today is torn between the past and the future. She appears most often as a "true woman" disguised as a man, and she feels herself as ill at ease in her flesh as in her masculine garb. She must shed her old skin and cut her own new clothes. This she could do only through a social evolution. No single educator could fashion a *female human being* today who would be the exact homologue of the *male human being;* if she is raised like a boy, the young girl feels she is an oddity and thereby she is given a new kind of sex specification. Stendhal understood this when he said: "The forest must be planted all at once." But if we imagine, on the contrary, a society in which the equality of the sexes would be concretely realized, this equality would find new expression in each individual.

If the little girl were brought up from the first with the same demands and rewards, the same severity and the same freedom, as her brothers, taking part in the same studies, the same games, promised the same future, surrounded with women and men who seemed to her undoubted equals, the meanings of the castration complex and of the Oedipus complex would be profoundly modified. Assuming on the same basis as the father the material and moral responsibility of the couple, the mother would enjoy the same lasting prestige; the child would perceive around her an androgynous world and not a masculine world. Were she emotionally more attracted to her father—which is not even sure—her love for him would be tinged with a will to emulation and not a feeling of powerlessness; she would not be oriented toward passivity. Authorized to test her powers in work and sports, competing actively with the boys, she would not find the absence of the penis—compensated by the promise of a child—enough to give rise to an inferiority complex; correlatively, the boy would not have a superiority complex if it were not instilled into him and if he looked up to women with as much respect as to men.° The little girl would not seek sterile compensation in narcissism and dreaming, she would not take her fate for granted; she would be interested in what she was *doing*, she would throw herself without reserve into undertakings.

I have already pointed out how much easier the transformation of puberty would be if she looked beyond it, like the boys, toward a free adult future: menstruation horrifies her only because it is an abrupt descent into femininity. She would also take her young eroticism in much more tranquil fashion if she did not feel a frightened disgust for her destiny as a whole; coherent sexual information would do much to help her over this crisis. And thanks to coeducational schooling, the august mystery of Man would have no occasion to enter her mind: it would be eliminated by everyday familiarity and open rivalry.

Objections raised against this system always imply respect for sexual taboos; but the effort to inhibit all sex curiosity and pleasure in the child is quite useless; one succeeds only in creating repressions, obsessions, neuroses. The excessive sentimentality, homosexual fervors, and platonic crushes of adolescent girls, with all their train of silliness and frivolity, are much more injurious than a little childish sex play and a few definite sex experiences. It would be beneficial above all for the young girl not to be influenced against taking charge herself of her own existence, for then she would not seek a demigod in the male—merely a comrade, a friend, a partner. Eroticism and love would take on the nature of free transcend-

---

°I knew a little boy of eight who lived with his mother, aunt, and grandmother, all independent and active women, and his weak old half-crippled grandfather. He had a crushing inferiority complex in regard to the feminine sex, although he made efforts to combat it. At school he scorned comrades and teachers because they were miserable males. [Author's note.]

ence and not that of resignation; she could experience them as a relation between equals. There is no intention, of course, to remove by a stroke of the pen all the difficulties that the child has to overcome in changing into an adult; the most intelligent, the most tolerant education could not relieve the child of experiencing things for herself; what could be asked is that obstacles should not be piled gratuitously in her path. Progress is already shown by the fact that "vicious" little girls are no longer cauterized with a red-hot iron. Psychoanalysis has given parents some instruction, but the conditions under which, at the present time, the sexual training and initiation of woman are accomplished are so deplorable that none of the objections advanced against the idea of a radical change could be considered valid. It is not a question of abolishing in woman the contingencies and miseries of the human condition, but of giving her the means for transcending them.

Woman is the victim of no mysterious fatality; the peculiarities that identify her as specifically a woman get their importance from the significance placed upon them. They can be surmounted, in the future, when they are regarded in new perspectives. Thus, as we have seen, through her erotic experience woman feels—and often detests—the domination of the male; but this is no reason to conclude that her ovaries condemn her to live forever on her knees. Virile aggressiveness seems like a lordly privilege only within a system that in its entirety conspires to affirm masculine sovereignty; and woman *feels* herself profoundly passive in the sexual act only because she already *thinks* of herself as such. Many modern women who lay claim to their dignity as human beings still envisage their erotic life from the standpoint of a tradition of slavery: since it seems to them humiliating to lie beneath the man, to be penetrated by him, they grow tense in frigidity. But if the reality were different, the meaning expressed symbolically in amorous gestures and postures would be different, too: a woman who pays and dominates her lover can, for example, take pride in her superb idleness and consider that she is enslaving the male who is actively exerting himself. And here and now there are many sexually well-balanced couples whose notions of victory and defeat are giving place to the idea of an exchange.

As a matter of fact, man, like woman, is flesh, therefore passive, the plaything of his hormones and of the species, the restless prey of his desires. And she, like him, in the midst of the carnal fever, is a consenting, a voluntary gift, an activity; they live out in their several fashions the strange ambiguity of existence made body. In those combats where they think they confront one another, it is really against the self that each one struggles, projecting into the partner that part of the self which is repudiated; instead of living out the ambiguities of their situation, each tries to make the other bear the abjection and tries to reserve the honor for the self. If, however, both should assume the ambiguity with a clear-sighted modesty, correlative of an authentic pride, they would see each other as equals and would live out their erotic drama in amity. The fact that we are human beings is infinitely more important than all the peculiarities that distinguish human beings from one another; it is never the given that confers superiorities: "virtue," as the ancients called it, is defined at the level of "that which depends on us." In both sexes is played out the same drama of the flesh and the spirit, of finitude and transcendence; both are gnawed away by time and laid in wait for by death, they have the same essential need for one another; and they can gain from their liberty the same glory. If they were to taste it, they would no longer be tempted to dispute fallacious privileges, and fraternity between them could then come into existence.

I shall be told that all this is utopian fancy, because woman cannot be "made over" unless society has first made her really the equal of man. Conservatives have never failed in such circumstances to refer to that vicious circle; history, however, does not revolve. If a caste is kept in a state of inferiority, no doubt it remains inferior; but liberty can break the circle. Let the Negroes vote and they become worthy of having the vote; let woman be given responsibilities and she is able to assume them. The fact is that oppressors cannot be expected to make a move of gratuitous generosity; but at one time the revolt of the oppressed, at another time even the very evolution of the privileged caste itself, creates new situations; thus men have been led, in their own interest, to give partial emancipation to women: it remains only for women to continue their ascent, and the successes they are obtaining are an encouragement for them to do so. It seems almost certain that sooner or later they will arrive at complete economic and social equality, which will bring about an inner metamorphosis.

However this may be, there will be some to object that if such a world is possible it is not desirable. When woman is "the same" as her male, life will lose its salt and spice. This argument, also, has lost its novelty: those interested in perpetuating present conditions are always in tears about the marvelous past that is about to disappear, without having so much as a smile for the young future. It is quite true that doing away with the slave trade meant death to the great plantations, magnificent with azaleas and camellias, it meant ruin to the whole refined Southern civilization. The attics of time have received its rare odd laces along with the clear pure voices of the Sistine *castrati,*° and there is a certain "feminine charm" that is also on the way to the same dusty repository. I agree that he would be a barbarian indeed who failed to appreciate exquisite

---

°Eunuchs were long used in the male choirs of the Sistine Chapel in Rome, until the practice was forbidden by Pope Leo XIII in 1880. The operation of castration caused the boy's soprano voice to be retained into adulthood, and it was performed for this purpose. [Translator's note.]

flowers, rare lace, the crystal-clear voice of the eunuch, and feminine charm.

When the "charming woman" shows herself in all her splendor, she is a much more exalting object than the "idiotic paintings, overdoors, scenery, showman's garish signs, popular chromos," that excited Rimbaud; adorned with the most modern artifices, beautified according to the newest techniques, she comes down from the remoteness of the ages, from Thebes, from Crete, from Chichén-Itzá; and she is also the totem set up deep in the African jungle; she is a helicopter and she is a bird; and there is this, the greatest wonder of all: under her tinted hair the forest murmur becomes a thought, and words issue from her breasts. Men stretch forth avid hands toward the marvel, but when they grasp it it is gone; the wife, the mistress, speak like everybody else through their mouths: their words are worth just what they are worth; their breasts also. Does such a fugitive miracle—and one so rare—justify us in perpetuating a situation that is baneful for both sexes? One can appreciate the beauty of flowers, the charm of women, and appreciate them at their true value; if these treasures cost blood or misery, they must be sacrificed.

But in truth this sacrifice seems to men a peculiarly heavy one; few of them really wish in their hearts for woman to succeed in making it; those among them who hold woman in contempt see in the sacrifice nothing for them to gain, those who cherish her see too much that they would lose. And it is true that the evolution now in progress threatens more than feminine charm alone: in beginning to exist for herself, woman will relinquish the function as double and mediator to which she owes her privileged place in the masculine universe; to man, caught between the silence of nature and the demanding presence of other free beings, a creature who is at once his like and a passive thing seems a great treasure. The guise in which he conceives his companion may be mythical, but the experiences for which she is the source or the pretext are none the less real: there are hardly any more precious, more intimate, more ardent. There is no denying that feminine dependence, inferiority, woe, give women their special character; assuredly woman's autonomy, if it spares men many troubles, will also deny them many conveniences; assuredly there are certain forms of the sexual adventure which will be lost in the world of tomorrow. But this does not mean that love, happiness, poetry, dream, will be banished from it.

Let us not forget that our lack of imagination always depopulates the future; for us it is only an abstraction; each one of us secretly deplores the absence there of the one who was himself. But the humanity of tomorrow will be living in its flesh and in its conscious liberty; that time will be its present and it will in turn prefer it. New relations of flesh and sentiment of which we have no conception will arise between the sexes; already, indeed, there have appeared between men and women friendships, rivalries, complicities, comradeships—chaste or sensual—which past centuries could not have conceived. To mention one point, nothing could seem to me more debatable than the opinion that dooms the new world to uniformity and hence to boredom. I fail to see that this present world is free from boredom or that liberty ever creates uniformity.

To begin with, there will always be certain differences between man and woman; her eroticism, and therefore her sexual world, have a special form of their own and therefore cannot fail to engender a sensuality, a sensitivity, of a special nature. This means that her relations to her own body, to that of the male, to the child, will never be identical with those the male bears to his own body, to that of the female, and to the child; those who make much of "equality in difference" could not with good grace refuse to grant me the possible existence of differences in equality. Then again, it is institutions that create uniformity. Young and pretty, the slaves of the harem are always the same in the sultan's embrace; Christianity gave eroticism its savor of sin and legend when it endowed the human female with a soul; if society restores her sovereign individuality to woman, it will not thereby destroy the power of love's embrace to move the heart.

It is nonsense to assert that revelry, vice, ecstasy, passion, would become impossible if man and woman were equal in concrete matters; the contradictions that put the flesh in opposition to the spirit, the instant to time, the swoon of immanence to the challenge of transcendence, the absolute of pleasure to the nothingness of forgetting, will never be resolved; in sexuality will always be materialized the tension, the anguish, the joy, the frustration, and the triumph of existence. To emancipate woman is to refuse to confine her to the relations she bears to man, not to deny them to her; let her have her independent existence and she will continue none the less to exist for him *also:* mutually recognizing each other as subject, each will yet remain for the other an *other.* The reciprocity of their relations will not do away with the miracles—desire, possession, love, dream, adventure—worked by the division of human beings into two separate categories; and the words that move us—giving, conquering, uniting—will not lose their meaning. On the contrary, when we abolish the slavery of half of humanity, together with the whole system of hypocrisy that it implies, then the "division" of humanity will reveal its genuine significance and the human couple will find its true form. "The direct, natural, necessary relation of human creatures is the *relation of man to woman,*" Marx has said.° "The nature of this relation determines to what point man himself is to be considered as a *generic being,* as mankind; the relation of man to woman is the most natural relation of human being to human being. By it is shown, therefore, to what point the *natural*

°*Philosophical Works,* Vol. VI (Marx's italics). [Author's note.]

behavior of man has become *human* or to what point the *human* being has become his *natural* being, to what point his *human nature* has become his *nature."*

The case could not be better stated. It is for man to establish the reign of liberty in the midst of the world of the given. To gain the supreme victory, it is necessary, for one thing, that by and through their natural differentiation men and women unequivocally affirm their brotherhood.

From PSYCHOLOGICAL REFLECTIONS

Carl Jung (1875–1961)

MAN AND WOMAN

So far as we know, consciousness is always ego-consciousness. In order to be conscious of myself, I must be able to distinguish myself from others. Relationship can only take place where this distinction exists.
44:326°

Although man and woman unite they nevertheless represent irreconcilable opposites which, when activated, degenerate into deadly hostility. This primordial pair of opposites symbolizes every conceivable pair of opposites that may occur: hot and cold, light and dark, north and south, dry and damp, good and bad, conscious and unconscious.   72:192

For two personalities to meet is like mixing two chemical substances: if there is any combination at all, both are transformed.   63:163

[All that pertains to the opposite sex] has a mysterious charm tinged with fear, perhaps even with disgust. For this reason its charm is particularly attractive and fascinating, even when it comes to us not directly from outside, in the guise of a woman, but from within, as a psychic influence—for instance in the form of a temptation to abandon oneself to a mood or an affect.   114:244

The young person of marriageable age does, of course, possess an ego-consciousness (girls more than men, as a rule), but, since he has only recently emerged from the mists of original unconsciousness, he is certain to have wide areas which still lie in the shadow and which preclude to that extent the formation of psychological relationship. This means, in practice, that the young man (or woman) can have only an incomplete

---

°The numbers following the selections refer to the major works by Jung from which the material was excerpted. See *Psychological Reflections*, edited by Jolande Jacobi (Princeton University Press), for the key to the sources.

From *C. G. Jung: Psychological Reflections: A New Anthology of His Writings, 1905–1961,* selected and edited by Jolande Jacobi. Copyright 1953 by Bollingen Foundation, new edition copyright © 1970 by Princeton University Press, Published by Princeton University Press. Reprinted by permission of Princeton University Press.

understanding of himself and others, and is therefore imperfectly informed as to his, and their, motives. As a rule the motives he acts from are largely unconscious. Subjectively, of course, he thinks himself very conscious and knowing, for we constantly overestimate the existing content of consciousness, and it is a great and surprising discovery when we find that what we had supposed to be the final peak is nothing but the first step in a very long climb.   44:327

Why is it that we are especially interested in psychology just now? The answer is that everyone is in desperate need of it. Humanity seems to have reached a point where the concepts of the past are no longer adequate, and we begin to realize that our nearest and dearest are actually strangers to us, whose language we no longer understand. It is beginning to dawn on us that the people living on the other side of the mountain are not made up exclusively of red-headed devils who are responsible for all the evil on this side of the mountain. A little of this uneasy suspicion has filtered through into the relations between the sexes; not everyone is utterly convinced that everything good is in "me" and everything evil in "you." Already we can find super-moderns who ask themselves in all seriousness whether there may not be something wrong with us, whether perhaps we are too unconscious, too antiquated, and whether this may not be the reason why when confronted with difficulties in sexual relationships we still continue to employ with disastrous results the methods of the Middle Ages if not those of the caveman.   33:xif*

Since [in the Middle Ages] the psychic relation to woman was expressed in the collective worship of Mary,° the image of woman lost a value to which human beings had a natural right. This value could find its natural expression only through individual choice, and it sank into the unconscious when the individual form of expression was replaced by a collective one. In the unconscious the image of woman received an energy charge that activated the archaic and infantile dominants. And since all unconscious contents, when activated by dissociated libido,° are projected upon the external object, the devaluation of the real woman was compensated by daemonic features. She no longer appeared as an object of love, but as a persecutor or witch. The consequence of increasing Mariolatry° was the witch hunt, that indelible blot on the later Middle Ages.   69:399

Although we are still far from having overcome our primitive mentality, which enjoys its most signal triumphs just in the sphere of sex where man is made most vividly aware of his mammalian nature, certain

---

°*Mary*: Adoration of the Virgin Mary among Roman Catholics reached its peak during the Middle Ages;

°*dissociated libido*: i.e., instinctual energies and desires are thwarted from natural expression in the outside world

°*Mariolatry* is a term of reproach meaning excessive veneration of Mary.

ethical refinements have nevertheless crept in which permit anyone with ten to fifteen centuries of Christian education behind him to progress towards a slightly higher level. On this level the spirit—from the biological point of view, an incomprehensible psychic phenomenon—plays a not unimportant role psychologically. It had a weighty word to say on the subject of Christian marriage and it still participates vigorously in the discussion whenever marriage is doubted and depreciated. It appears in a negative capacity as counsel for the instincts, and in a positive one as the defender of human dignity. Small wonder, then, that a wild and confusing conflict breaks out between man as an instinctual creature of nature and man as a spiritual and cultural being. The worst thing about it is that the one is forever trying violently to suppress the other in order to bring about a so-called harmonious solution of the conflict. Unfortunately, too many people still believe in this procedure, which is all-powerful in politics; there are only a few here and there who condemn it as barbaric and would like to set up in its place a just compromise whereby each side of man's nature is given a hearing.   33:xiif*

What can a man say about woman, his own opposite? I mean of course something sensible, that is outside the sexual programme, free of resentment, illusion, and theory. Where is the man to be found capable of such superiority? Woman always stands just where the man's shadow falls, so that he is only too liable to confuse the two. Then, when he tries to repair this misunderstanding, he overvalues her and believes her the most desirable thing in the world.   114:236

The elementary fact that a person always thinks another's psychology is identical with his own effectively prevents a correct understanding of feminine psychology.   114:240

Psychology guarantees real knowledge of the other sex instead of arbitrary opinions, which are the source of the uncurable misunderstandings now undermining in increasing numbers the marriages of our time.   33:xiii*

The discussion of the sexual problem is only a somewhat crude prelude to a far deeper question, and that is the question of the psychological relationships between the sexes. In comparison with this the other pales into insignificance, and with it we enter the real domain of woman. Woman's psychology is founded on the principle of Eros, the great binder and loosener, whereas from ancient times the ruling principle ascribed to man is Logos.   114:254f

Whereas logic and objectivity are usually the predominant features of a man's outer attitude, or are at least regarded as ideals, in the case of a woman it is feeling. But in the soul it is the other way round: inwardly it is the man who feels, and the woman who reflects. Hence a man's greater liability to total despair, while a woman can always find comfort and hope; accordingly a man is more likely to put an end to himself

than a woman. However much a victim of social circumstances a woman may be, as a prostitute for instance, a man is no less a victim of impulses from the unconscious, taking the form of alcoholism and other vices.
69:805

Women are increasingly aware that love alone can give them full stature, just as men are beginning to divine that only the spirit can give life its highest meaning. Both seek a psychic relationship, because love needs the spirit, and the spirit love, for its completion.   114.269

The love of woman is not sentiment, as is a man's, but a will that is at times terrifyingly unsentimental and can even force her to self-sacrifice. A man who is loved in this way cannot escape his inferior side, for he can only respond to the reality of her love with his own reality.   114.261

As long as a woman is content to be a *femme à homme*,° she has no feminine individuality. She is empty and merely glitters—a welcome vessel for masculine projections. Woman as a personality, however, is a very different thing: here illusion no longer works. So that when the question of personality arises, which is as a rule the painful fact of the second half of life, the childish form of the self disappears too.   66:355

The woman who fights against her father still has the possibility of leading an instinctive, feminine existence, because she rejects only what is alien to her. But when she fights against the mother she may, at the risk of injury to her instincts, attain to greater consciousness, because in repudiating the mother she repudiates all that is obscure, instinctive, ambiguous, and unconscious in her own nature.   67:186

It is a woman's outstanding characteristic that she can do anything for the love of a man. But those women who can achieve something important for the love of a *thing* are most exceptional, because this does not really agree with their nature. Love for a thing is a man's prerogative. But since masculine and feminine elements are united in our human nature, a man can live in the feminine part of himself, and a woman in her masculine part. None the less the feminine element in man is only something in the background, as is the masculine element in woman. If one lives out the opposite sex in oneself one is living in one's own background, and one's real individuality suffers. A man should live as a man and a woman as a woman.   114:243

The conscious side of woman corresponds to the emotional side of man, not to his "mind." Mind makes up the "soul," or better, the "animus" of woman, and just as the anima of a man consists of inferior relatedness, full of affect, so the animus of woman consists of inferior judgments, or better, opinions.   112:60

For a woman, the typical danger emanating from the unconscious

---

°*femme à homme*: A man's woman; her identity is contained within man's ideas of her, definitions of her—she sees herself only in relation to man, a fulfillment of his needs.

comes from above, from the "spiritual" sphere personified by the animus, whereas for a man it comes from the chthonic° realm of the "world and woman," i.e., the anima projected on to the world.   97:559

Unconscious assumptions or opinions are the worst enemy of woman; they can even grow into a positively demonic passion that exasperates and disgusts men, and does the woman herself the greatest injury by gradually smothering the charm and meaning of her femininity and driving it into the background. Such a development naturally ends in profound psychological disunion, in short, in neurosis.   114:245

No man can converse with an animus for five minutes without becoming the victim of his own anima. Anyone who still had enough sense of humour to listen objectively to the ensuing dialogue would be staggered by the vast number of commonplaces, misapplied truisms, clichés from newspapers and novels, shop-soiled platitudes of every description interspersed with vulgar abuse and brain-splitting lack of logic. It is a dialogue which, irrespective of its participants, is repeated millions of times in all the languages of the world and always remains essentially the same.   3:29

Indeed, it seems a very natural state of affairs for men to have irrational moods and women irrational opinions. Presumably this situation is grounded on instinct and must remain as it is to ensure that the Empedoclean game of the hate and love of the elements shall continue for all eternity. Nature is conservative and does not easily allow her courses to be altered; she defends in the most stubborn way the inviolability of the preserves where anima and animus roam. . . . And on top of this there arises a profound doubt as to whether one is not meddling too much with nature's business by prodding into consciousness. things which it would have been better to leave asleep.   3:35

When animus and anima meet, the animus draws his sword of power and the anima ejects her poison of illusion and seduction. The outcome need not always be negative, since the two are equally likely to fall in love (a special instance of love at first sight).   3:30

No man is so entirely masculine that he has nothing feminine in him. The fact is, rather, that very masculine men have—carefully guarded and hidden—a very soft emotional life, often incorrectly described as "feminine." A man counts it a virtue to repress his feminine traits as much as possible, just as a woman, at least until recently, considered it unbecoming to be "mannish." The repression of feminine traits and inclinations naturally causes these contrasexual demands to accumulate in the unconscious. No less naturally, the imago of woman (the soul-image) becomes a receptacle for these demands, which is why a man, in his love-choice, is strongly tempted to win the woman who best corresponds to

---

°chthonic: of the underworld, non-spiritual.

his own unconscious femininity—a woman, in short, who can unhesitatingly receive the projection of his soul. Although such a choice is often regarded and felt as altogether ideal, it may turn out that the man has manifestly married his own worst weakness.   104B:297

Every man carries within him the eternal image of woman, not the image of this or that particular woman, but a definite feminine image. This image is fundamentally unconscious, an hereditary factor of primordial origin engraved in the living organic system of the man, an imprint or "archetype" of all the ancestral experiences of the female, a deposit, as it were, of all the impressions ever made by woman—in short, an inherited system of psychic adaptation. Even if no women existed, it would still be possible, at any given time, to deduce from this unconscious image exactly how a woman would have to be constituted psychically. The same is true of the woman: she too has her inborn image of man.
                                                              44:338

Every mother and every beloved is forced to become the carrier and embodiment of this omnipresent and ageless image, which corresponds to the deepest reality in a man. It belongs to him, this perilous image of Woman; she stands for the loyalty which in the interests of life he must sometimes forgo; she is the much needed compensation for the risks, struggles, sacrifices that all end in disappointment; she is the solace for all the bitterness of life. And, at the same time, she is the great illusionist, the seductress, who draws him into life with her Maya°—and not only into life's reasonable and useful aspects, but into its frightful paradoxes and ambivalences where good and evil, success and ruin, hope and despair, counterbalance one another. Because she is his greatest danger she demands from a man his greatest, and if he has it in him she will receive it.
                                                              3:24

The persona,° the ideal picture of a man as he should be, is inwardly compensated by feminine weakness, and as the individual outwardly plays the strong man, so he becomes inwardly a woman, i.e., the anima, for it is the anima that reacts to the persona. But because the inner world is dark and invisible to the extraverted consciousness, and because a man is all the less capable of conceiving his weaknesses the more he is identified with the persona, the persona's counterpart, the anima, remains completely in the dark and is at once projected, so that our hero comes under the heel of his wife's slipper. If this results in a considerable increase of her power, she will acquit herself none too well. She becomes inferior,

---

° *Maya*: the mother of the Buddha; she dreamed his conception
° *persona*: originally, the mask worn by an actor. For Jung, it is "the individual's system of adaptation to, or the manner he assumes in dealing with, the world"; the role a person plays, usually in terms of his profession, in relating to people. "One could say ... that the persona is that which in reality one is not, but which oneself as well as others thinks one is"; man's conscious idea of himself, usually an idealized image.

thus providing her husband with the welcome proof that it is not he, the hero, who is inferior in private, but his wife. In return the wife can cherish the illusion, so attractive to many, that at least she has married a hero, unperturbed by her own uselessness. This little game of illusion is often taken to be the whole meaning of life. 104B:309

The psychiatrist knows only too well how each of us becomes the helpless but not pitiable victim of his own sentiments. Sentimentality is the superstructure erected upon brutality. 105:184

Archetypes are complexes of experience that come upon us like fate, and their effects are felt in our most personal life. The anima no longer crosses our path as a goddess, but, it may be, as an intimately personal misadventure, or perhaps as our best venture. When, for instance, a highly esteemed professor in his seventies abandons his family and runs off with a young red-headed actress, we know that the gods have claimed another victim. 10:62

Most of what men say about feminine eroticism, and particularly about the emotional life of women, is derived from their own anima projections and distorted accordingly. 44:338

Perfection is a masculine desideratum, while woman inclines by nature to *completeness* . . . a man can stand a relative state of perfection much better and for a longer period than a woman, while as a rule it does not agree with women and may even be dangerous for them. If a woman strives for perfection she forgets the complementary role of completeness, which, though imperfect by itself, forms the necessary counterpart to perfection. 7:620

Woman's consciousness has a lunar rather than a solar character. Its light is the "mild" light of the moon, which merges things together rather than separates them. It does not show up objects in all their pitiless discreteness and separateness, like the harsh, glaring light of day, but blends in a deceptive shimmer the near and the far, magically transforming little things into big things, high into low, softening all colour into a bluish haze, and blending the nocturnal landscape into an unsuspected unity. 48:223

It needs a very moon-like consciousness indeed to hold a large family together regardless of all the differences, and to talk and act in such a way that the harmonious relation of the parts to the whole is not only not disturbed but is actually enhanced. And where the ditch is too deep, a ray of moonlight smoothes it over. 48:227

All that feminine indefiniteness is the longed-for counterpart of male decisiveness and single-mindedness, which can be satisfactorily achieved only if a man can get rid of everything doubtful, ambiguous, vague, and muddled by projecting it upon some charming example of feminine innocence. Because of the woman's characteristic passivity, and the feelings of inferiority which make her continually play the injured innocent, the man finds himself cast in an attractive role: he has the privilege of putting up with the familiar feminine foibles with real superiority, and yet with forbearance, like a true knight. 67:169

Emptiness is a great feminine secret. It is something absolutely alien to man; the chasm, the unplumbed depths, the *yin*. The pitifulness of this vacuous nonentity goes to his heart (I speak here as a man), and one is tempted to say that this constitutes the whole "mystery" of woman. Such a female is fate itself. A man may say what he likes about it; be for it or against it, or both at once; in the end he falls, absurdly happy, into this pit, or, if he doesn't, he has missed and bungled his only chance of making a man of himself. In the first case one cannot disprove his foolish good luck to him, and in the second one cannot make his misfortune seem plausible. "The Mothers, the Mothers, how eerily it sounds!" ° 67:183

The girl's notorious helplessness is a special attraction. She is so much an appendage of her mother that she can only flutter confusedly when a man approaches. She just doesn't know a thing. She is so inexperienced, so terribly in need of help, that even the gentlest swain becomes a daring abductor who brutally robs a loving mother of her daughter. Such a marvellous opportunity to pass himself off as a gay Lothario° does not occur every day and therefore acts as a strong incentive. This was how Pluto abducted Persephone from the inconsolable Demeter. But, by a decree of the gods, he had to surrender his wife every year to his mother-in-law for the summer season. 67:169

Human relationship leads into the world of the psyche, into that intermediate realm between sense and spirit, which contains something of both and yet forfeits nothing of its own unique character. Into this territory a man must venture if he wishes to meet woman half way. Circumstances have forced her to acquire a number of masculine traits, so that she shall not remain caught in an antiquated, purely instinctual femininity, lost and alone in the world of men. So, too, man will be forced to develop his feminine side, to open his eyes to the psyche and to Eros. It is a task he cannot avoid, unless he prefers to go trailing after woman in a hopelessly boyish fashion, worshipping from afar but always in danger of being stowed away in her pocket. 114:258*f*

It is an almost regular occurrence for a woman to be wholly contained, spiritually, in her husband, and for a husband to be wholly contained, emotionally, in his wife. One could describe this as the problem of the "contained" and the "container." 44:331c

The question of relationship borders on a region that for a man is dark and painful. He can face this question only when the woman carries

---

°From Goethe's *Faust,* Part II, Act I.

°*Lothario*: a seducer (name of a character in *The Fair Penitent* by Nicholas Rowe)

the burden of suffering, that is, when he is the "contained"—in other words, when she can imagine herself having a relationship with another man, and as a consequence suffering disunion within herself. Then it is she who has the painful problem, and he is not obliged to see his own, which is a great relief to him. In this situation he is not unlike a thief who, quite undeservedly, finds himself in the enviable position of having been forestalled by another thief who has been caught by the police. Suddenly he becomes an honourable, impartial onlooker. In any other situation a man always finds the discussion of personal relations painful and boring, just as his wife would find it boring if he examined her on the *Critique of Pure Reason*. For him, Eros is a shadowland which entangles him in his feminine unconscious, in something "psychic," while for woman Logos is a deadly boring kind of sophistry if she is not actually repelled and frightened by it.   114:256

In the eyes of the ordinary man, love in its true sense coincides with the institution of marriage, and outside marriage there is only adultery or "platonic" friendship. For woman, marriage is not an institution at all but a human love-relationship.   114:255

Relationship is possible only if there is a psychic distance between people, in the same way that morality presupposes freedom. For this reason the unconscious tendency of woman aims at loosening the marriage structure, but not at the destruction of marriage and the family.   114:273

We deceive ourselves greatly if we think that many married women are neurotic merely because they are unsatisfied sexually or because they have not found the right man or because they have an infantile sexual fixation. The real reason in many cases is that they cannot recognize the cultural task that is waiting for them. We all have far too much the standpoint of the "nothing but" psychology, that is, we still think that the new future which is pressing in at the door can be squeezed into the framework of what is already known.   89:668

Most men are erotically blinded—they commit the unpardonable mistake of confusing Eros with sex. A man thinks he possesses a woman if he has her sexually. He never possesses her less, for to a woman the Eros-relationship is the real and decisive one. For her, marriage is a relationship with sex thrown in as an accompaniment.   114:255

Traditionally, man is regarded as the marriage breaker. This legend comes from times long past, when men still had leisure to pursue all sorts of pastimes. But today life makes so many demands on men that the noble hidalgo, Don Juan, is to be seen nowhere save in the theatre. More than ever man loves his comfort, for ours is an age of neurasthenia, impotence, and easy chairs. There is no energy left for window-climbing and duels. If anything is to happen in the way of adultery it must not be too difficult. In no respect must it cost too much, hence the adventure can only be of a transitory kind. The man of today is thoroughly scared of jeopardizing marriage as an institution.   114:248

Woman nowadays feels that there is no real security in marriage, for what does her husband's faithfulness mean when she knows that his feelings and thoughts are running after others and that he is merely too calculating or too cowardly to follow them? What does her own faithfulness mean when she knows that she is simply using it to exploit her legal right of possession, and warping her own soul? She has intimations of a higher fidelity to the spirit and to a love beyond human weakness and imperfection.   114:270

Do our legislators really know what "adultery" is? Is their definition of it the final embodiment of the truth? From the psychological standpoint, the only one that counts for a woman, it is a wretched piece of bungling, like everything else contrived by men for the purpose of codifying love. For a woman, love has nothing to do with "marital misconduct," "extramarital intercourse," "deception of the husband," or any of the less savoury formulas invented by the erotically blind masculine intellect and echoed by the self-opinionated demon in woman. Nobody but the absolute believer in the inviolability of traditional marriage could perpetuate such breaches of good taste, just as only the believer in God can really blaspheme. Whoever doubts marriage in the first place cannot infringe against it; for him the legal definition is invalid because, like St. Paul, he feels himself beyond the law, on the higher plane of love. But because the believers in the law so frequently trespass against their own laws, whether from stupidity, temptation, or mere viciousness, the modern woman begins to wonder whether she too may not belong to the same category.   114:265

Secretaries, typists, shop-girls, all are agents of this process, and through a million subterranean channels creeps the influence that is undermining marriage. For the desire of all these women is not to have sexual adventures—only the stupid could believe that—but to get married. The possessors of that bliss must be ousted, not as a rule by naked force, but by that silent, obstinate desire which, as we know, has magical effects, like the fixed stare of a snake. This was ever the way of women.
114:251

It is no longer a question of a few dozen voluntary or involuntary old maids here and there, but of millions. Our legislation and our social morality give no answer to this question. Or can the Church provide a satisfactory answer? Should we build gigantic nunneries to accommodate all these women? Or should tolerated prostitution be increased? Obviously this is impossible, since we are dealing neither with saints nor sinners but with ordinary women who cannot register their spiritual requirements with the police. They are decent women who want to marry, and if this is not possible, well—the next best thing.   114:248

It is a bad sign when doctors begin writing books of advice on how to achieve the "perfect marriage." Healthy people need no doctors. Marriage today has indeed become rather precarious. In America about a quarter of the marriages end in divorce. And the remarkable thing is that this time the scapegoat is not the man but the woman. She is the one who doubts and feels uncertain. It is not surprising that this is so, for in post-war Europe there is such an alarming surplus of unmarried women that it would be inconceivable if there were no reaction from that quarter.   114:248

Since the aims of the second half of life are different from those of the first, to linger too long in the youthful attitude produces a division of the will. Consciousness still presses forward in obedience, as it were, to its own inertia, but the unconscious lags behind, because the strength and inner resolve needed for further expansion have been sapped. This disunity with oneself begets discontent, and since one is not conscious of the real state of things one generally projects the reasons for it upon one's partner. A critical atmosphere thus develops, the necessary prelude to conscious realization.   44:331b

Seldom or never does a marriage develop into an individual relationship smoothly and without crises. There is no birth of consciousness without pain.   44:331

AH! SUN-FLOWER

William Blake (1757–1827)

Ah, Sun-flower! weary of time,
Who countest the steps of the Sun,
Seeking after that sweet golden clime
Where the traveller's journey is done:

Where the Youth pined away with desire,   5
And the pale Virgin shrouded in snow
Arise from their graves, and aspire
Where my Sun-flower wishes to go.

WORKS IN *Short Story Masterpieces*

D. H. Lawrence, *The Horse Dealer's Daughter*

OTHER SUGGESTED WORKS

Emily Brontë, *Wuthering Heights*
Thomas Hardy, *Tess of the D'Urbervilles*

John Fowles, *The French Lieutenant's Woman*
Henrik Ibsen, *A Doll's House*
Sherwood Anderson, *Sophistication*
Leo Tolstoy, *Anna Karenina*
D. H. Lawrence, *The Rainbow*
  Women in Love
  The Man Who Died
Doris Lessing, *The Golden Notebook*

QUESTIONS

1. Compare Shakespeare's Description of his beloved's eyes with Wordsworth's description of his "phantom of delight." How is Shakespeare's woman different?

2. What does Blake mean by "the lineaments of Gratified Desire"? Why is the same answer given for both women and men? In what do both share equally? What is the reality of "Desire" that places it beyond personal theories and opinions?

3. According to Blake, Sappho, Whitman, Sexton, and Ciardi, what is essential to profound human relationships? What do men and women seek in each other? How is "Love" defined? How is "Eros" different from lust or sexual fantasies, pornography, or ideas of feelings? How does it bind people together?

4. Discuss the imagery that Shakespeare uses to describe Love. What is a "true mind"? Why can only "true minds" marry? How is "the marriage of true minds" different from the marriages in Part III?

5. Compare Shakespeare's imagery with Whitman's in *A Woman Waits for Me*. What is an essential element of Eros? How is the way in which Whitman defines sexuality different from the way Bromion views it? (Refer to the treatment of Oothoon in *Visions of the Daughters of Albion*.) What saves Whitman's man from "palely loitering"? What is his woman that La Belle Dame can never be?

6. What kind of woman is Mabel in D. H. Lawrence's *The Horse Dealer's Daughter* (in *Short Story Masterpieces*)? What is significant about her being a horse dealer's daughter? Why does Lawrence use the image of horses and horse-dealing? What are the brothers really giving up? Why is this destructive to their sister? Why does she want to die? What kind of man does Mabel need? What is wrong with her brothers? What saves her life? Discuss the nature of the relationship between Mabel and the doctor. (Compare with the woman and man in *Us* and *A Woman Waits for Me*. Explain how the doctor is different from Michael Robartes.) How does this story illustrate what Sappho says about Eros? What draws these two people together and binds them?

7. How is Emanuel's "the bridal pair" different from his "we" watching? Discuss the nature of "the wreckage," the "tough little monuments" left by years of actually living together. What is "the Paradise that seldom was"? Contrast the "tough little monuments" with the fingers lightly touching. What is the "Eden" from which the young couple wave? What do the hands of the older couple remember? To what are the "young horns" blaring farewell? Discuss the difference between marriage as an institution, a static place or condition (like The Garden of Eden), and marriage as a relationship, a vital connection between two people that carries them into new experiences, rather than being an absolute experience in itself.

8. Why is Ciardi's image of an arch appropriate for a real marriage or union of opposites? What is joined and upheld? How can "two weaknesses . . . lean into a strength"? What third force is created by this union?

9. The man and woman in *Us* get rid of what "impediments" that stand in the way of their union? How do they free themselves and make themselves honest for and open to Love? What enables them to "harvest"? Why is harvesting an appropriate image? What is its connection with "the Horn of Plenty" in Yeats's *A Prayer for My Daughter*? What is the nature of the ceremony that they must perform before they can harvest?

10. Discuss what Jarrell respects and admires in women. What judgments from Urizen's world does he defend them against? What is woman's relation to Law and Love? (What restrictions must the woman in *Us* get rid of before she is free to love?)

11. Discuss *The Mental Traveller* as a description of the evolution in human consciousness. Describe the stages through which the human being passes in the process of becoming a unique individual. (Refer back to images in earlier poems to illustrate each stage.) What is "the frowning babe" at the end of the poem? Why do the people flee from it? Discuss the effect that growth in consciousness has on man/woman relationships. What happens to the individual as he/she moves from a primitive, unconscious state of existence to a more sophisticated, more highly conscious state of awareness? Discuss the kinds of Body-Knowledge and Intellectual Knowledge that are essential for creative growth. What forces oppose this growth?

12. How are the "Daughters of Los" different from Urizen's Daughters? What effect does Imagination have on Reason? Compare Los's "wondrous golden building" with "The Golden Hall of Urizen." Why do Los's women find "intoxicating delight" in their work? Who are the Spectres "that they work for always"? What is the nature and significance of what Los's women are creating? Why don't men understand "the distress and the labour and sorrow" that these

women endure? What is the nature of "the Interior Worlds"? Can only women dwell there? What do women have to offer from those worlds?

13a. Explain how Yeats's Dancer, Jane Harriman, and Susan Sutheim are all "Daughters of Los." What is the nature of their "Interior Worlds"? What do the men in their lives fail to understand? Discuss the nature of each woman's suffering and how she endures and transcends it. What keeps her from becoming like Urizen's pale, reclining woman?

b. What kind of prison is Harriman describing in her story? What enables her to escape the would-be jailors? How is she different from the helpless victims in Part III? What formidable obstacles in Urizen's world resist her courageous efforts to be herself? (Compare her with Oothoon in *Visions of the Daughters of Albion*.)

c. Discuss the nature of the anger expressed in Sutheim's poem. What is healthy about women being angry, being aware that they are angry, and expressing it? Why must woman find herself before she can find man? What is man's "inevitable clumsiness" that woman no longer finds excusable? What in woman has he been blindly stepping on? (Refer back to Jarrell's image of man "as a polar bear on roller skates.")

d. How is Michael Robartes like the men who cannot understand what takes place in "the Interior Worlds"? How is he stepping on the Dancer's head? What kind of person is he? What masculine quality does he represent? What do the Dancer's replies reveal about her? What does she know that Michael cannot understand? What is the "dragon" in women that men do not like and want to kill? Compare Michael's lengthy speeches with the Dancer's brief replies. Why is her "wretched dragon" right to be perplexed by what Michael is saying? Why does he place so much importance on proof and scholarly references? What is ironical about his method of praising the physical?

e. Contrast Michael's style and tone with his message. What is the wisdom that he wants the looking glass to teach his lady? Why doesn't the lover want to see anything besides what is reflected in the mirror? (Refer back to *The Mask, The Lady of Shalott,* and *Christabel.*)

f. Discuss Michael's views of education for women. How would he answer Sappho's *An Uneducated Woman*? What kind of knowledge is he describing that a "mere book" cannot provide? What knowledge is contained in "that beating breast, That vigorous thigh, that dreaming eye"? Is woman aware of this knowledge, too, or do men only assume that women possess a mysterious knowledge as part of their physical being? What level of consciousness is woman being denied?

g. What do "Paul Veronese and all his sacred company" represent? Why does Michael refer to them and also to "Michael Angelo's Sistine roof"? What kind of argument is he making for the superiority of the body? What is the "great danger in the body"? What are people (particularly women) taught about their bodies? What does Michael mean by: "I have principles to prove me right"? Why is this statement absurd? Can a "Latin text" know anything about the nature of women? What has the Dancer learned at school? If she were indeed like Michael's description of women, how could she say what she does? How could such a dialogue be possible? Why is it significant that it is a dialogue rather than a monologue? What two elements are really conversing?

14. Discuss *A Dialogue of Elf and Mole* as a response to what the men in *A Prayer for My Daughter* and *Michael Robartes and the Dancer* are saying about woman's role. Discuss the difference between how women serve men and how they serve themselves, and how they live independent of men's projections. Why must woman shatter the looking glass in order to be herself? Why can't she be satisfied with being man's source of inspiration?

15a. Discuss what Virginia Woolf means by "androgynous mind." Why is such a mind necessary? Why is Woolf bored by Alan in Mr. A.'s story? What in man tends to obliterate woman, and makes him blind to her true nature? Discuss what Woolf means by: "For Alan had views and Phoebe was quenched in the flood of his views." (Refer back to *Michael Robartes and the Dancer*.) Why can't anything grow within the arid shadow of the masculine "I"? (Why couldn't Yeats's "green laurel" flourish there?) What impedes the one-sided, masculine mind? "Being honest as the day and logical as the sun," what is the only thing that such a man can do when he encounters a woman?

b. Discuss what Woolf means by "self-conscious virility" and why it is the problem of modern men. What do these men lack? How is their experience of emotion different from woman's? According to Woolf, what is essential to "the act of creation"? What kind of "marriage of opposites" is she talking about? (How is this like Shakespeare's "marriage of true minds"?)

c. What is the difference between "the world of reality" and "the world of men and women"? Do you agree that "it is much more important to be oneself than anything else"? What is involved in being fully oneself? What does it mean to "think of things in themselves"? How is this different from thinking of the mirrored images of things? (Refer back to how Urizen thinks and what his spectres represent.) What reality lies beneath artifice and intellectual theories? What unites Body and Mind? What does the image of Shakespeare's unknown sister signify? What must women do in order for the unknown sister to be born? In what way is she inside every woman?

16a. Discuss Simone de Beauvoir's essay in terms of the works read in Parts II, III, and IV. How has woman been lied to? How has she been taught to view herself and the world? Discuss the influence of upbringing on what woman becomes and on how she feels about herself. Discuss de Beauvoir's distinction between viewing oneself as subject and viewing oneself as object. (Refer back to the question raised in Part II: Why do women spend so much time in front of mirrors?)

b. What connection is de Beauvoir making between action and transcendence, passivity and immanence? How are these terms used? Why does de Beauvoir place so much emphasis on "doing," on relating to things in the outside world? Discuss the relation between "self-realization" and "work." Why does de Beauvoir consider idleness self-destructive? What does man gain by discouraging woman from being active? Discuss the nature of the slavery to which such a woman is condemned.

c. What is the relation between "slave" and "queen," "mask" and "self-mutilation"? Why can't there be "equality in inequality"? Why isn't "irresponsibility" a desirable "privilege"? What does de Beauvoir mean by "bad faith" and how does she define "evil"? Discuss how woman is "a product elaborated by civilization" and not just "a creation of nature." Explain what is meant by: "in human society nothing is natural." How do women become jailors? Compare them with the men jailors in the works in Part III. Discuss how the liberation of women will also free men. Compare de Beauvoir's vision of liberty, equality, and self-realization with Woolf's vision of androgynous selfhood and creativity. What is the "brotherhood" that men and women must affirm?

17. How does Jung's psychological interpretation dovetail with Woolf's and de Beauvoir's insights and observations about the nature of man/woman relationships? Discuss Jung's distinction between the Logos and Eros functions, and the difference between sexuality and Eros. What awareness do one-sided Logos men lack? How does this blindness cause them to misunderstand women? (Refer back to Blake, Yeats, and Woolf.)

18. How is Blake's vision in *Ah! Sun-flower* appropriate to Woolf's, de Beauvoir's, and Jung's theories of the androgynous mind or psyche? What kind of union or wholeness must the feminine and masculine elements of the human psyche strive to attain? Why is the Sunflower an appropriate image? What is the nature of "that sweet golden

clime"? Compare it with the graves (or death-like existence) of the Youth and the Virgin. Discuss the nature of the journey that they must begin in order to achieve their desire. What do the Youth and the Virgin signify? What must happen to the unconscious (or innocent) man and woman for them to be reborn? How do they fertilize each other within their individual psyches and give birth to new life—to a creation beyond each one's separate existence?